MEMOIRS OF THE SECRET SOCIAL WORKER

I MET HUNDREDS OF VULNERABLE CHILDREN DURING my eighteen years of service. It was frustrating that this personal time was so limited. Sadly the reality is that direct work is never prioritised. I ended up despising the broken system which controlled what I could do. "Looked after children" were repeatedly denied the necessary safety and stability from the very professionals who are supposed to protect them.

I am sure many are still haunted by what they witnessed and endured. This novel is dedicated to all of them, with the sincere wish that life is now being infinitely kinder.

The Secret Social Worker
Somewhere in the north of England

Be careful
who you
trust!

MEMOIRS OF THE SECRET SOCIAL WORKER

A Novel

First published in 2023 by the Secret Social Worker
London
United Kingdom

Amazon paperback ISBN: 978 1 78846 298 3
eBook ISBN: 978 1 78846 297 6

Produced by Kazoo Independent Publishing Services
kazoopublishing.com

Kazoo Independent Publishing Services is not the publisher of this work. All rights and responsibilities pertaining to this work remain with Amanda Marcus.

Cover design by Andrew Brown

Disclaimer

THIS STORY IS WORK OF TOTAL FICTION. The novel is inspired by my general experiences of being a childcare social worker. Any resemblance to actual characters or cases is purely co-incidental.

Whilst Bill Clarke, Fenton's team manager is an invention, this malignant type does unfortunately exist in many local authorities. Detached and obsessed by his budget, he is totally unsuited to an environment where vulnerable children and their families face life changing decisions. The reputation of statutory social work is tarnished by those like him who personify all that is wrong with children's services.

THIS UNIQUE HARD-HITTING DEBUT NOVEL EXPOSES the dysfunctional world of a fictional frontline child protection team.

The reader is buoyed by a few successes, yet at other times plunged into despair by examples of neglect and incompetence.

At the heart of this story are the catastrophic injustices that result from unfit "tick box" social workers. This sensational fast-paced read brings up many moral dilemmas. When inaccurate assessments result in devastating consequences for generations of families, apologies and compensation are meaningless.

Follow the Secret Social Worker on:

The Secret Social Worker@thesecretsocia4

The Secret Social Worker

The Secret Social Worker (under the pseudonym, Amanda Marcus)

Glossary

Assessments – Under the Children Act 1989, local authorities undertake Social Work Assessments of the needs of individual children to determine what services to provide and action to take.

Care Order – Will last until the child turns eighteen but can be ended earlier by the court. The court may initially make an Interim Care Order. The care plan will be made within two weeks of a Care Order being issued and will be reviewed regularly. The child has the right to have their wishes and feelings expressed at these review meetings and to be informed of the main points of discussion. This is referred to as Looked After Child (LAC) Review meetings.

Contact centre – A safe and impartial place where children can see their relatives. They are categorised into two types of contacts – supervised contact or supported contact.

Fostering-to-adopt schemes – Where a young child in care is placed with registered foster carers who have additionally been approved as adopters. The programme is specifically to provide early permanence where the prognosis for rehabilitation to their birth family is poor.

Guardian Ad Litem – A person who is appointed by the Court to look after a child or young person's rights and interests during cases where Social Services are seeking an Order.

Life story work – All children in long-term care should be receiving an open and honest approach to understand their personal history. As regards adoption specifically, photographs of their birth family, later life letters and an accurate explanation of why they are being placed with a new family is paramount.

"Lift" – The jargon sometimes used to describe removing children from parents or care givers.

Looked After Children – Under the Children Act 1989, a child or young person who has been in the care of their local authority for more than twenty-four hours is known as a Looked After Child. This arrangement can be voluntary or by Order of the Court.

Police Protection Order – If a child is believed to be at risk of significant harm, they can be removed from their home without a Court Order and placed under police protection for up to seventy-two hours in a safe location, under the Children Act 1989.

Pre-birth Assessment – The main purpose is to identify the needs of, and risks of significant harm to, the child, and whether the parents are capable of recognising these and working with relevant professionals so that the needs can be met and the risk reduced with a package of support.

Section 17 – Financial assistance can be provided to a child, parent or carer under Section 17(6) Children Act 1989 to address identified needs to safeguard and promote a child's welfare where there is no other source.

Significant harm threshold – The Children Act 1989 introduced Significant Harm as the threshold that justifies compulsory intervention in family life in the best interests of children. Physical Abuse, Sexual Abuse, Emotional Abuse and Neglect are all categories of Significant Harm.

Special Guardianship Order – This is a private Law Order made under the Children Act 1989 and is intended for those children who cannot live with their birth parents and who would benefit from a legally secure placement. It appoints one or more individuals to be a child's "special guardian".

About the Author

The Secret Social Worker retired from practice in her early forties after serving over eighteen years across various local authority children and family teams.

She lives with her husband and rescue dog somewhere in the north of England. As a mother herself, she takes great issue with the fact that children in the care system are let down by the very people entrusted to protect them. The corporate parent, in her eyes, does not exist practically or emotionally.

Forced to leave the profession by a toxic work culture and a morally bankrupt modus operandi, the Secret Social Worker has established a Facebook page for those struggling to navigate the system. Crucially it has attracted other like-minded professionals who offer support too. Receiving a notification that her page has contributed towards reuniting a family makes the effort worthwhile.

One

Monday 7th July 2003

Most child protection social workers find it distressing when tasked with removing children from their parents or caregivers. But power-crazy Wayne Nunton has no issue with it. He acknowledges that it can be an unpleasant business, but it has to be done. He hurtles around at breakneck speed, determined to save lives, and secretly hopes that one day his efforts will be recognised in the form of an OBE for his services.

Wayne is one of the few to make a reasonable income from social work. He chooses to locum as opposed to becoming employed by any city council. That way, he makes far more money and can escape rapidly when the formal complaints get too frequent for his liking.

Today was his first day at Fenton Childcare Services Area Team Three. There was no point hanging about waiting for droplets of advice in the form of some inferior induction. Instead he had simply delved into his predecessors' filing cabinet. It was here that he discovered Kyle and Brandon Leigh's file stuffed at the back. As he heaved it out, scraps of paper fell to the floor. He stooped to pick them up.

Handwritten notes appeared at first glance to span back years. "Children storing food in their pockets," said one. Another undated post-it note read, "Kyle distressed that his mother was locked in by his father." There were further reports that both children appeared to be fearful of their father at nursery pick-up time. Wayne shook his head despairingly.

An experienced worker, he knew too well that witnessing long-term domestic violence combined with systematic emotional abuse at such a young age would be having a devastating effect on these boys' wellbeing. It took only five minutes of grim reading to decide that these innocent four-year-old twins should have been removed from their parents some time ago.

Fortunately for these children, Wayne considered himself more robust than the previous trail of his ineffectual colleagues. Annoyingly though, he knew there were the statutory procedures to jump through first. It appeared that no social worker had visited the property for over six weeks and, appallingly, there appeared to be no chronology to hand. It therefore fell to him to go through the motions of inspecting the home conditions and record his findings.

He realised that this would purely be a box-ticking exercise, but now was as good a time as any, as the boys were in nursery that morning. It would be less traumatic for them that way.

He slammed the filing cabinet drawer shut and sighed in familiar despair. It was now 9.15am, a full half-an-hour after the official start time, and no one had arrived yet. He had guessed as much at his interview the previous day. He had unfortunately begun work at yet another substandard social work team.

What was evident straight away was that the twins' father had managed to intimidate professionals to such an extent that it had been easier just to leave things be. There was little point in hanging around, begging his scared colleagues to accompany him. In any event, he preferred to work alone. That way, he could speak to clients in any way he deemed fit.

Forty minutes later, he knocked on the white PVC door, glancing around him as he waited. A bulging bin bag had ripped slightly and lay on the side of the weed-infested path, its contents poking out. Debris was strewn over the paved front, and a small downstairs window had been boarded up. Certainly the 1960s Barnham Hill crime-ridden housing estate had a dismal feel to it.

Dressed casually in a white linen shirt and stone coloured chinos, a tan leather briefcase slung over his shoulder, he barely waited before knocking again. With a standard heavy caseload to wade through, he was impatient to begin. It was frustrating enough that he was going to have to linger longer than necessary in order to gain the evidence to move things forward.

"Hello, Mark, Saira, are you at home?" he called through the letterbox, pulling himself up as a hard-featured lanky male came into view.

The door opened, and the keen new locum social worker smiled as he introduced himself. This gesture wasn't returned. Instead, Mark Leigh stared at the newly-printed identity badge hanging round his unwanted visitor's neck. "Not you lot again!" he uttered before moving aside to allow Wayne to enter the premises.

Attempting to make polite conversation, Wayne acknowledged the boarded-up window in what he felt was a concerned manner. But his client responded harshly with, "Can't you lot sod off and go and help kids that need you?"

This offensive statement was about trying to redress the clear power imbalance, and Wayne had heard it many times over the years. He took his responsibilities extremely seriously and, as usual, needed to work quickly and methodically. There was no time for niceties or he would be there all day!

Choosing to ignore the fact that he was not welcome, he followed Mark into the living area.

"Is it OK to sit down?" he asked, trying again to sound sociable. Not waiting for a response, he positioned himself strategically on the couch, leaving the door open as an escape route. Mark Leigh's bullying tactics had clearly worked to date. But for his colleagues to give in and allow children to live like this? This was unacceptable.

The front room had a grim feel to it. To his right sat a gaunt but attractive looking young Muslim woman, her thick dark hair falling over her shoulders. She had been staring at a television chat show in an almost trance-like state, but turned to him now and smiled. Perhaps she was used to professionals turning up unannounced. Gentle mannered, she apologised that she was still in her dressing gown.

Although it was warm outside, the curtains and windows were

closed. The property had a transient feel to it and there were few indicators of what kind of people lived here. There were no wedding photographs, or souvenirs from day trips, for example. A broken chair lay on its side, and the coffee table was covered with bills and dirty food containers.

Skilled at assessments, he wasn't going to be sidetracked by what he felt to be time-wasting pleasantries. "Is it OK to have a look round?" he asked, trying to sound bright.

But Mark had picked up on the insincerity. "Not really," he responded dourly, adding, "There is no point in you being here!"

"I won't be here long," Wayne explained, continuing to make light of his presence.

But Mark Leigh was firm. "I've told you lot so many times!" he spelt out, his voice measured and holding his own. "The nursery staff are happy with the twins' progress."

This absurd statement couldn't have been further from the truth, but Wayne knew not to antagonise his client so early in the home visit.

"Look, mate!" Mark offered, softening his approach. "We don't do drink or drugs. I am sure there are plenty more deserving kids you could be helping."

This familiar assertion was wasted on Wayne, who prided himself on his opinion that parents must never be pandered to. "I need to see round the house now!" he announced. For good measure, he used one of his own phoney stock phrases, "I'm sorry about this, but it's just my job!"

"I said no!" his client told him emphatically. But Mark's resistance didn't faze him. He had read about his troubled background. Sadly, like many other clients he had to deal with, the twins' father had been brought up in the system. "Brought up" was an extremely generous term for it. An only child, Mark had learnt to protect himself from authority and played his care background to his advantage.

Used to dealing with social workers his entire teenage years, he was on to them, and their little techniques to try and worm their way into his private family life. How he loathed their patronising attitude and invasive presence! Since becoming a father, he had demanded they pay him respect. To book an appointment in advance, so that he had time to prepare for any of their "little inspections." He despised their hidden agendas, and so far had been successful in firing off complaints to their ineffectual team manager, Bill Clarke.

But this latest cocky new social worker sitting before him seemed totally undaunted. "If you don't allow me, I will return with the police!" Wayne now threatened, boldly holding eye contact until his client looked away. He meant it.

This real warning worked and instantly, Mr Leigh, as he asked to be addressed, backed down. A rather grateful-sounding Wayne got up, thanking him for his co-operation. "Let's start with the kitchen. I will follow you," he said, as cheerfully as he could muster given the circumstances.

"So have you made any plans for the summer holidays?" Wayne enquired, posing the question casually as he opened the fridge door, noting the near empty shelves. Excellent. More evidence to record. He usually found that, if he made polite conversation, clients were diverted from the power that he had over them.

"There isn't much in. I'm going to the shops later," Leigh muttered. But Wayne had moved on.

No one had ever trained him in the practicalities of spotting abuse signs. He had created his own strategies since qualifying for spotting abuse and to be fair, he was extremely thorough. He worked rapidly, opening and shutting each cupboard, mentally registering the contents. Then came one of his "party tricks." He looked in the bin and was relieved to see empty yogurts and a cereal box. Proof, perhaps, that the children had been fed something. However, in this occupation he knew assumptions were dangerous. He needed undeniable hard facts.

Without asking permission, he bounded up the stairs, turning at the landing to ask which room the boys slept in. It was an absolute mess. Mark leant on the doorframe, his arms folded as he watched Wayne observing his surroundings. This wasn't good. This new social worker was too self-assured, stampeding through his home. In a vain attempt to stall things he queried why he hadn't received notification of an appointment. Yet Wayne simply shrugged. There was no obligation to justify any of his actions to this child abuser.

None of those pathetic creatures in Fenton Childcare Services had bothered Mark for a while. Now, all of a sudden, this latest piece of filth arrived. He usually made the children tidy up before a visit, and now he had been caught out.

Wayne ignored the stares, and concentrated on the job in hand. The room hadn't been aired in some time and clothing and underwear were strewn over every surface. Then he spotted something of significant concern. The double wardrobe was closed with a key in the lock.

He paused a moment before opening it. The uneasy feeling was back and was threatening to overwhelm his thought process. He knew he had a strong disposition, but he was now uncomfortable about being alone with this unpleasant character. How stupid of him for not bringing a colleague with him. As usual, he had rushed out without making his own enquiries. He prayed that he would not discover anything sinister.

But there it was. He took a deep breath as he spotted several empty bags of crisps in amongst the clutter. It was an indication. A mere suggestion that the twins could have been locked in there. And what about Saira? Was she forced in there too?

He had no idea how often or if it even happened at all. It was just a gut feeling. But like other experienced social workers, he knew to listen to his intuition. He couldn't rely upon it completely, as he was supposed to be assessing evidence-based risk. But his feelings hadn't changed from the moment he had begun reading about the twins. There was not much he could do to protect Saira without her consent, however, as for his charges, he didn't want them staying here another night.

Two

"Why do you have a key in here?" He looked at the twins' father directly, demanding an answer. None was forthcoming. Sickened, he asked, "Why is the wardrobe empty?"

Challenging him on any parenting issues was a lost cause. He needed to leave the house now. He would give no explanation, but head straight for the twins' nursery. He intended to call emergency services for back-up on route and meet the police there. All he needed was the police protection order and he was in business. Obviously, there was no approval for an emergency foster placement lined up, but this wouldn't hinder him. He could always bring the children back to his office in this short interim period whilst arrangements were made. This was a crisis, but nothing that he hadn't dealt with before.

But then Mark came back with, "Because the door keeps swinging open. It's broken, you weirdo!"

Not trusting a word of what he was hearing, Wayne swung the door open several times, discovering that this was indeed the case.

Experience had taught him to defuse a situation, and he quickly turned his attention back to the client.

He needed to calm the tone down and therefore changed the subject. Attempting to sound supportive, he suggested a local charity that provided second-hand, free furniture. Due to the fact that he was dealing with a volatile character, he felt he had pushed this particular matter as far as he could. The wardrobe was still a worry, but Mr Leigh had come up with what felt like a satisfactory explanation.

The children could still, of course, have been locked in the wardrobe, but the probability was less likely. This meant that the legal threshold of "significant harm" could not be met realistically without further evidence.

This was obviously frustrating as there would now be a delay. For starters, there would be the laborious paperwork to complete, and a chronology to create. The hoops to jump through to justify a request to place the children into local authority foster care. The Leigh family dynamics were complex and, on the surface, he couldn't justify an instant removal.

It was easy to understand why Brandon and Kyle had slipped through the net. The various social workers who had picked up their case over the years had seemingly all struggled to work with them. Each transfer or closing summary cited unbearable pressure from Mark, threatening legal action and such like.

Wayne didn't care for lengthy dialogue on any aspect of the care of the children. However, he had to remain in the house, continuing to dip in and out of the multitude of concerns. The conversation and observations were only a tool to fill out the documents required for the next stage.

Changing the subject, he now asked, "I read in the file that the family support service had delivered the children's bedding. Where is it?"

"Not more bloody questions!"

"I need to know!"

"No clue. Saira deals with all the washing," Mark retorted, before turning his back on him and walking downstairs.

This dismissive attitude suited Wayne and he made the most of the brief time offered from the prying eyes. He worked swiftly, checking under both boys' beds and noted that the mattresses smelt of urine. He rifled through the piles of clothing and located what seemed like fresh pillow cases and separated them from the rest. Age-appropriate toys were evident, but on closer inspection many appeared to be broken. He briefly entered the bathroom which was acceptable.

Once satisfied with his examination, he returned to the lounge to continue his assessment. Saira turned away from the television and smiled sadly in the direction of her visitor. She was probably glad of the company, but there was no point in making small talk above the din and the daytime quiz show host was off-putting.

"Would you mind turning off the TV?" he politely asked her. She obliged instantly, reaching for the remote control, when her husband intervened offering a compromise, an agreement to reduce the volume!

Getting a superficial feel of how Saira functioned, Wayne randomly asked her how the boys had enjoyed the art set that had been supplied by the department six weeks earlier. He noted instantly how Saira stared at her hands, appearing to examine her wedding band.

"So where are the crayons now?" Undeterred, he pursued the matter. He knew how to catch out clients with his careful probing. "Carmel, your previous social worker, dropped them off the last time she visited."

"I threw them away!" Mr Leigh interjected. "The little shits were colouring on the walls!" His harsh tone and foul language regarding the alleged behaviour of his young children spoke volumes.

Saira seemed broken and didn't speak up. Wayne stayed quiet too, as he thought out his next strategy. Did he really need to ask where the damage occurred? At last, he was hearing the perfect padding to his impending court application! Mark Leigh was falling nicely into his own dark crevices, and it wasn't his role to lift him out. Wayne sat back on the sofa and allowed him to take control. It was rather unpredictable behaviour. Mark was suddenly presenting as more open and unaware that he was being judged on every aspect of his parenting.

"And the board games you lot sent were no good. Can't you get us better ones?" he whinged on, seemingly ignorant that Kyle and Brandon were dangerously close to being removed from the family home.

What was he supposed to be now? A toy shop? He privately despaired. How exactly was he to deal with all this micro managing? It was only his first morning and he was already emotionally exhausted. He absentmindedly ran his left hand through his neat buzz cut haircut as he decided how best to respond. He resented this side of the family support role. He hadn't counted them yet but he was probably personally responsible for at least eighteen families on his caseload. Each and every one of them would be relying on him to deliver services.

He hated how clients threw their problems at him, expecting instant solutions. It only served to overwhelm him, when all he cared about was returning to his own agenda. There was the crucial matter of whether these young children slept on bare mattresses. Ignoring Mark, he tried engaging Saira.

"Do you know where the extra bedding is?" he asked her directly. "I know that Carmel ordered four sets," he volunteered, studying her reaction. Indeed she looked terribly fragile as she stared at her hands silently.

"You need to make up their beds after I leave!" Wayne told them both, assuming the worst. "It's not acceptable for them to sleep on mattresses without adequate sheeting."

He began lording it over them, repeating himself and generally enjoying the power this role gave him. For good measure he added, "You need to put their clean clothes away."

Saira finally spoke up and offered that all the bedding had been put in the wash that morning. As directed by her rather smug husband, Wayne got up to verify these statements, and true enough, there was a door he hadn't noticed, leading to a small utility room. Again he had been shown up. No wonder it had been so problematic to move this case on. He returned to the lounge and muttered an apology.

It made no difference in the scheme of things. Even if the children had never been locked in the wardrobe, even if they slept in clean bedding every night, the evidence against their general wellbeing was damning. He continued in his dogmatic lecturing style, hoping Mark would slip up again. He ventured on, telling them both, "There was nothing wrong with the board games. Did you show the twins how to play? Did you join in?" He talked at them both, lacking inclination and time to engage them properly.

Yet in Mr Leigh, he had finally met his match. For he too had become skilled at distraction tactics, and began inappropriately enquiring about his sexuality, openly asking him whether he was gay! Disgusted, Wayne firmly responded that this matter was private and that he wished to keep things professional.

But smirking, Mark chose to persist, taunting him with, “Well, I would put money on it. You haven’t got kids so what do you know?”

This time Wayne chose not to respond. Instead he busied himself delving into his briefcase and gathering his pen and notebook. He wrote furiously, nodding at what Mark was telling him, perhaps giving the impression that he was agreeing with him. He listened as he reeled off previous social workers’ names, describing how they constantly harassed him, invading his right to a private family life.

Leigh’s warped opinion of Fenton Childcare Services were irrelevant. This misogynist needed punching in the face. There were no words for how the children and their mother were having to exist.

With this type of home environment, there were endless more issues than could reasonably be challenged in one single visit. He did not dare mention the huge elephant in the room. The multiple referrals indicating the likelihood of domestic violence towards Saira. What was the point? She didn’t even own her own mobile phone. Her safety would, most likely, be compromised the moment he left the property.

There was, however, an issue he needed to address. There was Saira’s family to think of. If he was placing the children into care, the first choice would be to see whether her extended family could be approached. In usual circumstances, they could be assessed as potential carers. Whilst he had only skimmed the file before rushing out, he had seen documentation to say that she had refused to provide any details on her relatives.

He was duty bound to do something, and therefore came up with a reasonable strategy. He made what sounded like a casual suggestion that Saira return with him to the offices. His idea was to talk to her alone, and try and persuade her to put her children first and accept help.

But predictably her husband interrupted, demanding what Wayne wanted with her in private. Before he had a chance to think up a plausible excuse, Saira shook her head firmly, offering only that she didn’t go out much. Disappointed, he observed Mark lean back and nod at her. This response must have been his preferred answer, and it had clearly pleased him.

This home visit was tiresome but he needed to continue, if only to tick the boxes. He recalled from previous reports that assistance had been offered repeatedly to Saira in the form of a refuge. She had consistently refused to engage.

The case history had made sad reading. It appeared that Mark had "gaslighted" her away from her close Muslim community over a hundred miles away. No thanks to him, she had become estranged from them, increasing her vulnerability. The eleven year-age gap was significant, and it was symbolic too that neither child had Muslim first names.

The visit had gone fairly well. The introduction evidenced how Mark was in denial that the family needed support. The inspection had been thorough. Usually there would be some sort of wrapping up. Perhaps a support package would be addressed. But in this case, there would be no promises of returning, and emphatically, he refused to answer Leigh's demand that the case be closed. The twins clearly met the threshold of being at risk of "significant harm". There was no need to dwell for the sake of it. He glanced at his watch and abruptly made his excuses.

Relieved to be out of that oppressive and abusive environment, his mood lifted somewhat. It was a beautiful day and in a few hours the boys would return to that awful dwelling that could never be described as a home. He knew nothing about their routine, or whether they had any social interaction with other children outside of nursery. None of this, he felt, was important at this stage. He just had to get the paperwork concluded and signed off, for their immediate needs were not being met.

Next on his frantic agenda was to visit Kyle and Brandon at their nursery. It was only a short walk, but he didn't relish leaving his car outside the Leigh family home, so he drove the three hundred metres down the road.

He rushed through this visit too. Mark was right in one aspect. Wayne wasn't a natural with children. He tended to revert to social work jargon and asked closed questions. In the five minutes he spent with them, he made little attempt to get to know them, preferring to engage with their key staff who, as predicted, were deeply frustrated by the lack of progress.

Concerns were raised repeatedly by their nursery manager. The twins were reportedly withdrawn and had few friends in their class, preferring to play with each other. They were observed to grab at food and store it in their pockets on occasions. The situation was unacceptable, she argued, and she literally begged him to do something. As they said goodbye, he shook her hand and promised her that he would be escalating this case with immediate effect.

The next four hours were taken up completing the core assessment. It was a large document and workers often undertook this task over a period of a month. It was supposed to be a meaningful tool, but he felt perfectly justified by racing through, copying and pasting the same information on each page. The facts were undisputable, but still he had to provide a detailed analysis. The impending court application would need hard proof.

Then there was the problem of persuading Bill Clarke of his plans and getting the form signed off. Every decision always came down to precious financial budgets. Children being removed from their caregivers and placed in foster care was an expensive business, and one always had to justify this. But Wayne read people well and had grasped immediately how inept and uninterested his new manager appeared to be. He hoped he wouldn't be the type to notice any gaps or inconsistencies.

Suddenly something else threatened to sabotage all his hard work. He smiled when Bill approached him, assuming that, finally, he would be offering some level of induction, perhaps providing him with some background material as to his new charges. But instead, he was notified that Mr Leigh had just hand-delivered a letter of complaint.

Given his client's lackadaisical attitude towards the basic care of his young children, Wayne openly expressed his disgust as he followed Bill into his tiny windowless office, and sat waiting impatiently for the usual time-wasting council bureaucracy to begin. He hoped that he wouldn't get suspended pending further investigations into alleged malpractice. This wouldn't look good on his first day! In fact, Bill would probably just sack him on the spot.

He soon grasped that this tiresome grievance tactic was clearly

Mark's signature dish, to divert social workers and keep them at bay. Right now, Wayne had more pressing concerns than fighting to hold his good name. He used one of his favourite stock phrases and announced confidently that he wasn't there to be liked. "It's a shame that Mr Leigh hasn't chosen to use his free time to ensure his children are fed properly!" he reiterated sourly.

As his new manager read the contents of the letter out loud, he wondered whether this criticism would be well received. Troubled, Wayne insisted that they needed to discuss a plan for the urgent removal of the twins and didn't have time for all this. But he needn't have worried.

"Just listen to this!" Bill said eagerly. "Don't ever send that social worker out to our house again!" he read aloud, clearly finding the contents amusing.

Wayne's new team leader cut a sad figure in every sense of the word. His full head of grey hair with an unfashionably long fringe, the thick beard begging to be trimmed and his general shabby attire gave the impression that he was unloved. It was obvious that he didn't care about the children either as he was happy to be so easily diverted. So Wayne leant forward and tried to explain that the team were accountable for the fact that these preschool twins had been seriously neglected for some time. But all Bill could respond with was that this was how it had always been.

Desperate, he felt now was a good time to add forcibly that he didn't appreciate Mr Leigh's homophobic comments. But Bill shrugged this complaint off too.

"You know how it is, Wayne, we get abused by our clients every single day!"

But instead of the usual complaints procedure being implemented, he was shocked to observe Bill rip up the letter and drop it into his waste paper bin. What light relief. Wayne prided himself on being a good judge of character, and had correctly assessed Bill's lack of decency. How tiresome it must be, to have to respond to the constant protests from dissatisfied clients!

With this matter dealt with, Wayne proudly handed him the core assessment to sign off. He stood for a moment, assuming he would be congratulated on his swift progress on such a troublesome case. But no praise was forthcoming.

It was clear that his manager fell short of what was expected from a child protection manager, so Wayne took the initiative to instruct him to sign off the material as a matter of urgency.

He left the document with him and approached one of his new colleagues. Siobhan was a gym-gear-clad woman in her late twenties with unappealing frizzy hair. He had met her briefly the previous day after his interview. She had been wearing a similar outfit then and as a big-boned woman, the Lycra look wasn't particularly flattering. The inappropriate dress code was a strong indication that she avoided clients, choosing, if she could, to hide behind her computer screen.

Smiling at him, she stopped tidying her top drawer and enquired how his first day was going. Social workers tended to be outgoing by nature, and Wayne began relaying what he had discovered at the Leigh home. He had already gleaned from the file that she knew them too, and assumed that she would be alarmed and show concern for Kyle, Brandon and Saira's immediate welfare.

But she too began sniggering at the very mention of Mark Leigh. Animated, she told him, "That loser has ideas above his station!" She then launched into an account of an incident when she had threatened Bill with going on indefinite sick leave unless she was immediately removed from the case!

Disappointed, Wayne turned his back on her, ending the conversation in mid-flow. It was clear she had nothing helpful to add to this horrendous situation. Indeed Siobhan, like every social worker who had touched this case, had shown themselves to be part of the problem. Innocent children's lives were being ruined and there was nothing remotely amusing about that.

Three

THE CORE ASSESSMENT SUMMARY MADE FOR UNPLEASANT Reading for Bill, but this wasn't because they were suffering abuse. Two more preschool children were about to enter the care system, which would add thousands of pounds each year to his unrealistically tight annual team budget. There was absolutely nothing he could do. The hard-hitting facts were unquestionable and he realised for the first time that Wayne was right. Mark Leigh should never have been pandered to. As team manager, he was solely responsible for this blunder, for it had been his signature on the closing of the case file time and time again.

With the paperwork now completed, Bill got up and approached Wayne, finally praising him for acting so promptly. He often handed out vacuous platitudes as it cost him nothing, but on this occasion, it wasn't so insincere. As team leader, it would have been him, not this rather good new member of staff, facing a drawn-out disciplinary hearing.

After an exchange regarding the way forward to remove the children, Bill returned to the cupboard that he generously described as his office. His latest locum seemed perfectly competent to manage things alone and there were his own stress levels to consider. With two years to go before he could take his pension, he would prefer to avoid the process of being suspended again. As regards his mismanagement of this seemingly straightforward case, the judge would definitely pick up on it.

Familiar with the ropes, he knew exactly how this would pan

out. A formal complaint would land on the Fenton's Director of Services desk. Several others would be copied into a lengthy email and moments later, his line manager, Dawn Smithers, nicknamed the "silent assassin" for good reason, would demand an immediate face-to-face meeting. She would harangue him, wanting to know all the little details which he wouldn't be able to recall nor care about. He would be made to feel like a naughty child. He was sick of it all and swore under his breath as he grabbed his cigarettes and headed off in the direction of the smoking shelter.

As far as Wayne was concerned, with Bill's rather dramatic tearing up of Mr Leigh's protest letter, and the core assessment signed off, he had the green light to proceed. He could set about the business of arranging the imminent removal of the twins. Good practice was to arrange a planning meeting of all the relevant agencies in the case. It was already late afternoon so this would need to take place ideally the following day.

There were pressing concerns that the children needed their basic care needs met somewhat until he was able to remove them in an organised way. The mornings for the next couple of days were not so critical as the nursery provided them with breakfast and a shower, but the evenings filled him with dread.

Despite the fact that the case had been known to the family support team, Wayne was instructed to make a laborious fresh referral highlighting the input he desired with immediate effect. He sighed repeatedly as he got on with faxing over a request for someone to attend the Leigh home that afternoon. The tasks identified were to ensure that they were fed and stimulated until bedtime. Desperate to minimise the damage of potential domestic violence, he literally begged the duty officer to make sure someone remained with them until they were tucked into bed. In the extenuating circumstances, the plan was approved on a very short-term basis. It wasn't foolproof, but it was the best he could do at this interim stage.

First in, he was now the last out of the building. It was now nearly 7pm and he hadn't made a start on studying the other cases he had inherited. He couldn't face opening the filing cabinet again so late in the evening. He didn't want to familiarise himself with any of his other new charges, fearing that every one of them would become personal to him. Then he wouldn't sleep well knowing he had let them down. The reality was he could only cope with one crisis at a time and needed a full-time assistant.

No one could accuse Wayne of not being diligent. He set himself high standards and vowed he would focus on them once Kyle and Brandon were safe. However skilled he was, Area Team Three was clearly understaffed and de-motivated. For now, he packed the Leigh file into his briefcase, in order to study the relevant reports at home that evening.

Whilst Wayne felt that child protection social work was his calling, one negative feature, was that, sympathetic though he might be, he did not relate to children as such. They were something more like clients to him than persons with whom he could become emotionally involved. He was pragmatic rather than emotional. This crucial aspect of his social work practice didn't concern him and he was selective whom he provided with a good service.

Of course something would have been gained by his being able to develop some relationship with Brandon and Kyle, but time was of the essence and there was so much organisation and planning to do for the urgent meeting that still had to take place. So far, he had only spent five minutes with the twins! Now, ironically, he somehow had to pave the way for them to have a secure and happy future.

It was gone eight o'clock when he finally got back to the flat he shared with his widowed mother. It suited her that her son had little in the way of a social life and he noticed her face light up when he walked in. They inevitably talked about the events of the day and he shared all the details. It didn't occur to him that he was breaching client confidentiality. In the dated kitchen she stood next to him whilst he microwaved two jacket potatoes for their supper. It had been an intense day and she was starting to pester him. Surely she could do her jigsaw or watch a television programme. He was thankful that he had more work to do, a genuine excuse to escape her questions.

The following morning he nodded to Bill as he passed him at the designated smoking area. He wasn't a pretty sight. His mid-life spread, bound by a worn-out belt, was forced inside his shiny black trousers, stretching a tad above his ankles. He wore a short-sleeved polyester shirt, looking the very epitome of a used-car salesman. The man was an embarrassment and Wayne felt somewhat repulsed by him. The expression "rot starts at the top" came to mind and what with two members of the staff on long-term sick leave, his negative persona was clearly having a domino effect on his team.

But Wayne was used to working alone, and first in again, he picked up the phone to make preliminary inquiries into a foster placement for Kyle and Brandon. He learnt instantly that all the placements within the borough were at maximum capacity. No surprises here. There were more "looked after children" than local authority foster carers, and therefore, a private placement outside of the area was the only option. The significant cost to Fenton Childcare Services of this outsource wasn't his concern.

Within the private fostering sector, there was much more choice, but still there were no potential individuals free who matched the twins' cultural background. His only concern was to pick experienced carers. Ian and Brenda were grandparents in their early sixties who had won awards for fostering over forty children in their career.

Although satisfied to hear this news, he cut their link worker short. He just needed the twins placed some distance away from their home and this location matched his criteria. Hopefully Mark would find it impossible to trace them and arrive unannounced on their doorstep. There was no time to read their details and he agreed to the match on the spot. He had to trust the private fostering agency. That's what they were paid to do. He was already on to his next task.

Next on his ever growing to-do list was to make contact with the foster carers to introduce himself. Ian answered and sounded the jovial sort. Wayne became so absorbed with telling him how stressed he was about the impending removal that he had to butt in and ask for more details about the children. This was where Wayne stumbled. He didn't know them in any real sense and had no idea about routines or food preferences for instance. But Ian wasn't fazed and said that they had variety packs of cereals in stock just in case!

With the fast-paced nature of child protection, it was usually impossible to arrange for the children to meet with their new carers prior to being placed into the care system. But at least he had ensured that Ian and Brenda were on standby so that the twins could arrive at any time of day or night. As always, though, the obligatory stack of paperwork had to take precedence!

With this placement secured, Wayne's task now was to focus on arranging an urgent meeting. This would assist him in the physical planning arrangements. He would need to identify who had to be invited and made a list: the police, the duty solicitor from Fenton Childcare Services, the Family Support Team Link Worker and the relevant nursery staff would suffice. More repetitive information to fill out and fax.

He now needed to consider a suitable venue. It would make sense to hold the meeting at the nursery, for he hoped that it was here that the removal would be initiated. The staff who cared for them on a day-to-day basis would surely be the best placed to aid him. Moreover, he hoped that they would assist him in the actual transporting of the twins. He worked methodically as usual and, within half an hour, had called everyone on his list. They all understood the severity of the situation and offered to rearrange appointments to attend at short notice. Such was the nature of child protection.

It would make sense, too, if he saw Kyle and Brandon for a couple of minutes after the meeting. It would be impossible that day to try and establish anything meaningful, though. This was always a pretext with him. Most social workers liked to get to know the children on their caseloads, perhaps take them out, so that they wouldn't feel like strangers to them. But this was a luxury he couldn't ever justify. He was always short of time. Duplicating reams of paperwork and ticking what he deemed as pointless boxes was always a higher priority than doing one-to-one work with children. Nothing ever changed there.

Now that he had informed the participants that he would be chairing the meeting, and that it would begin at 1pm that same day, he spent several minutes drafting an agenda. This was a relatively straightforward case and he whittled the entire four years of social work involvement into a few bullet points.

"Meeting to discuss the plan for the removal of Kyle and Brandon

Leigh." He typed in bold, adding the date and the time.

"Issues to discuss:

Preparing the children for the move.

Potential assistance needed with regard to transporting the children to their new foster placement.

Police backup needed to inform Mr and Mrs Leigh."

There was nothing else worthy of mention. His reasoning was unambiguous. He wasn't going to give any of the invited professionals ammunition to detract from what needed to happen. He had chaired too many of these types of meetings to know that conversations often tended to drift into histrionics.

As he printed off copies of his agenda, he was fully aware that the major difficulty in this operation would be the careful handling of Mr Leigh. It was obvious why no one wanted this case and as a result it had been passed around for years. But this was no excuse. He felt tense but determined. This swiftly-formulated action plan was long overdue.

At 12.45pm, Wayne found himself the first to arrive at the Barnham Hill Nursery. Situated in the heart of the estate, this prefabricated low-rise building was in need of more than a lick of paint. But for two years, it had served as a lifeline to neglected twins Brandon and Kyle.

With a little time to spare, he didn't think to use this time to get to know the twins better. Instead he had a look around. The door was open to the shower room and he stepped inside. On a long row of shelving he could see that staff had carefully labelled towels and toothbrushes. He moved closer and recognised Kyle and Brandon's names.

This excellent provision provided significantly more to these children than just a preschool education. Next door in the utility room, he could hear the sound of the washing machine reaching its spin cycle. Neatly folded fresh clothing was stacked on open shelves. The boys, he had heard from staff, occasionally arrived wearing dirty items that they might have slept in. It saddened him to think that the nursery was propping up a situation that Bill had had a duty to resolve many months, if not years, earlier. Surely he gave his staff regular supervision. What was going on?

He now located the meeting room and sat down. A mural depicting a pastel rainbow looked tired. The happy sounds of children playing outside served as a sharp contrast to the depressing house he had visited the day before. In the far corner of the room, red beanbags lay on a rug depicting a town map. Brightly-coloured books in different sizes were stacked haphazardly on cheap Formica bookcases. The vivid images of the broken chair and locked wardrobe were following him everywhere, hanging round his neck, demanding he did the right thing.

He assumed Kyle and Brandon were engaged with their classmates outside, but he didn't get up to observe them. He barely recalled what the identical twins looked like and didn't want to have to have them pointed out. As usual, he was only focused on achieving his desired outcome: moving them to a foster placement in a planned way.

If he had bothered to look out for them, he would have spotted them, standing silently against a wall. Unbeknown to him, that morning their father had refused to give them a drink and had screamed at their mother when she had tried unsuccessfully to intervene. So traumatised by their abusive home life, at that moment, they were only able to watch their other peers playing.

The participants now arrived and Wayne made brief conversation as he handed out copies of his agenda. He assumed that everyone knew the ropes. After they introduced themselves, each professional chose to state their involvement with the case. The family support worker, in particular, was rather loquacious.

Why weren't they all adhering to the agenda? He couldn't have made it more concise. Everyone seemed to be adding things that, as far as he was concerned, were not relevant. The police officer mentioned that Saira had no previous convictions. There was only one caution relating to Mr Leigh concerning a verbal confrontation with a neighbour some years ago. Wayne glanced at his watch several times. This was a waste of precious time.

Saira now became the topic of conversation. Was he supposed to be chairing the meeting? At this point he found himself struggling to get a word in. He feigned limited interest and wrote some notes as the discussion took its own flowery path. Frustrated, he felt disempowered. He had called this meeting. If he had wanted this aspect of the case discussed, he would have written it down on the agenda!

The nursery manager now turned on him, her tone accusing. "I'm surprised to learn that the plan is foster care," she announced rather curtly. In her opinion, Saira should be offered one last chance at being assisted to move to a women's refuge with the children. She added that the Muslim community could assist with practical and emotional support and she would be happy to try and engage with her again in private.

There was no time for Wayne to respond, as her two key staff (her protégés) appeared to jump on the bandwagon. They spoke enthusiastically about Saira's strengths. "Yes, she is passive, but there are positives," they said, taking it in turns to speak.

"If she was to care for them on her own, they would probably thrive."

"The children adore her."

"She really loves them."

The nursery manager joined in earnestly, backing her staff. She clearly had ambitions to become a social worker, he considered cynically, taking an instant dislike to her. He was mindful that they were all going round in circles. This offer had been made on many occasions. In his mind, Saira had also neglected her children. Things were far too serious. He suggested that in the future, this could be addressed, but only when the children were safe and secure.

He was forced to abandon his agenda when the child protection police officer politely interrupted him, voicing his agreement with the nursery manager and her staff. Wayne masked his fury when he too offered his support if Saira needed protection to escape to a place of safety.

On and on. Wayne continued to write his notes as they would serve as the minutes and would save time. He was convinced that the nursery manager was attempting to show him up and this was feeling like a personal attack on him. He found himself unable to look at the so-called professionals around him, hearing only the odd word here and there. "Empowered … a new start …"

He knew that he should be guided by them but their attitude was unrealistic. He was only concerned for the welfare of Kyle and Brandon. Giving their mother a final chance didn't make sense considering the level of neglect his young clients were exposed to every single day. Besides, Saira had specifically said that she did not want any support from her Muslim community or her extended family.

Enough of this pandering! He tried politely to steer the conversation away, but the nursery manager stormed on ahead. He butted in rudely, interrupting her in mid-flow.

"In the last four years, there has never been any indication that Saira has taken any advice seriously," he said, speaking firmly. "How can we trust her not to disclose which safe house she would be taken to?" He glanced round the room at everyone, announcing forcibly, "Now we need to move on."

This last statement seemed to have an impact and both the police officer and the nursery staff fell silent. There was now only one attendant who felt differently. The family support worker told everyone that she felt she was making headway with Mr Leigh.

"He was fine with me last night," she announced, rather too confidently for Wayne's liking. "I think he likes me, as he doesn't see me as a threat," she added, sounding incredibly inexperienced and naïve.

But Wayne wasn't going to waste time debating the irrelevancies of her subjective opinion. This family support worker clearly didn't have the first clue about childcare law. He did.

So far, the duty solicitor from Fenton's local authority legal team had been intent on making notes. She hadn't uttered a word other than to introduce herself. She lifted her head now, catching Wayne's stare, and gave a discreet nod. He only cared for her approval. The threshold of significant harm to the twins had been reached. She had seconded this. He would be removing the children and making an immediate court application and no one else's opinion actually counted for anything.

After nearly an hour of time wasting, he was relieved to be able to return to address his agenda. The detail of the plan needed to be discussed. It was agreed that the physical removal of the twins would occur the very next morning. Wayne was reluctant even to let the twins stay another night at home. Based on what he felt was an accurate assumption, Saira, Kyle and Brandon were petrified of Mark Leigh. Yet another night of going to sleep, fearful for themselves and their mother. But it was deemed prudent to carry out the removal in a less dramatic fashion. He wanted to avoid a scene where two impressionable children would be dragged from their home, with their father shouting abuse or threatening violence. Or worse!

Eventually, the plan of action was approved. The next morning, Wayne would be notified once the boys had been dropped off at nursery and they had ensured that their father had safely left the premises. The twins would not be taken to have their usual shower, as there would be no time. Instead, the staff would take them directly to the quiet reading area and give them breakfast whilst they waited for him. He would then have the arduous task of attempting to explain to them why they would not be returning home that afternoon.

It was unusual that a social worker could be so passionate about improving the lives of vulnerable children, yet feel uneasy in their company. He appreciated, on a surface level, the intense emotions of the ordeal that Kyle and Brandon would be going through. But he could not, on a practical level, cope with the anxiety that the twins were likely to show. He was anxious too that they would not deal well with their terror at being taken away by a relative stranger. Perhaps they would become hysterical with fear and physically resist his efforts to persuade them to get into his car.

So it was with some relief that he accepted the offer of help from one of the nursery key workers to accompany the twins on the journey. Over the years he had encountered several instances of his charges sobbing in the back of his car and being unable to console them. It hadn't been easy.

As the meeting drew to a close, the tone became less fraught. There could even be said to be a sense of comradeship. The nursery workers offered to take photographs that afternoon of the twins playing and would create albums for them. They would also arrange a signing of farewell cards from the staff as a keepsake.

The family support officer stated that she would call Mark straight after the meeting to say that she would be taking the boys to the park and then out for tea that evening.

The idea was to minimise the time they would spend in their home that evening and that way, at least the children wouldn't go to sleep hungry. There was a concern, naturally, that Mark might become suspicious but there was nothing anyone could do about this. The timing of the "lift" was crucial to avoid further trauma to Kyle and Brandon.

Even the representative from the police now became useful, offering to send two officers to flank him for the unenviable task of informing the twins' parents that their boys were not coming home to them in the near future.

Feeling safe now in the knowledge that the meeting had gone to plan, he now led a disingenuous tribute to Saira. It didn't cost anything other than a couple of minutes and it made him sound quite human. Everyone nodded in agreement that she was an affectionate and loving mother, but they acknowledged that this wasn't enough. She had failed to protect her children.

The whole situation was pitiful and largely avoidable. Without Mark Leigh in her life, she probably would have thrived. She was a victim of systematic domestic violence; she was broken and isolated. The decision to remove her beloved children could send her over the edge. But she was a grown woman, and she had made her decision. Kyle and Brandon needed to be put first. And with that statement, he ended the meeting.

As for Mark Leigh, Wayne wasn't looking forward to delivering the news. He wasn't usually afraid of confrontation but there was something terribly unpredictable about this individual. He was going to need support!

Four

Wednesday 9th July 2003

As the moment edged nearer, Wayne dreaded telling the Leighs that they were about to be deprived of their children. In the early hours he woke up thankful to escape from the nightmare. The scene played out vividly: he felt himself cowering in the corner of their grim lounge with his back forced against the wall. The TV was blaring and the curtains were closed. Mark Leigh was standing over him, his tattooed knuckles almost white as he gripped the broken chair leg with such force.

This was all too real! It was just 5am. In nine hours' time he would indeed be facing this vicious and intimidating client, and the scene might not be too dissimilar. Stressed, he was effectively alone in dealing with this crisis. He tried to think of alternative options. Perhaps he could ask another social worker from a different area team to attend with him for support. But this would have to be a colleague who hadn't met Mark before. No one would exactly be running to help him.

He sipped from the glass of water next to his bed and tried to persuade himself that everything would work out well. He knew the ropes, having done this many times over. He was used to manipulative clients, but Leigh seemed to be sharper than most of them. The police would be flanking him when he announced the news to the boys' parents, but he realised that it would be best not to go into the property. It wouldn't be professional or sensitive to discuss such a confidential matter on the front door step, but surely his safety came first.

There were other issues, such as his overly-ambitious tight schedule. The police could be running late. Or he could face traffic delays and not yet be back in time.

He realised that his beloved planning meeting hadn't covered a back-up plan. If there was going to be a delay, an unsuspecting Mark Leigh would set off to pick up the children from nursery. He would surely go insane with fury when he discovered the truth and no doubt there would be a horrific scene played out in front of the other parents and children.

Unsurprisingly, he struggled to fall back to sleep and when his alarm went off several hours later, he felt shattered. It wasn't a good start to the day!

He forced a can of Diet Coke down; the caffeine rush instantly worked. Charged with adrenalin, he drove to work, keeping his work mobile on the passenger seat, willing it to ring. After the nightmare, he decided it would be sensible to fill in the Whereabouts diary with his plans for that day. From experience, all kinds of unforeseeable problems could arise. And quite possibly things had already gone awry. Perhaps one of the twins was ill, and Leigh had kept them at home that morning.

Siobhan had arrived before him and was busy on her mobile booking an aerobics class! When she had dealt with that, she turned and asked him about his plans for dealing with the twins. She seemed to listen, nodding now and then. But then she simply blurted out, "Saira will get a right good battering from the bastard once he gets her on his own!"

No wonder, he thought (not for the first time in his career), that social workers suffered from such poor press coverage. Siobhan wasn't fit for purpose, and her comment wasn't, he felt, worthy of a reply. She had made it plain that this case wasn't her problem anymore. He breathed in deeply in an attempt to brace himself for an extremely nerve-wracking day.

Soon Wayne learnt that Leigh had been late dropping off the twins and had now left the building. It was safe to make his way over as planned. The turnaround time was tight and he knew he would have to be focused to achieve what he needed to do within the given timescale.

Once at the nursery, he was told to wait for one of the staff to meet him. He distracted himself by looking at the patch repairs to the well-worn industrial carpet. Artwork strung up with such pride on the walls offered some colour and love to the tired building. He was greeted after a while by the nursery manager, her tense expression giving away her anxiety.

She showed Wayne into the room where, the day before, the removal plan had been drawn up. The twins, as planned, had been separated from their nursery group. Looking relaxed, they sat on the red beanbags listening intently to a story. He recognised the nursery key worker from the previous day. She had kindly volunteered to assist with the removal. The boys sat close to her, eating their buttered toast, unaware of what was about to happen. The only real safety they had was here in this building. They loved their mother but their world was about to be ripped apart.

He brought over a child's plastic chair and sat down opposite the twins. The alternative would be to sit on the play mat and that would be even less comfortable. But he put aside these petty worries. The most important thing right now was to try and engage with them.

He recognised that he was now going to threaten those things that the twins had always taken for granted. That sense of familiarity to which they were accustomed. He could, however, absolutely justify what was about to happen. His eyes were drawn to Kyle's dirty nails. His grease-marked orange t-shirt was slightly too small. He noticed the hurried manner with which the boys ate their toast. Wayne took a deep breath and signalled for the storytelling to stop.

"This is going to be really hard for you to understand," he started to say in the gentlest tone he possessed. Uneasy with children, he gave them too much information for them to process in one sentence. He told them bluntly, "I am going to take you to a new home, away from your mum and dad, because they have not been looking after you properly."

Brandon didn't seem to understand what Wayne was saying

but Kyle did. He immediately responded boldly with: "They are looking after us." His face fell as he spoke. It was almost as though his family secret had been cruelly exposed.

"Everyone has been worried about you both," Wayne stepped in, trying to explain what would be impossible for two small children to comprehend. "We are going to take you to meet two very nice people," he said, sounding cheerful. "They are called Brenda and Ian and they are excited to meet you."

He spoke slowly and picked his words carefully.

"Their garden has a trampoline and a football net," he offered enthusiastically, adding, "I am sure there will be loads of toys as well."

He sounded inappropriately upbeat, and reiterated, "You are not going back to your home today! I am going to take you to live with Brenda and Ian."

"So we are all moving there? Us and Mum and Dad?" Brandon asked, looking hopeful.

Wayne realised that he hadn't made himself at all clear because Kyle then stated, "I only want my mum to come," clearly agitated as he began to absorb the terrifying news. "I don't want my dad taking my toys away. He won't let me play on the trampoline either."

At this distressing comment, the key worker looked visibly upset. She picked up Kyle and put him on her knee. The nursery manager had now arrived and briefly turned her back on them all. She didn't want the boys seeing her tears.

"You are both going to share a room," Wayne offered, trying in vain to reassure them. "But your mum and dad are going to stay at your old house. I will make sure you see them very soon, though."

The boys looked shocked and confused, and stared at him, struggling for clarity. But their new social worker was unable to pick up on this, and was set on racing through his agenda.

Wayne hadn't noticed that the nursery worker was staring at him, perturbed. She could have done a better job herself. It was obvious that he was panicking about the turn-around time, but he seemed unaware that his charges were only four years old! Now he launched into another issue that was irrelevant at that exact point in time. He said he would be visiting them regularly to ensure that they were happy with their new foster carers.

How could the children process this overwhelming news?

"I want my mum to come with us," Kyle cried out, leaving Brandon and the nursery key worker to try and comfort him.

"It's not your fault. You are four years old. You need to be cared for properly," Wayne said, almost relishing the power that this role gave him at that moment. "You have done nothing wrong," he reiterated.

"If we tell Dad we are sorry, can we go home?" asked Brandon hopefully. "We need to stay at home with Mum as we look after her," he insisted. He sounded older than his years and it was pitiful.

Kyle stopped crying momentarily. "Don't tell him that! Tell no one anything. That's what Dad told us. Don't you remember?"

Wayne needed to store this crucial evidence for his court application. But he had no time to interview the children properly and record what they were saying. He was all over the place, jumping from one topic to another. He raced on, raising the issue of the boys seeing their parents in a supervised contact centre. He did, however, pick up on the fact that they might feel frightened of meeting their father on their own. "You are going to see your Mum and Dad together in a few days," Wayne continued, in a more upbeat tone. He felt it appropriate to clarify that the contact sessions would not be at their own house, but that they would be taken to a new place with lots of toys.

There was far too much information for the twins to deal with. Bombarding them further, he expanded on the contact centre process. He told them that a member of staff would stay in the room with them there, in order that they wouldn't get into any trouble.

Understandably, both children became equally distressed, each feeding off the other's anxiety. Eventually, it dawned on him that nothing was to be gained at this time by continuing with this line of conversation. He needed to get things over with. Drawing on his experience, he knew that once they met Ian and Brenda, they would hopefully feel somewhat calmer. "Shall we talk about this in the car?" he said, whilst struggling to get up from the low chair.

With that, the nursery staff gently took the empty plates away from the boys and took them by the hand to the entrance. The manager went into her office and came out with various items for the twins. She handed them each a carefully wrapped gift, a bar of chocolate and cards. She knelt down to embrace them, telling them softly that they could open their gifts once they were strapped safely in the car. Her parting words were that she had their new telephone number and would call them that night to say hello.

This diversion worked and the boys' fear had now temporarily abated as they looked at their presents. Wayne was impressed. He had been concerned with the practical tasks, such as remembering to borrow the booster seats from the office store cupboard. He hadn't thought of any strategies to persuade the twins to get into his vehicle. The nursery worker climbed in, positioning herself between the two children, helping them with their seatbelts. So far so good, he thought, as they all waved goodbye. Wayne took a deep breath. They were such sweet caring children and he was under no illusions. They were going to need a significant amount of play therapy to recover from their ordeal.

The fifteen-mile journey was to prove the first problem. Wayne had studied the directions earlier in the morning but still had to resort to pulling over constantly to check his A–Z again and again. He asked the nursery worker if she had good map-reading skills but she replied that she would feel nauseous if she had to try reading anything whilst the car was in motion! He tried to hide his stress but Kyle and Brandon picked up on it and momentarily became quiet.

Soon though, their treats had been eaten, and the novelty of the new toys had worn off. For his part, Wayne's stress levels were rising. He hated anyone consuming anything in his precious GTI. He always kept it spotless. But now he could imagine chocolate finger marks all over the windows and the seat fabric. Their repeated mantra, asking when they would see their mother again, was also grating on his nerves. No wonder he was getting lost. He glanced at the key worker in the mirror, willing her to deal with these constant questions, but she was silent. What use was she?

"You will go to a special centre where staff will make sure

everyone has a nice time," he told the boys, absentmindedly, whilst trying to focus on the motorway driving. But the questions were persistent so he added for good measure, in a firmer tone, "You won't be going home at the moment!" The boys had exhausted his patience.

"Our mum will cry if we don't go home. Dad will get very angry with us. We need to go home," Brandon told him, as he tried to pacify his distraught twin brother.

"I am going to talk to your parents and explain everything," Wayne offered, trying to sound engaged. He told them not to worry, which he recognised was a nonsensical statement considering the children were preschool age.

He was desperate to tell the boys to shut up. And the nursery worker was irritating him too. All she was doing was blocking his rear view. She was next to useless as she wasn't able to pacify them either. He needed to focus on the driving. With all these distractions he realised that he had missed the motorway turn off.

At times like this he hated his job. As the questions were unrelenting, he stopped replying. All he was focused on was trying to find when the next turn-off was. He started to sweat and swigged from his second can of Diet Coke that morning as he stared at the road ahead and gripped the steering wheel. This was hopeless. At this rate he was never going to be back at Fenton Police Station for 1.45pm. It was now gone half past eleven and time was ebbing away as he drove the extra six miles in the wrong direction!

It was with a real sense of relief that he finally reached their destination. He parked outside a 1930s nicely-maintained semi-detached house with a pleasing front garden. On the opposite side of the road an allotment stretched across the entire length of the street. The nursery worker lifted Kyle out of the car, leaving Wayne to assist Brandon. As he did, he realised that the little boy had wet himself. He tried not to think about what that would mean for his precious Golf GTI. He would have to persuade Bill to pay out of petty cash the cost of having the car internally cleaned. Just now he had to reassure the children that all would be well. He needed to fight this other battle later.

Before they even got past the gate of the house, a well-built woman in her sixties opened the front door and was walking down the path to greet the children. It was Brenda. Her streaked blond hair framed her face and she had a pleasing smile. He felt an instantly positive vibe emulate from her. It was like an angel had been sent to rescue them all from what was so far an extremely challenging morning.

"We have been so excited all morning to meet you both," were her warm opening words. "It's lovely to meet you all," she said gently as she bent down to their level. Wayne noted that the boys instantly seemed at ease with her. They responded politely when she enquired if they were hungry, and told them that she had made sandwiches.

Taking an instant liking to their new foster carer, Wayne discreetly made it clear that there had been a little accident and Brandon would need to change his clothes. Brenda nodded and told Wayne that they had a full stock of clothing items for emergencies such as these. The boys followed her upstairs to see their new room.

But the pressure was on, and Wayne could think of nothing else but the need to get back to Fenton. He glanced at his watch repeatedly, wondering how long he should stay without seeming extremely rude. He knew it was bad practice just to drop his terrified young charges and go, but he had mistimed things. It seemed like ages before Brenda shouted down that they could chat "later on!" Her voice sounded relaxed, but with this major cock-up, Wayne realised that there would be no "later!"

Whilst they were all upstairs, he waited impatiently in the hallway. Then he overheard loud laughter coming from the direction of the kitchen. On an occasion like this one would expect that the arrival of two traumatised children would have been the focus of attention. Being absorbed in a private phone conversation was hardly appropriate.

"Sorry about that!" Ian, Brenda's husband, said as he emerged, having terminated the call. He offered his hand to Wayne, announcing, "I was just on to our eldest daughter," he said, adding, "She only lives round the corner and we see her every day."

Unimpressed, Wayne didn't reply. He struggled to understand why, as a designated carer, Ian had chosen to be diverted at such a significant moment in Kyle and Brandon's lives. He should have slammed the phone down the moment they arrived in the house. Wayne didn't have great depth into children's emotional needs, but he knew enough to know that this harrowing day would remain in their memories for ever. Their needs should have come first.

However, Ian soon redeemed himself, and Wayne's first impressions of him changed when he stood at the kitchen window several minutes later, watching Ian interacting with Kyle and Brandon. They seemed to take to him instantly and allowed him to help them get on to the trampoline. Ian too seemed completely at ease in the presence of children. Unlike Wayne. It was a basic skill that he realised he was lacking and he now felt despondent about his own weaknesses.

Whilst the boys' nursery worker updated Brenda on the children's needs, Wayne rather abruptly refused an offer of a drink. Despite being encouraged to sit down, he refused. He glanced at his watch again anxiously. It was now 12.25pm. Time to go. He had to allow for the fact that he might get lost again on the way back!

"I will be available on my phone later on, or tonight," Wayne interrupted the conversation, adding that he needed to get to see the twins' parents before their father set off to nursery. Enjoying the sound of his own voice, he told Brenda, "It's not fair on the staff if they witness the father kicking off."

There was nothing he could do about his cryptic style of conversation. He literally had no time to expand. He watched as Brenda's expression changed when he told her that the paperwork would not be completed there and then.

"We are normally given all the information when the children arrive," she complained, too assertively for Wayne's liking. "We don't know anything about their routine," she added. "We don't know if they are allergic to anything."

Of course Brenda was within her rights to complain. This wasn't good practice and, quite ashamed, he averted his eyes to the baby pink carnations stuffed into a large ceramic jug on the spotless work surface. He prayed he could afford another minute or so, and forced himself to sit down at the pine kitchen table. His body language said it all, as he folded his arms whilst deciding on his exit strategy.

He began apologising profusely. After all, it cost him nothing. A technique he had learnt over the years always worked. He promised he would ring them both after he had seen Mr and Mrs Leigh. That was the best he could do. He told Brenda he had only just picked up the case and their safety had been his immediate concern. Being familiar with their day-to-day routine came very low down on his agenda. As far as he was concerned, he told Brenda, braving eye contact with her, the Barnham Hill nursery staff had been the children's carers.

He watched as the twins' key worker opened her mouth to speak, and rudely dismissed her, using a hand gesture. He needed to head off and take her with him.

It was then that another option came to him. Perhaps the boys' nursery worker could stay here with them all, and assist them further. It wouldn't take much in the way of arrangements. She could take a taxi to the nearest train station, and make her way back to Fenton town centre in her own time. But it would probably be a no go.

He had got the feel of Bill, and felt fairly pessimistic that he would approve this expense out of his precious Section 17 annual budget. Just in case, though, Wayne quickly dialled his manager's number. What a surprise, it was turned off! The lazy idiot was probably at the smoking shelter!

There was nothing more he could do. He had delivered the twins safely to their new home and they were together. So something had been achieved already. Sadly though, pandering to their aggressive birth father had to be prioritised above settling two extremely traumatised young children.

He could not delay leaving any longer, and fifteen minutes after they arrived, he and the nursery worker went outside to say their goodbyes to Brandon and Kyle. Thankfully they were so engrossed on the trampoline that they didn't really acknowledge them. It was better that way.

The journey back was straightforward. After he dropped off the nursery worker, he realised there was no time for lunch and, instead, he ran into a newsagent's, purchased two bars of chocolate and ate them in succession.

At 1.45pm, an extremely tense and exhausted Wayne arrived

at the police station. As planned, the two uniformed officers were waiting for him in reception. Confrontational scenes never usually fazed him, but there were limits! He gave them both a brief indication of the aggression issues and finally, at 2 pm. prompt, he stood on Mr and Mrs Leigh's doorstep flanked by them.

An alarmed Mark opened the front door and was obviously disconcerted by what greeted him.

"Not again! You social workers just don't get the message," he said, trying to contain his anger. "And what's this with the police, for fuck's sake?"

"Can we come in? It is highly confidential," Wayne asked calmly. He couldn't believe this. How was he supposed to deal with Mark when a wave of nausea washed over him? It was a combination of tiredness and fear, but thankfully the episode passed as quickly as it had arrived.

"No. Say what you have to say here!" Mark held his own. He added, "The kids aren't here anyway."

This suited Wayne. He had no desire to enter the property after his vivid nightmare. He began talking and calmly advised Leigh that there were concerns about the level of care provided to Kyle and Brandon, that they had been neglected, and that it was important to speak to Saira too.

"Not this rubbish again," Mark interrupted him, clearly irritated. "I've told you lot. The nursery are happy with them."

Wayne was silent whilst thinking of what to say next. His priority right now was to see Saira. She had parental responsibility and was at risk herself of harm. But Mark insisted that his wife was in bed. Trying to sound accommodating, Leigh offered, "I can give her a message when she wakes up!"

But now the children had been placed into local authority care, Wayne was sure they were out of immediate danger. He felt his usual inner strength return and refused to allow Leigh to abuse him any longer. He looked into the dimly-lit narrow hall. It was hard to work out what colours the walls had been painted, it all looked so grubby. Since his visit, only two days previously, the door to the lounge appeared to be hanging off its hinges. His eyes were drawn to an empty pint of milk which lay on its side, the lid off, a few drops of liquid escaping onto the concrete paving slabs. None of this mattered anymore. He reminded himself he was on a mission. He regained his confidence and, keeping eye contact, he demanded to see Saira immediately. In the silence that followed, Wayne made reference to both police officers and calmly stated that they would all enter the property if Mark refused access.

"Saira, get here now!" Mr Leigh now bellowed.

The twins' mother edged her way through the broken door frame. She hadn't been upstairs in bed at all. She must have been listening to the conversation from the lounge. She looked petrified.

Leigh told her: "This freak has just claimed that the level of care provided for the kids is not satisfactory. That we have neglected them." His sneering impersonation of Wayne's nicely-spoken accent was rather good.

Choosing to ignore the attempt at mockery, Wayne intervened again. "Decisions have been taken by our legal team together with the police to remove Kyle and Brandon to a foster placement."

This time the twins' father's jaw dropped open. Wayne then delivered even harder-hitting news.

"There is now a police protection order in place," he announced rather proudly, not caring to explain the context. As far as he was concerned, he was just ticking the boxes. In his usual style, he launched into how Fenton Chidcare Services' legal department would be applying to the courts for an interim care order within the next seven working days.

Just as Wayne had overwhelmed the frightened children, he now bombarded their parents with information. That the final decision of where their children would live would lie with the judge, and that the outcome of the case would not be known for many months, possibly up to a year.

This felt like revenge but it wasn't. Still Wayne felt a certain satisfaction – Leigh deserved to be hit hard with every single word he had to say.

Wayne did, however, have more sympathy for Saira as he watched her pitifully tug on her husband's arm, pleading with him to help get the children back. It was a dreadful situation. But he struggled as to why she appeared to be genuinely surprised by his announcement. Surely they had both known this day would finally arrive.

"Why are they doing this?" Saira spoke to Mark in a low flat tone, obviously traumatised by the years of living in such an abusive relationship.

"I haven't a fucking clue," he responded, adding for effect, "This faggot social worker is telling me a load of bollocks."

The two police officers raised their eyebrows as they glanced across at each other. Still they didn't intervene.

Wayne was disgusted with the homophobic comments but didn't feel this was a good time to challenge Mark. He was used to being verbally abused by clients, and had more critical things to worry about. Focused only on containing Mark's fury, he heard him announce, "I'm going to the nursery now to find out why they allowed my kids to be taken without speaking to me first!"

As he spoke, he yanked Saira's arm away from him and turned to her, hissing, "You bitch, this is your fault for not looking after them whilst I'm out."

He tried to push past them all but both officers blocked his way and grabbed him by the arm. One of them got out his handcuffs in anticipation that they would be necessary. The younger officer spoke out, warning him firmly, "You are not to go to the nursery. The doors are locked and the staff are not prepared to discuss the case with you!"

Wayne added for clarity purposes, "The children are placed some distance away. They will not be returning here. You are banned from the premises."

For a moment, Mark appeared to be more submissive. He even tried to comfort his wife, who had broken down, her hands covering her face. Wayne forced himself to adopt a more kindly tone for Saira's benefit.

"I advise you to instruct a family solicitor to represent your views in court," he told them both. As a goodwill gesture, he tried to be helpful. "You will be legally aided so there will be no cost to yourselves. You need to look in the Yellow Pages."

With that, Mark ordered Saira to get back in the house, and he turned too, slamming the door in their faces aggressively. To

Wayne's relief the meeting was over. He breathed out slowly, gesturing to the police that it was time to leave.

The worst was over, and Wayne was rather proud of what he had achieved in an extremely short time. He vowed to himself then that he would ensure that they would never return. Well, as long as he remained in Fenton Childcare Services, as their allocated social worker. Who knew what a new caseworker would plan for them?

Interrupting his thoughts, Mark ended up having the final word, and Wayne jumped when he heard his client's voice.

"You fucking queer! No one speaks to me like that!" he ranted at the top of his voice from the upstairs bedroom window. Controlling even to the very end, he added for good measure, "What do you call yourself? Warren, William, or whatever?"

Wayne avoided eye contact with the police and looked behind him uncomfortably. Hopefully the neighbours in the cul-de-sac weren't listening.

Leigh continued raising his voice, "What the hell do you know about children? You haven't even got any!"

With that, Wayne increased his pace, desperate to get away from Leigh. These comments were targeted specifically at him and were grossly offensive. He tried hard to shrug them off, but seated in the back of the police car, he felt totally unsupported by the young officers.

It had been an unbearably stressful day, and the tiredness caught up with him. He pictured his single bed in his mother's flat and desperately wanted to be in it. Sadly the day wasn't over, and there was the cumbersome business of the fostering paperwork to complete back at the office.

As he was driven the short journey back to the police station to pick up his car, he stared out of the window, reflecting on how the day had gone. Leigh had been correct in one observation: he had no real understanding of how to relate to children. And with this thought, he wondered, not for the first time, whether he was indeed suited to social work.

Five

A Year on: 9th July 2004

With the protracted court proceedings going on for the course of a full year, this only meant more uncertainty for Kyle and Brandon. At last, though, the date for the final hearing loomed. Court work always appealed to Wayne. Here he could really show his expertise. He enjoyed, too, the whole experience of mixing with people of considerable prestige. Barristers and solicitors all mingled in the ground-floor café and he loved rubbing shoulders with them. There was always the possibility, he thought, of making real social connections with one or two of them. The reality was that this rarely happened, but the fact that it ever happened at all was a real incentive.

Wayne, too, was very efficient in his preparations of the relevant reports pertaining to typical cases such as the Leighs. There was really very little to it. There was no statistical data to research. It was just about presenting the hard facts. It also helped that he saw himself as skilled when being cross-examined in the witness box. He loved the opportunity to wear his only suit. In fact, he loved the whole sense of drama that inevitably was present in a court of law where the expert facts and arguments were perfectly shaped to suit their case.

On a great number of occasions, he had been instrumental in swinging cases in his favour because of his rigorous knowledge of the case in question. Within each family, of course, each dynamic was unique. However, the different types of child abuse underpinning each case were, by nature, terribly similar. But neglect cases were often the hardest to deal with. The facts were ambiguous and, with good legal representation, could be disputed.

The Leigh case was a mix of domestic violence and neglect issues. This didn't faze him. However, the prospect of dealing with such an abusive character in court was quite daunting.

There were further problems. It had been impossible to try and locate Saira's estranged family as she had refused to co-operate in this regard. Wayne had no idea where her home town was and assumed that Saira had been gaslighted by Leigh. By rights, he was entitled to overrule her privacy in this regard, but contacting mosques would have been a mammoth task and, he had already spread himself too thinly.

As regards Mr Leigh's extended family, Wayne assumed that they would not be suitable as potential kinship carers. He had been brought up in the care system so that was the end of that. He wasn't going to spend any more time analysing the case. It was simply not necessary. His opinion was that this case was as clear-cut as it could get. An adoption verdict would be entirely in Kyle and Brandon's best interests. He had looked forward to Friday July 9th and had kept the day clear in his diary for over three months now.

It was a relief, though, to have received notification from his solicitor that the case had been listed for only one day. The judge had presided over all the previous hearings. Wayne was persuaded that the final hearing would be totally straightforward and all would be settled once and for all. He had had to wait a whole year for this day and he deemed that totally unnecessary. But Mr Leigh had been effective in dragging the whole thing out. There was no need to call expert witnesses, for example. As always, it was morally wrong to waste taxpayers' money on allocating more hours than was required.

In anticipation of a satisfactory outcome, Wayne had a bottle of Lambrusco chilling in the fridge. As the months had progressed, he had stopped feeling so intimidated by his client. Still, it wouldn't be pleasant to be cross-examined by him. He felt pleased that his involvement would be coming to an end, and that would be a cause for celebration in itself. Even Wayne's mother knew all about Leigh's narcissistic personality. She had shown a keen interest in how the case had been developing.

As he parked in the court car park, he went over the issues again in his mind. This was not just about neglect of the children's basic needs. Emotional abuse of the children and domestic violence towards Saira had been evidenced many times over. Surely the judge would just be going through the motions.

The twins were five years old now and Wayne had got to know them better over the course of the year. He had visited them regularly, and had noted how secure they had become with their carers. He had arranged for them to see a play therapist, and they were making progress. The key issue was that they missed their mother desperately. How could he answer their questions as to whether they would ever be returning to their old home, when the court hadn't made a decision yet? What did five-year-old children understand about final judgements and assessments that dragged on for a year? Kyle and Brandon urgently needed to know what would be happening to them.

Privately, he was looking forward to telling the children that they would always be safe from their father. It would surely be a good outcome for them, and then the search could really begin in earnest to find them a forever family. Perhaps it would be a single parent, or a family that already had children placed with them. But either way, it would be permanent.

He waited in the court café for his local authority solicitor to arrive. The judge's final verdict, he assumed, would certainly be one that favoured adoption. His legal representative would strongly object to the possibility of a formal appeal against the inevitable judgement. After all, there were no fresh grounds to justify this process. He could see no reason why Mr Leigh could ever expect that his children could be reunited with him. He had even taken precautions to deal with any outburst of rage on Leigh's part when the verdict was read out. Experienced unfortunately in handling similar situations over the years, he had requested that security staff have their surveillance cameras trained on Courtroom 37 and the surrounding corridors.

The proceedings began promptly at 9.30am. As in all but one of the previous hearings, Saira's absence was noted. As the allocated social worker, it was usual that Wayne was called first to give evidence. Standing tall in the witness box, he avoided eye contact with Mr Leigh. As trained, he directed all his responses towards the judge.

Entirely focused, he answered in detail the questions put to him. He told the court the twins had made good progress in their placement and had settled comfortably at their new school. He reported, too, how they were close to their foster carers' grandchildren. He tended to slip into social work jargon and was not concerned whether Mr Leigh understood or not.

Then it was Mr Leigh's turn to cross-examine Wayne. Wearing a black tracksuit instead of his usual grey one, he began firing questions. It was an unusual, unorthodox situation. When the children had been removed from their parents' care, Mr Leigh had instructed a solicitor. But continuing on his path of self-destruction, he had quickly dismissed him as incompetent. In fact, he hired and fired time and time again.

In the absence of counsel, Mr Leigh began studying family case law at the city library. Once he established the facts, he took an interest in reading other case studies. He didn't understand some of the content, but he could get the gist of it. It gave him a sense of direction he had never experienced before. He made meticulous notes, and before long became obsessed with making bizarre complaints to the local law society.

Fenton wasn't a large town. It was here that Mr Leigh set a unique precedent. It only took a matter of weeks before word got out and all the local childcare solicitors took a stand, and refused to represent him in the case he was fighting against Fenton Childcare Services. Mr Leigh became one of the few clients eligible for legal aid to represent himself!

Wayne had clearly underestimated Mr Leigh's intellect. The fact that he had probably not continued into further education was irrelevant. His tireless research had seemingly paid off. He hurtled question after question at Wayne, until eventually he began to tie Wayne in knots. He succeeded in opening up gaping flaws in his social work practice. In the end, Wayne had no choice but to admit that he had not encouraged the twins to see their parents during the period that they had been in the care system.

But to be fair to Wayne, he had good reason for not promoting the contact. After Kyle and Brandon had been removed from their parents' care, he had gone to the trouble of arranging a one-hour long supervised contact. But sadly Saira had failed to attend. The interaction between the father and his sons had not gone well. Mr Leigh at one point had whispered something into Kyle's ear and made him cry. Then there was an altercation in which one of the supervisory officers correctly refused to allow Kyle's father to take him to the toilet alone. The staff had tried to speak calmly to him, but Leigh's over-reaction proved to be a negative force on both boys.

There were reports from the boys' foster carers, that they had returned from this particular contact session inconsolable. As well as witnessing the altercation, they had expected to see their mother and that night had cried themselves to sleep. Furthermore, over the period of that entire year, they consistently said to their guardian ad litem, to Wayne and to their foster carers, that they were frightened of seeing their father.

The judge listened intently as Wayne explained that he had wanted the boys to see their mother. But there were always difficulties in contacting her. Wayne spoke calmly and clearly, as he informed the presiding judge that he had received verbal and physical threats from Leigh. He had made the decision that it was not safe to go to the family home any longer. To add to his argument, he expanded, announcing that none of his colleagues were prepared to accompany him either.

As regards to Saira, Wayne explained to the court that as she did not possess her own mobile phone, his only viable choice of communication had been to write to her, requesting that she call into the offices or reverse the charges on a pay phone. Nothing came of this plea.

Wayne had duly made some attempts to write to Saira over the past year. He had also sent her the minutes of the Looked After Children reviews in order that she would read exactly how the boys were progressing in their new school and foster placement.

He had not received a single response. He hadn't left the situation to drift exactly, but had to admit that he didn't know whether she had received any of the correspondence.

Unexpectedly he found himself squirming in the witness box. He couldn't own up that he had been too busy balancing his other cases to keep trying to reach out to Saira. The truth was more simple: to set up contact with her and the children would have been a nightmare to arrange. Furthermore, he had worried she would let them down. With this scenario in mind, it was easier just to leave it alone.

Seizing this opportunity, Mr Leigh called into question the whole nature of Wayne's practice. It was, Wayne contemplated morosely, Leigh's finest hour! He had expected that the judge would intervene, but, instead, he watched the cloaked bespectacled gentleman who he guessed was in his early sixties simply lean forward and stare at Wayne intently. Experienced at giving evidence, Wayne correctly interpreted the judge's body language to mean that this aspect of the case was highly relevant.

"My wife," said Mr Leigh, "doesn't go out much. She hasn't the confidence to get the bus to the contact centre on her own."

Wayne nodded impotently, choosing to stare at the clock on the back wall. Anything other than to look at his vile client.

"You should have picked her up yourself," continued Leigh.

This was ridiculous, thought Wayne. "I hold a full caseload," he said politely. "I just don't have the time."

But Leigh appeared to have a response for every possible scenario.

"Then you should have arranged for a family support officer to take Saira. That's your job, you lazy weirdo!" He then spoke to the judge directly, telling him that it was unfair that the children had been allocated such a useless social worker. That he had written a formal complaint demanding a new social worker but this request had been ignored.

It suddenly occurred to Wayne that perhaps Leigh had been consulting with other parents in the Barnham Estate, who had also experienced their children being taken from their care. The twins' father seemed to know too much. After an hour in the witness box,

Wayne was worn down. Without realising it, was nodding his head in agreement.

That unfortunate act of surrender opened the flood gates for more criticism.

"You shouldn't have suspended the contact sessions with me, should you?" Leigh barked at him.

Wayne managed a sip of water and gathered his strength. This matter was something he felt totally secure on. From the previous court hearings, he recalled that his legal team had hammered home the point that Mr Leigh had refused to see his children if the visit had to be supervised. But this crucial fact now seemed to become lost, owing to his client's measured tone.

The judge's body language itself, as he sat back nonchalantly in his chair, did not encourage Wayne, who was now perspiring. He gave himself a pep talk. He couldn't be bullied by him, like the other social workers before him. Facing the judge, he cleared his throat and spoke clearly. "I am Kyle and Brandon's social worker, I am not their parents' social worker," he announced, adding, "These young boys feared seeing their father!"

Giving evidence was not going as Wayne had hoped it would. The pressure was mounting as now it was the turn of the guardian ad litem's solicitor to question him. He had anticipated there would be difficulties giving evidence about incidents that had taken place prior to his appointment at Fenton Childcare Services, and he had been right to worry. The guardian's manner was curt as she challenged him as to why, in four years, no action had been taken to safeguard Kyle and Brandon. "I am astounded," she said, "that the children were removed from the At Risk Register on several occasions."

There was nothing Wayne could say, so he remained silent and stared down at his hands. He was trapped. What he was facing had been predictable from the moment he had read the case. He had ended up being held accountable for Area Team Three's historic incompetence. But what Leigh hurled at him were personal insults and he was now concerned that he would lose his reputation as an experienced and competent locum. He felt it harsh that the judge hadn't intervened at this point.

It should have been Bill who took the flak for this gross error of judgement spanning four years. He reminded himself that he had asked him to attend court with him, but this request had been refused. He recalled how, with his manager's usual insincerity, he had told him, "You will be fine!" He even remembered how Bill had showed him out of his office, keen, as usual, not to delay his cigarette break!

Wayne didn't feel particularly fine, as, predictably, he was asked to expand upon certain dates of when referrals were received by his team since the boys had been born. Of course, he could manage to some degree as he had carefully crafted the chronology himself. But more of the detail was lost in a miasma of confusion. He was only as good as the scant notes at his disposal.

As he continued to give evidence under oath, he skipped through endless repetitive scrawl by a variety of social workers, all of whom struggled to manage the Leigh case. He skimmed, too, through the multiple closing summaries. The less said about them, the better, he felt. The boys would have every right to sue Fenton Local Authority for damages when they were older!

Wayne dreaded the next question which would surely be to ask how many times the case had been open and closed. As the cross-examining continued, this issue became blatantly apparent. The barrister took off her rimless eyeglasses for maximum effect. She cleared her voice.

"You have made it clear that all your colleagues felt intimidated by Mr Leigh," she said. "Imagine, then, how his own children felt!" There was utter silence in the court room as she continued. "Yet instead of recognising their fears, and taking steps to protect them, Fenton District Area Team Three chose to close the case." She studied the judge's surprised reaction and added for extra measure, "This is beyond incomprehensible!"

Again, Wayne found himself with nothing he could respond with. She continued in what he considered to be a self-righteous fashion. "These vulnerable children were neglected for years. They were let down by people they should have been able to trust ... a flawed system ..."

As she spoke, Wayne watched Mr Leigh nervously. He removed

his tracksuit top and put it carefully on the seat next to him. He then folded his arms; his sharp features were relaxed, even smug. He was clearly enjoying watching the charade. Wayne, on the other hand, was struggling to respond to the questions put to him. Not one legal representative praised his swift actions the moment he had been allocated the case. As per usual, he was blamed repeatedly for the many failings of his colleagues.

There was more. The issue of engaging Saira was brought up again. He was now criticised for not making enough effort with her. Since the boys had been removed from her care, a year earlier, he had only seen her on one occasion. In September 2003, the boys' mother had attended court with her husband. She looked delicate and vulnerable. Furthermore, she looked like she had lost more weight, her plain white T-shirt billowing over her slight frame.

As ever with a razor-sharp memory, he recalled the details plainly. He had been pleased to see Saira and had demanded to talk to her without Mr Leigh present. He then asked that the children's guardian ad litem join them. The court security staff had guarded the interview room. It had been an opportunity to try and help her realise that she would never get the children back unless she separated from her husband. But it had proved fruitless. As soon as she had left the room, she could be overheard relaying everything to him.

His cross-examination finally over, he stepped down and took his seat behind his solicitor. It had been a heavy hour and a half in the witness box and he felt emotionally exhausted. But the day was far from over and he had every reason to be apprehensive as Mr Leigh was now called to give evidence. Swearing on the bible wouldn't mean anything to him. But he had given his lawyer plenty of material to throw at him. Key to this case, after all, was the safety of the children.

Wayne wrote on his notepad, and tore the sheet off, folding it carefully several times. He reached in front of him and tapped his solicitor on the shoulder. He watched as she put on her glasses to read his hastily written scribble. "Ask about the storing of food in their pockets!"

The young solicitor swiftly turned her back on the judge and mouthed: "Don't worry."

She was spot on. Mr Leigh's performance on the witness stand was almost farcical. His view on how to rear children came from Dickensian times. When asked to explain the claims that he had neglected to care for the boys properly, he defended himself by saying he brought them up to be independent!

Interestingly, Mr Leigh raised his voice several times whilst giving evidence, but the judge raised no objection to this. He seemed only too prepared to accommodate him. His refusal, too, to answer pertinent questions was not challenged. His steady complaints vacillated between feeling victimised by the social workers "who show up unannounced, just as I'm about to go food shopping," and protesting directly against Wayne: "That lazy freak has ruined all our lives, especially my children's." These were surprisingly tolerated. Wayne squirmed in his seat. He had been before more robust judges in his career! He could have at least attempted to rein him in.

After lunch, the children's guardian ad litem was cross-examined by Mr Leigh, who accused her of collaborating with Wayne. Fortunately, she was too skilled at giving evidence to falter. She spoke highly of how the children were now progressing, expressing her satisfaction particularly at how well they had settled into their foster placement. Without being asked, she volunteered her opinion that the only future for Kyle and Brandon would be adoption.

Avoiding Mr Leigh's cold stares, she spoke directly to the judge. "The boys' parents have not engaged with childcare services in any meaningful way." She expressed her disappointment, however, that the children had not been removed earlier.

With all key aspects of the case exhausted, the judge adjourned the proceedings for an hour. He needed time to write up his findings and prepare his judgement. They all stood up, and once he had left the room, they trooped out, gathering in the corridor. Wayne felt secure, surrounded by his legal team, and he glanced at Mr Leigh, who sat alone at some distance to them.

He recalled at that moment, the very first court hearing involving Kyle and Brandon. It was almost a year to the day when he had removed the children from their parents' care. He had faced

Leigh several days later, and had predicted an unpleasant scene. Even he had been surprised by the abusive tirade towards him. Mr Leigh had humiliated himself more than him, though, when he had gestured towards anyone within earshot, "Look at that bastard social worker over there! Needs to shut his mouth. I'm going to get him struck off!" His solicitor at the time had tried to calm him down, but to no avail.

A year on, the court proceedings and being denied seeing his children had clearly taken its toll. Leigh looked exhausted and broken. Slumped in a chair, his tracksuit jacket in his hands, he didn't move or utter a word this time.

It was a relief to be called back into the courtroom only forty-five minutes into the break. There was silence as the judge entered the room and sat down. In his judgement he showed no sympathy for Mr Leigh. He did, however, thank him for attending court and his final words were saved for him. "You and Saira must move on with your lives."

In his summary of the case, the judge expressed his regret that Kyle and Brandon had been subjected to so much abuse in their lives until they were brought under the protection of the court. Predictably, he stated that social work standards in Area Team Three had consistently failed them and that he would be writing a detailed critical report of his findings. This would then be submitted with urgency to the director of Fenton Childcare Services.

Though he did not feel personally to blame for this damaging situation, Wayne was made to feel quite uncomfortable. However this didn't last long, as within minutes, he experienced an immense sense of release. The judge had finally delivered the long-awaited verdict: "Adoption. Placement Order."

From the moment that Wayne had created the chronology on the very sad start to the boys' life, he had only had one mission for them. It had been a long year of uncertainty for Kyle and Brandon. He knew that his role was not over, of course. Babies and toddlers were more in demand with adopters. Girls were more popular than boys. A sibling group was always more complex to place. But he would continue to do his best for them. There were no winners really, and he was conscious of the pain Saira would continue to suffer at the hands of Leigh, who had ruined her chance of bringing up her much loved children.

The hearing finished and the judge bowed slightly and left the room. Wayne smiled as he shook hands with his solicitor. He would normally say goodbye to the other legal representatives, as well as the guardian, but in this case he chose not to. In the case of the latter he had felt insulted that she had blamed him for issues that she knew full well were beyond his remit.

Overall, Wayne felt a sense of achievement. With his help, Kyle and Brandon could move on and leave the care system for ever. He felt quite elated. His sense of satisfaction, however, was suddenly spoiled by a line of abuse from Mr Leigh who had been waiting for him in the corridor.

"Oy, you fucking child-grabbing faggot," he shouted at Wayne, within earshot of several bystanders and court ushers. "You haven't heard the end of this!"

Six

Monday 13th July 2004, 11am
Washton Lane District Adoption Services

It was impossible for Wayne to ignore the bold sign that was sellotaped onto the entrance hall wall. What a welcome! It seemed the current building issues were a recurrence of previous problems. The flea infestation specialists were due back for a third treatment. And no one should eat at their desks due to the ongoing vermin issue. Repulsed, he tried to console himself that he was only visiting.

As a precaution, he decided to take the stairs to floor five just in case the dodgy lift broke again. He was feeling optimistic, but as always, impatient to get on with the job. He thrived on the fast pace of child protection work, and wasn't suited at all to the family finding work. He struggled with many aspects of it. He failed to understand, for example, why the twelve or so panel members needed to know every single detail of a prospective adopter's life. It was an invasion of their privacy and made the whole process laborious in the extreme.

He had skimmed many an adoption assessment over the years. If an applicant decided to drop out of a university course, or an injury stopped him or her from playing a particular sport, it felt irrelevant to him. He just wasn't interested enough in people to read such detail.

Of course, he appreciated that experiences would shape the way they dealt with children's disappointments. But in his opinion, all the potential adopters would be more than capable of encouraging any child to reach their potential. Why else would they undertake training and agree to open their hearts to a stranger? To share such intimate details about their fertility issues, for instance.

Wayne was purely focused on improving children's lives. He tended to see anything at all that diverted this process as deeply frustrating. Children would often languish in the care system waiting for new adopters to be approved and this fact made him feel very sad.

It was over the top, he felt, that adoption social workers were forced to spend six months or more interviewing prospective candidates. It wasn't so much an interview, it was more an interrogation. To the point, for instance, that the applicant would be asked such things as what time they woke up at weekends. To Wayne, all this banal information was surplus to requirements. So what if a candidate enjoyed a lie in? Most applicants had suffered years of horrendous disappointment. He was sure they would only be too glad to get up early once placed with a child. They were perfectly entitled to make the most of their freedom until then.

It felt like social workers were searching desperately for problems when there weren't any. They were looking for the perfect parent. And guess what? They didn't exist. The slightest negative factor would be magnified into a big issue. If an applicant appeared slightly set in their ways, for instance, the assessor may assume that he or she would struggle to adapt to the needs of a small child.

It could work the other way too. The protocol had changed in recent years and now applicants were actively encouraged to write large sections of the assessment themselves. They would naturally choose their close friends to provide glowing references. Everyone now presented as flawless with wonderful support networks. And in the case of couples, they seemed to be part of such a strong partnership that only served to thrive under such stress and uncertainty. He wasn't naïve. What a load of drivel! He wished he could believe it, but he was a realist.

The judgemental comments banded about by social workers

irritated Wayne even more. A colleague may comment that the house was too untidy. Or it would be too clean. Or a prospective adopter devoured too many novels in the evenings. Questions would be predictably raised about how this applicant intended to make time to bring up a child. It wasn't as if social workers were so perfect. He needed to look no further than his friend and colleague David as an example. For one reason or another, his two young children hadn't seen him for weeks.

Wayne truly hoped though that he would find what Kyle and Brandon needed. Stability, nurturing, love and positive reinforcement of their dual heritage background. His involvement with them had begun almost a year ago, and, in that time, he had met them some dozen times whilst they were living with Ian and Brenda, their foster carers. He had grown very fond of the children. It had been a heart-breaking time for them, as they constantly enquired as to what would happen to them. Would they have to go back to their home? They were certainly too young to have to live with so much unknown, and it saddened him that he wasn't able to comfort them with the news they wanted. He wished he could tell them that they would never return to their father's care, but until the court matter had been concluded, some four days ago, no permanent decision could be made.

The bulging files relating to Kyle and Brandon's story posed the familiar challenge to any adopter of older children. It may well be that the department would have to fund a private agency fee should there be no suitable candidates. There was never any bartering about this payment, as even at over twenty thousand pounds, it would be cheaper than keeping any child in a foster placement for the rest of their childhood. But no amount of money thrown at this problem would be able to get them an absolute cultural match.

Unfortunately for Wayne, he made his entrance into the adoption team offices as the weekly team meeting had begun. As he waited for the discourteous secretary to acknowledge him, he looked around him. He didn't know whether to be pleased or worried to see the strategically-placed poison boxes in every corner. There would be no one to assist him for an hour or so, he was curtly advised. There was no offer of a beverage either.

Guiding him to an empty desk, the secretary placed the paperwork in front of him and left him to it.

"What good is this?" he muttered to himself, once she was out of earshot. He was a practical man in many senses, and noticed instantly that there was no index on the front page. He hadn't even begun his search, and was frustrated already at the thought of trawling through the reams of paper. He estimated that there were at least eighteen approved adopters, practically every excruciating detail of their entire lives, alphabetised, hole-punched and rammed into two overstuffed lever-arch files.

He turned the pages impatiently, coming to the fast conclusion that the adopters with surnames beginning with A probably had the best chance of being matched. This was hopeless. He needed guidance and he wished he had checked first whether staff would be free to assist him before he had set off.

He hoped that he could count on Belinda Taylor to help him. He had called her after leaving court on Friday afternoon, and gave her a brief update on what he was looking for. The two colleagues' paths had crossed whilst working in a neighbouring authority and Belinda was a seasoned agency worker too. Now she had done well to achieve the position of locum team leader at Washton Lane Adoption Team.

Excitedly he had broken the news that the judge had granted permission to place Brandon and Kyle for adoption. But he could read into Belinda's silence in response to the information that these were older children. He knew this factor alone would make it hard for them to be placed, but this didn't curtail his enthusiasm. He offered to email the relevant information she required to her that weekend, so there would be no delay.

It wasn't his fault that he had been expected in the offices the day before, and hadn't had time to explain his absence. Now he was disappointed that Belinda hadn't arranged for some assessments to be left to one side for him to peruse. As predicted, the majority of the adopters were approved only to adopt one child, preferably under six months old. The children he was looking for were already of school age.

A plan formulated in his mind. He would look at the photographs of the potential adopters first. Whoever had kind-looking eyes would be in with a chance. He would then check whether they were approved for a sibling group. But, after looking at the first six or seven glossy photos, Wayne considered that they all had warm eyes, matched with genuine looking smiles. They all seemed on the surface to be good people.

He didn't really want to come back here if he could avoid it. He picked up the second lever-arch file and started to work backwards. It wasn't fair on the adopters with surnames that started at the end of the alphabet to miss out on being selected. This act was typical of Wayne, who prided himself on having a strong moral code of practice.

Wayne knew that he needed to search for an individual or a couple with experience of children. In any event, he had expected that Belinda would have at least sifted out approved adopters for a sibling group. There were many positives. The boys had made significant progress in the year they had lived with their foster carers, and were relatively settled.

Suddenly, he stopped turning the pages. He was drawn to an attractive well-dressed man who looked like he was in his early thirties. He scoured the page for crucial information. Gary Yates was thirty-four years old. He was approved to adopt one child, between the ages of four and six years old. He noted too that the adoption panel had approved him only four weeks ago, at the beginning of June. Which meant that his personal data was bang up to date!

He quickly looked around him and glanced at the time. It was just 11.15am. No one had entered the room, but he would have to keep an eye out. The team meeting could finish early. He knew the rules well. The family placement team took confidentiality seriously and no files were allowed to be removed from the office. He had to act swiftly. There would be questions raised if he was observed reading files that were irrelevant to his caseload.

Rummaging in his soft leather bag, Wayne lifted out his navy-blue work desk diary. On the back page, he wrote clearly. He then scribbled it out. If it got into the wrong hands, he would be in trouble. He didn't have long. He grabbed a piece of paper from the photocopier and carefully copied out Gary's name, address, and phone number.

The secretary was positioned at the far end of this large open-plan room. He glanced across at her but noted that she was absorbed in typing fiercely. He was safe, and it took him just under an hour to absorb the 25,000 words on Gary Yates' life to date.

In contrast to the dull and protracted assessments he hadn't found the energy to even skim, Wayne fully appreciated the lengthy, nicely-crafted report on Gary. He felt a little guilty. It was akin to spying on him. By now, he felt like he knew him. Whilst Gary lived just a couple of miles out from the town centre, he owned a large hairdressing salon in the heart of the shopping area.

He closed the file and carefully ran his right hand across his head. He wasn't due a haircut, so he would have to wait. He hoped Gary hadn't met anyone since the adoption assessment had been concluded. Wayne prided himself on thinking outside of the box. It wouldn't be too difficult to google "Gary Yates Hairdressers".

His thoughts on this new man, he allowed himself to wonder how his day was going. He imagined him chatting easily with his regular clients, remembering the names of their partners, asking them about their holiday destinations. Gary, he knew for sure, would be skilled at making his clients feel good about themselves. In that sense, they would have so much in common. But he didn't want to rush in. He preferred to plan his strategy: how best to meet him. He turned the pages over and began reading another assessment, but found it near impossible to concentrate.

Eventually, Belinda broke the silence as she bounded into the room. He hadn't seen her for a while and was shocked to see that she was now sporting a severe haircut. She hadn't bothered to remove the remnants of red dye at the top of her forehead and she was dressed in some sort of heavy maternity smock that didn't become her. A bedraggled-looking man and five other equally dowdy-looking social workers trailed in after her, sitting down quietly at their desks. There certainly wasn't any of the light-hearted energetic banter that his team so enjoyed.

A sickly smell of cheap body spray wafted across as Belinda now towered over him.

"I thought you were coming in yesterday, and I did tell you about our meeting this morning," she said, not attempting to hide her annoyance. She wasn't his line manager and had no right to speak to him in that tone but Wayne didn't dare answer her back. In this job he was used to people turning on him and generally speaking to him like shit. Instead, he stole a glance at his bag, placed now at his feet. He was reassured that the side pocket was zipped up securely. Gary Yates' details were safely tucked in there. He focused on the matter in hand – he needed Belinda to help him. He wanted out of this infested depressing tower block as soon as possible.

"I have a strong couple who are approved for two siblings," she said rather passively. "I've pulled their files from the rest and have it in my office for you to have a read." She then softened as she told him that she had tried to locate a cultural match but it had been impossible. She told him that she had met Maxine and Tom at the formal panel approval meeting the week before. They were a white couple, but this was the reality. She nodded at him, as if to say that would be the end of the conversation in that regard.

He couldn't get an ethnic perfect match, he knew this. But still this was good news, he considered optimistically, as he followed Belinda into her office and waited for her to locate what he needed to proceed. Her large desk was a mess with files stacked everywhere. The obligatory dirty mugs were most unappealing. He spotted a banana that had seen better days and recalled the sign about the flea infestation. How could she eat in here?

Belinda located what she needed and handed over the wad of papers to Wayne. Unashamedly, he instantly turned the pages to locate the glossy photograph. He absorbed the image of Maxine and Tom, a smiling tanned couple who looked like they were in their mid-thirties, sitting on a Cotswold stone wall, two golden Labradors by their sides. And indeed they were approved for school-age children. Wayne warmed to the couple instantly. He scanned some more details. They worked on a farm owned by Maxine's parents, and their references created a picture of a relaxed couple. It talked about how they saw the best in people. Not dissimilar to all the other adoption write-ups, Wayne reflected, but this particular assessment sounded perfect.

For a start, the prospective adopters lived at least twenty miles away from Brandon and Kyle's birth family. This rural life would be idyllic for the lively twins. He turned back the pages to study the photograph of them again. The picture had most probably been taken at the farm, and Wayne wondered whether they had built the stone wall themselves! He looked up briefly, truly excited at the prospect of discussing them with Belinda. Shocked, he observed she was absorbed in circling job adverts in that week's edition of *Community Care* magazine. He didn't want to disturb her!

Despite being diverted by Gary temporarily that morning, he generally took his work seriously. He had already had the misfortune of becoming involved with a traumatic adoption breakdown some years previously. He had blamed himself. After all, he had chosen the individual. The innocent toddler had spent less than two weeks in her new home before Wayne had been instructed to pick her up immediately. Bearing this in mind, he had come to the conclusion that glowing references meant absolutely nothing.

But Belinda now refocused on the matter in hand, and turned her attention to Wayne again. She explained that the link worker for Maxine and Tom was off sick, so she would get her duty worker to contact them and arrange for Wayne to visit them over the next few days.

This just wasn't good enough. The familiar wave of anxiety hit him in the stomach. He had learnt many years earlier that social workers saying they would do something and actually doing it were two very different things. It wasn't that they were intentionally negligent. It was just that something more urgent always seemed to take priority.

It was a well-known fact that newly-approved adopters could be grabbed the moment they came out of the panel meeting room. He needed to meet Tom and Maxine and see for himself whether it would be a good match. To discover they were approved for school-age sibling groups was rare. To read that they lived and worked on the family farm was too good to be true. He had to act now, and hoped he had made himself clear that this was urgent. He repeated his concerns for good measure.

"Just leave it with me. I will get someone to call soon," Belinda responded, her tone firm and detached.

This was beyond ridiculous. Here he was, moments away from securing a forever family for Brandon and Kyle. All Belinda had to do was pick up the phone that sat inches away from her. He would do the rest. He felt himself perspiring. How could a team leader of an adoption team treat this as a nine to five job? She was insistent on delegating a task which would take all of three minutes. All she had to do was set up a meeting. Or hand the phone to him.

This was all about control and the power of becoming team leader had clearly gone to her head. Maxine and Tom's panel-approval was now out there. Every local authority adoption team within a forty-mile radius had been faxed their details. He wasn't the only social worker to have a hard-to-place sibling group on his caseload. Experience told him that he needed to act extremely quickly.

He had a responsibility to these children, his clients. He cared deeply for their welfare. The twins had been through enough in their short lives. It was a shame that Belinda Taylor was too busy securing her next locum placement to give a damn!

Belinda was nothing to him and he was not going to let her get away with her blasé behaviour. However, it was clear to him that the meeting was over, and he had little choice but to smile falsely at her when she told him to close the door behind him.

Trying to fight back, he decided to give her an hour before pinging an email across to her. He would mark it urgent in the header. The wording would be polite but he would ask for an immediate response. This felt like bullying. Belinda, like Bill, were miserable excuses for managers. He had met enough of them in his time. Just inadequate social workers with no management training. He knew full well that someone else may have already bagged Maxine and Tom whilst she was only focused on circling job vacancies.

And what if Belinda didn't reply? He needed a plan. He would have to turn to Bill and ask him to email her on his behalf. But this wasn't Bill's style. The captain of delegation, he would probably advise him that it would make no difference, and that the protocol was that social workers should arrange the visits between themselves. He didn't usually run to Bill, but as he was so close to permanency for the boys, he could not allow Belinda to ruin it. He would stand over Bill and make him do it. It was easier to bully his own manager.

With this plan of action in place, he tried to stop panicking and consciously made an effort to think more positively. He visualised the short but significant adoption celebration service in the family courtroom. The smiling usher taking photographs of them all. Brandon and Kyle dressed smartly in suits, standing proudly on each side of the smiling judge. Maxine and Tom and their respective parents looking ecstatic.

After the hearing, Maxine and Tom would ask him to walk with them all to the car park. There they would ply him with gifts. Perhaps an expensive bottle of red wine or Belgian chocolates. He knew he wasn't permitted to accept vouchers, but it would be rude not to. Most meaningful, though, were the thank you cards. The carefully chosen words that made him feel he had made a difference. He cherished them.

He thought back to when he had first come across Kyle and Brandon's file, a year before. The scraps of paper dropping out of the file. The drip drip. The unacceptable years of emotional neglect. But he had managed to save them and it would be a fine ending. This was why he loved this godforsaken job. To leave his mark on this world. For moments like these.

Seven

Tuesday 13th July 2004

The positive energy soon dissipated; after all, Wayne was a realist. Just four days after the court case was concluded, he stormed out of Washton Lane District offices, fuming. It had been such a slow and traumatic year for the twins, but now this hard-faced, so-called "childcare professional" was actively ruining their hopes of becoming adopted quickly. Belinda, like so many others he had come across, was an absolute disgrace to the profession.

He knew just how vital it was to get out to Maxine and Tom's home before any other social workers in the borough got their hands on what he deemed to be a perfect assessment. He was only as good as his colleagues involved in the matching process and that lethargic adoption team manager was holding him back from achieving what his young charges desperately deserved. They were screaming out for security. To know what would happen to them.

Aggravated, he duly completed his mileage form before starting the engine. He swore repeatedly to himself as he drove out of the car park. Absentmindedly, he reached across to the glove compartment where he knew the packet of chewing gum was located. He needed to relax somehow. He switched on the radio but quickly found that the dated pop songs from the 1980s grated on his nerves. He couldn't stand the gibbering of the overly enthusiastic DJs. Even the Classic wavelength made little impact on his anxious mood.

Opting for silence, he attempted to think of other things, but Gary Yates' photograph lingered still. He knew it was wrong to try and see him, given that he was a potential adopter and it wasn't the first time he had taken advantage of his position and read personal files purely for interest.

Back in his office, he flung his briefcase on his chair and noted that a couple of items of post had arrived for him. All this could wait though, as he targeted his rather fine-looking colleague and friend David Lindley, for advice about how to go about connecting with Gary. He had become close to him over the past year, and wheeled his office chair across to where his colleague was absorbed in eating a tuna sandwich. The fishy smell permeated the area around his desk and in true Wayne style he instructed him to get a move on and finish his lunch. He was keen to relay what had happened in the Washton Lane offices and needed a diversion from dealing with Belinda, if only for a few minutes.

He pushed a spare chair to be nearer David and leant forward whilst launching into how he had found the details of what he hoped would be his potential new lover whilst searching for adopters for Kyle and Brandon. He pointed to his leather briefcase proudly and grinned as he told his trusted colleague that he had recorded Gary's private details and that he knew his workplace in the heart of Fenton town centre.

"I'm going to book an appointment," Wayne announced in his usual dramatic style. "I need a strategy. It's a big salon. I want to ask specifically for him, but would that sound obvious?"

David until now had said nothing. He prided himself on his good table manners and didn't talk with his mouth full. He could wait no longer though and covered his mouth with his hand as he blurted, "Are you totally mad?"

"Lower your voice, will you!" Wayne hissed, rather taken aback.

Over the course of the past year, the two men had become firm friends. Both lonely, they tended to see each other frequently outside work. But now David's tone was curt. Wayne wasn't impressed. After all, what double standards David had! Nobody had forced David to sleep with Natasha, the social work student, so he was hardly in a position to judge professionalism in the workplace!

Siobhan moved towards them, sensing the impending gossip. She welcomed any interruption to her never-ending paperwork and listened intently to Wayne, repeating the events of that morning. She was fond of Wayne, and even though she clearly found the story entertaining, she too put a dampener on it.

"Have you heard of client confidentiality?" she preached sarcastically.

David interjected again, advising him that he could end up being struck off the social work register.

It felt like they were ganging up on him as Siobhan declared, "Why can't you meet men through the normal channels?"

"Look, I will be really careful!" Wayne said, refusing to give in to the pressure. "I won't mention I'm a social worker. Come with me, Siobhan," he pleaded as he stared at her hair which added years to her age.

"Absolutely not! I am not having anything to do with this," Siobhan declared assertively. She added, "I think I know that salon. It's too upmarket for me."

Wayne and David smiled knowingly at each other. They knew what the other was thinking. Siobhan was in dire need of a good hairdresser. The long dull brown frizz that framed her face was most unflattering.

Seemingly unaware, she continued lecturing Wayne. She pointed out, "You will make a slip-up and this Gary bloke will wonder why you know so much about him."

"We have warned you!" David butted in again.

Wayne realised that he shouldn't have expected anything else from him. After all, he knew full well the high price that his friend had paid for his one-night stand with Natasha. But with Siobhan he had hoped for a more sympathetic and enthusiastic response.

He walked back to his desk in the full knowledge that he could ask everyone in the building and their answers would be unanimous. He would have to give it more serious thought. Still thinking about the striking image of the man who graced the front page of his adoption assessment, he absentmindedly began opening his post.

"What the hell does he want?" he asked loudly, as he instantly recognised the familiar handwriting style.

Wayne

Give Brandon and Kyle a message.

To be near the school gates at every break.

I know where their foster carers live (87 Wilson Park Road) and have worked out which buses to take. There are four primary schools nearby, so I will just go from one to the other. They probably each have their breaks at the same sort of time, so I can't give a definite day or time.

The judge said I should move on with my life, but I can't do that.

You don't have any kids. You don't know anything. You think that you can get them adopted, but it won't work. I will trace them and get them back home. I mean this. They belong to me. I don't care how many years it may take. I will be phoning every school in the country to find them.

It won't be difficult to locate identical twin boys.

I've heard through my cousin that you lot didn't get his kids adopted. This was over two years ago now. So he has seen his solicitor, and he has applied to the courts to get them back. I've heard that's the law now, but I'm going to the library to check this.

I've told you before. I don't have my visits to my children supervised. So I'm not going to the goodbye visit that you wanted to arrange. Neither is Saira. I will be seeing them next week at school anyway.

I'm cancelling your visit on Friday to pick up photos that you wanted of our family. I'm not helping you with your little "life story" project that you keep banging on about. Brandon and Kyle don't need a book made up about their lives with us. All they need is their mum and dad back.

I will never ever give up my fight to get my children home.

Mr Leigh

Wayne slumped in his chair, covering his face with both hands. Totally out of character, he swore repeatedly under his breath.

The morning had started out so well. How elated he had been to achieve a possible match for Brandon and Kyle so quickly after the court had released them for adoption. The impending meeting with their prospective new forever family was about to be set in motion. Now this plan had been sabotaged indefinitely. Aghast, he forced himself to reread the contents of the letter.

The facts were that the Leighs had lost their parenting rights, but this had not deterred them from continuing to assert them. The court case was over. Why did it feel that it was continuing? Wayne doubted Saira had any idea about the plan, and if she did, would she be going along with it? It had taken Wayne a year, but he realised now that he had underestimated this extremely troubled man. Within those deeply disturbing threats, he had played his trump card.

It was obvious that Mark Leigh had the determination and initiative to track the twins down at some point in the future. Wayne briefly wondered whether it would assist if the police issued a restraining order. He imagined that he would take the risk of being incarcerated if it meant getting to see his children.

But reading between the lines, was this letter really about getting his boys home? Or trying to control their fate? After all, in all those early years, he couldn't even attempt to clean the house when he knew social workers would be knocking on his door to undertake spot checks.

He liked to see the good in human beings and hadn't predicted this scenario at all. Totally absorbed in this crisis, he unconsciously leant forward, placing his head in his hands. Far from being naïve, he knew exactly the significant implications of such threats. He didn't need to ask Belinda what chances the boys now had of being placed with a forever family. He knew full well that very few adopters would be willing to take the chance of coming face to face with such an abusive birth father, either in the school playground, or worse still, banging on their own front door.

He dragged himself up and stormed into Bill's office. But as usual, he found him to be absent in every sense. Only a packet of cigarettes lay open on his tidy desk, his trademark blue lighter missing!

As usual, it would be left to Wayne to work out what to do next. He wondered whether it may be worth going back to see Mr Leigh. To plead with him to let things go. Naturally, he knew he would be made unwelcome, and that any dialogue may have to take place on his front door step. But in his heart he realised this would be yet another fruitless trip. Yet more precious time wasted in that depressing home with its broken chair reminding anyone who entered that damage can never be fixed. A symbol of everything that had gone so terribly wrong.

Over the past twelve months, there had been so much that he had wanted to say. Many a time, he had felt the urge to scream at Leigh. It had been unacceptable and disappointing that Bill hadn't been interested in challenging Leigh's homophobic abuse targeted at him. Furthermore, being accused of being lazy in front of the entire court hadn't been too pleasant an experience either. But as a social worker, it was part of the job. He had to be professional and calm at all times. And that included taking personal insults from irate and disempowered clients.

But reading the letter for a third time, Wayne was close to tears.

Had it not been enough to deny Brandon and Kyle a secure and loving childhood? Their father seemed intent to continue destroying them in any way they could. Wayne questioned whether Leigh was capable of love. If he was, surely he would have attended the supervised contact sessions. He would have engaged with social care staff in a more proactive manner. In the many years he had worked in social care, he had come across many manipulating birth parents but this miserable excuse for a human being was in a league of his own.

One simple contribution Leigh could have made was to provide details of his own family background, to be included in "life story work". This was such an essential element in the adoption process. Creating meaningful "life story books" was Wayne's piece de resistance. It was vital in helping to establish a child's identity. It helped avoid that often desperate search for the truth when the child became an adult. They should be provided with a realistic picture of what had happened to them. The truth often hurts but if the material details were recorded sensitively, they could only gain by knowing the real facts behind their being taken into care.

A memory came back to him of an instance, some years ago. A guardian ad litem had been so impressed with his beautifully presented and detailed work, that she gave it credit in her court statement. The judge noted the comments, and requested that it be brought to the adoption hearing for him to see too. Wayne had been delighted to receive a notification from the Director of Social Services which referred to the commendation from the judge. Furthermore, he had been thrilled to read that this high standard should be used as a model of good practice.

None of these qualities would be called on in this particular case. The twins' father saw himself as a victim, behaving so selfishly and failing to recognise the consequences of his actions. The boys showed several symptoms of trauma and Brandon wet the bed every night. They had already received six months of play therapy and everyone involved had been pleased with the signs of improvement. But now they would need more specialist input. There would be no guarantees that professional help would ever be enough to assist these insecure and vulnerable boys in life.

The present scenario filled Wayne with fear. Mr Leigh was entirely correct. He and Saira would be entitled to make a fresh application to the courts if the local authority failed to place Kyle and Brandon for adoption within two years of the order being made. In that case, the parents' circumstances would be reassessed and Wayne recognised that he would be long gone from Fenton Childcare Services by then. It would take an extremely robust and experienced social worker to deal effectively with such a vicious character.

Wayne stared at the letter miserably. The ramifications were heart-breaking. He wished he could tear it up and assume Leigh was bluffing. But he wasn't naïve. He would have to make a number of calls immediately. He didn't know where to start, so he began making a list of names. Belinda. Brenda and Ian. The twins' headmaster. The police. The fostering team.

He would have to set up a meeting between all the professionals. He knew, though, what would happen. He would need to move the boys to an alternative foster placement. The further away the better.

Brandon and Kyle would never get to live with Maxine and Tom on their farm. Instead, he feared they would spend the rest of their childhood being shuttled between different foster placements. As a result of this, their education would also be constantly disrupted.

It was bad enough that they would languish in the care system, but they would soon learn that their father was searching for them. What would happen to them once they were in high school? No one could keep them safely locked up inside playground gates then.

He stared at his phone, unable to pick it up. He wasn't ready. He dreaded having to tell Brandon and Kyle. He knew it wasn't his fault, but he wished he hadn't rushed to tell the boys the good news that previous Saturday morning. The court case had finished that Friday afternoon and he had been desperate to share the wonderful outcome. Ecstatic for them, he had explained what had happened in court. He told the twins he would be looking for a forever family for them. That they would be together and safe. That they didn't need to worry anymore. They would never be going back to their old house. He nearly fell back on the deckchair as the boys ran to Brenda, wrapping their arms round her. He had glanced at Ian, who had taken off his sunglasses and was wiping his eyes.

His thoughts were with Brenda and Ian too. They were such good people. Fostering wasn't a job to them. They had grown to love the twins and were utterly dedicated. Their own children and grandchildren included them in every family event, and always bought them gifts when they visited. Brandon and Kyle were so settled there. In fact, one of the things that he had wanted to talk to Maxine and Tom about was whether they would be prepared to keep in touch with the boys' foster carers. But of course, all his good intentions were now just pipe dreams. This meeting would never take place.

Nothing would change. Until their birth father became so unwell that he could not physically fight on, he would remain a negative force in Brandon and Kyle's lives indefinitely.

Devastated, he put his head in his hands. There was nothing more he could do. Leigh somehow had won. It was over.

Eight

Tuesday 13th July 2004

As Wayne was consumed by the devastating news, he failed to notice that David had sneaked out of the office, seemingly for the rest of the day. On the spur of the moment, he had lied in the whereabouts book. An entry claiming a doctor's appointment covered his tracks.

David indeed felt liberated as he walked quickly out of the building. In the far right, he could see Bill, smoking alone in the designated area. He felt entitled to take the afternoon off and justified it by the fact that it was a one off. He stared in the direction of his ineffective team leader. What a terrible role model he was.

To be fair, this unpredictable behaviour was most unlike David. He worked late most evenings, trying to keep his paperwork up to date, thus relieving himself of added work stress. Like all his colleagues, his caseload was overwhelming, but his team had additional challenges. The more able social workers had transferred to Amin's team across the corridor to escape from Bill. Siobhan didn't pull her weight and Yotunde was distracted. It clearly suited their own needs to stay put. Things had deteriorated when Carmel suffered a breakdown. She had now been off work for a year and was unlikely to return imminently. The pressure was unbearable at times, with both Wayne and him constantly playing a game of catch-up.

The issue he begrudged was that there was no concept of claiming overtime in the social care sector and applying for time in lieu was deeply frowned upon. The only difference between him and most other child protection workers in the country was that he did his extra hours in the office. They were all university educated, on government salaries that had been frozen at an extremely low point, being forced to do hours upon hours of unpaid work each week, just to keep afloat. Today, he just felt like looking after himself for a change.

Childcare social work had always been his calling. With each case, of course, came different problems with their particular dynamics. Working with younger children was where he experienced most job satisfaction. He worked tirelessly to try and get them adopted or settled with special guardianship orders before the damage sustained by spending their childhood enmeshed in the care system was irreversible.

All of his cases were multifaceted and tragic. With each child he worked with, David could almost predict the long-term outcomes. Their cheeky faces and personalities would leave their mark on him. He knew exactly how this would evolve. As they progressed to high school, the problems would start, often escalating quickly. The predictable path to self-destruction: multiple changes of foster carers, threats of exclusion, mental health referrals, criminalised behaviour ... The cycle would often repeat itself in each generation. Soul-destroying.

He knew he should be using his precious time doing something therapeutic, but the darkness that surrounded him during his free time was proving impossible to shake off. Soon enough, he found himself back in his bedsit with absolutely no incentive to do anything productive for the rest of the afternoon.

It was his workload that gave him the greatest boost and it was the only stable force in his life at that moment. Pouring himself a glass of wine, he felt annoyed with himself for taking the decision to come home that day. If the "silent assassin", Bill's supervisor, discovered his unauthorised absence, it would result in a suspension. Now he queried why, like everyone else in the building, he hadn't just taken a day's holiday. He was owed enough. But this was his downfall. He tended to act impulsively.

At that precise time nothing seemed to matter. Even work took second place. He poured himself another drink and stared around the bare room almost in disbelief. He was forty-three years old. What was he even doing here? He had made no attempts to personalise this rented studio flat in Fenton city centre. He sat in the only armchair in the room, staring at the blank newly-decorated brilliant white walls, waiting for the effects of the alcohol to relax him somewhat. There was nothing else for it but to wallow in his many mistakes.

It was now three o'clock and all he felt capable of was pouring himself a third glass of wine. This was pathetic, he knew. The weekend before had not gone well and he had drunk far too much. His clients always put up a hard fight for their children. But he was stuck in a dark hole and seemed unable to find inspiration to even call his own. It was more complicated than picking up the phone. There was the harsh rejection that was too much right now.

The mood swings were the hardest to live with. It took physical energy to get up and change his bedding and put it in the washing machine. There was nothing else for it, as he chose to refill his glass. He couldn't take a chance and drive back to the office now. Being available for clients had always been his saviour. Despite all the issues, he never felt lonely whilst being so needed. He recognised that it was vital to keep occupied. He sat with his head in his hands, recalling how Wayne had been grating on his nerves earlier that day. In hindsight, his reaction had been childlike.

The truth was that the only people that needed him were his clients and other professionals involved with the cases. Long gone were the days when he would rush out of work, eager to pick up his two boys from football practice. The summer evenings now stretched far ahead of him. For some strange reason, he had started skipping meals. He would now wait until he felt the first pangs of hunger before giving in.

Since moving out of the family home three months earlier, he had adopted a predictable pattern. He would walk to Asda to select a sandwich, a packet of biscuits, and a bag of ready salted crisps for his evening meal. Being a vegetarian made it even more difficult, as by the time he reached the store, there wasn't much choice left.

He would half-heartedly glance at the ready meals but he knew that he couldn't face the effort of warming them up. Walking down the aisles, he knew that his monotonous existence outside of work was pitiful.

He tended not to answer his mobile phone these days, even if old friends called. It was always poignant arriving back at his rented first floor bedsit. He knew the term was rather dated perhaps. These days it was known as a studio flat. Either way it was a stark reminder that he had hurt his children. He hadn't meant to. It was only a one-night stand. An immature obsession with his social work student. Now he was alone and only had himself to blame.

The Victorian terraced house in the small village outside Fenton had initially been David and his girlfriend Gina's pride and joy. Obviously, they could never have afforded such a nice area, but the prices in 1995 had been low and his parents had thankfully put down a generous deposit. In the early months together, he would try and share his day with Gina. He would tell her plenty of detail, in the safe knowledge that she wasn't the type to repeat things. She would make the right noises, before telling him to change the subject. Her reasons were always the same. It was just too upsetting to listen to.

He lived and breathed for the children on his caseload. He knew as well that there were downsides to the job. But to achieve a positive outcome was worth everything to him. Gina, though, would repeatedly tell him that he wasn't paid enough for him to worry in his own time!

Looking back now, he realised that Gina had never been interested in any aspect of his life. Why had he ignored his gut feelings, preferring to obsess about twenty-one-year-old Natasha, his social work student? He was leaving a trail of errors in his life and he questioned whether leaving the family home was another one of them. He missed opening the little wooden gate that he would religiously repaint baby blue every year. He would walk down the tiny cobbled path, checking that the plants were not drooping over it too much. The small garden he had created at the front of the house had been tended with such devotion. When the kids were asleep, he used to spend many a summer evening out there, chatting to the odd passer-by who would inevitably praise his achievements.

The inside of the house wasn't as aesthetically pleasing. The kitchen and bathroom were tired, and Gina used to tell her friends she felt embarrassed to have them round. But he hated DIY, and actually wasn't very good at it. Furthermore, his meagre salary didn't cover the cost of workmen and new carpets. He recalled one particular instance when she was shouting at him through the upstairs window to forget the deadheading and get inside and hoover. Mortified, he was convinced his neighbours had overheard her.

Gina interpreted the fact that he refused to apply for any social work management positions as a lack of ambition. She was like a stuck record.

"If you can't see that the extra increments will make such a financial difference, you are thick ... Who cares if management is not for you? It's a cushy number," she would scream at him. "There are football boots to buy and holidays to pay for!"

He would turn his back on her but the words stung: "Your kids are suffering due to your little indulgence, you idiot."

David knew her tirade off by heart the moment she started shouting at him. But his job made him happy and he refused to give in.

It was crucial that he kept himself busy. He didn't want to face his own dire circumstances any more than he had to. The shame he had brought on himself ate away at his whole being. It was not so much the way he had humiliated Gina. He could live with that. But he had wrecked their boys' chance of a family life. It was distressing, too, that on the odd occasion when he saw them, they seemed wary of him. His ex-girlfriend had done an excellent job of parent alienation. So full of regret about his children, he felt it easier to keep a low profile.

Obviously, the relationship would have ended at some point, but his obsession with Natasha had only served to bring about the timing earlier. He knew it was irrational to still think about his ex-social work student, but he couldn't help himself. The university graduation ceremonies were held this time of year. How he would have loved to have been by her side celebrating.

He used to be quite outgoing. Now, though, he found it hard to face the people that had respected and cared about him. He wasn't sure that he respected himself anymore! He had made a decision to distance himself from his parents. Always vocal, they hadn't felt the need to hide their disappointment in him. They didn't need to berate him every time they saw him, David had told them. Speaking to him like a spoilt teenager, they had repeatedly told him, "There will be no more handouts, and you can fend for yourself!" His reply was always the same. "I heard you the first time!"

Clearly embarrassed by their irresponsible son, instead, they stepped in and offered both financial and moral support to Gina and the children. She had always got on well with his parents and this was the one thing he didn't hold against her. For he certainly didn't have a good income or significant savings to fall back on. Gina had now returned to work full-time and he learnt that his newly-retired father picked his grandsons up from school every day. They had even taken them to their static caravan for an entire week. Everyone, it seemed, had moved on. Except him.

He had always been immature and self-centred. He couldn't understand why his parents were not loyal to him. He felt they should be offering to pay for a solicitor. They could clearly afford it.

Bizarrely, David had made no attempt to enquire about his rights to see his children. He knew, of course, how to use Google and type in eligibility criteria for legal aid. He had signposted many a client to the Citizens Advice Bureau, yet he couldn't face queuing up himself. He reasoned that taking official legal steps would fuel Gina into poisoning the kids to say they didn't want to see him. And this catalyst, he fretted, may send him over the edge.

It seemed that all he ever did was prioritise: which case to deal with next? Which phone call to return more urgently? Right now it was far easier to put his workload first rather than face his own family crisis.

One of his many passions had been running. But living in down-at-heel Fenton town centre wasn't the same as pounding through quiet residential streets and the woodlands near his old home. He would go through the motions of putting on his trainers, but lacked both the emotional and physical energy to even tie the laces! The only get-up-and-go he had was now reserved for his caseload.

His doctor hadn't been much use. All he had offered was to write out a sick note. This wasn't an option. The flatness would worsen if he was left to his own devices. The fact that he was overworked was a welcome diversion. It kept him sane, but it felt like a vicious circle. The more he focused on his paperwork, the harder it became to switch off from it. Sunday nights were usually the worst as he fretted about what impending crisis may have blown up on his caseload over the weekend.

Time passed slowly, so it made sense to catch up on some much-needed sleep. Two hours later, it was still light outside and he knew it would be sensible to get some fresh air. But his loneliness only heightened if he walked the streets aimlessly. It felt like longer than three months ago since he had voluntarily left the family home. The atmosphere had been toxic and it hadn't been fair on the children. The anti-depressant tablets should have started to kick in now, but he still felt quite unstable.

Looking around the open plan kitchen, he knew that he would never get used to living on his own. The fact that it was furnished made him feel even more unsettled, but at the time he had felt desperate. And what was the point of spacious surroundings, such as a balcony or a room to entertain?

He had no confidence in any of his decisions these days and spent hours with his memories, taunting himself. How he missed his south-facing garden, the full-size football net ruining the view. The children had helped him put it together. He was always forced to stand in goal, the yelling getting on his nerves. He hadn't appreciated it at the time and used to steal glances at his watch, feigning enthusiasm. The kids shouted that he should concentrate on the game but all the while he had been secretly concerned about the expanding area of bare soil that lay in front of him. All that grass feed had made no difference.

Now, he stared intently at the combination microwave balanced on top of the washing machine. The spin cycle was too high and the glass plate was in danger of breaking as the machine now vibrated.

There was the important matter of returning to his house to collect some personal belongings before they ended up binned.

He hoped that his Dire Straits *Brothers in Arms* record hadn't been touched. It held special memories of his losing his virginity. If she had binned it, he would be livid. He had come to terms with the fact that the split was permanent, but seeing the children and having to explain everything to them again was too hard. For this reason, he had delayed contacting her. He knew that she would take pleasure in making this a drawn-out and uncomfortable experience for him.

He contemplated Gina in her trademark flesh-coloured sports bra that she wore on a daily basis. The sexless item, its wide straps digging into her skin. Their sex life had become predictable years ago and he felt lucky if it was more than once every couple of months. Even then, it morphed inevitably into the perfunctory missionary position, lasting a maximum of ten minutes. It was, he came to think, marginally better than nothing.

How had he allowed himself to fall so far? As a teenager, he recalled, he had had everything going for him. He attended an all-boys private school with extensive playing fields. He had loved school life and had been a talented athlete. He had taken pride in his large bedroom, plastering posters of cars and 1980s pop stars all over the walls. His bookshelves were stacked with cheap medals dangling down from a multitude of differing-sized bronze and silver trophies engraved with his name and sporting event.

He never won an academic prize but he didn't care. Parents' evenings were always a trial for his parents who, whilst waiting in the queue, listened in as other pupils were being advised about the forthcoming Oxbridge entrance exams. Instead, his mother would despair when she caught sight of his untouched A-Level textbooks, lying tidily on an otherwise empty desk. His popularity with other pupils, together with his love of competitive sports, the teaching staff assured her, would enhance his confidence.

It had been a happy childhood and he tended to reminisce about it. Now he couldn't remember the last time he had truly laughed out loud. All his friends had young families that occupied their free time and he didn't fit in anymore.

Oddly, he found himself more at ease if he met with Wayne occasionally, outside work. There was no putting on a show for him, particularly as he was open about his own issues forming relationships. There were times when he got on his nerves, like today, and he wished he wouldn't wear those creased linen shirts! But in David's time in need, Wayne had proven himself to be a good listener and in turn, he knew he should be grateful.

Picking up the remote control, he began skipping through the TV schedules. There was nothing to interest him. He couldn't think of anything to occupy his time and it was easier as usual to dwell on his caseload than focus on his own crisis. He wondered what had happened to Tracey Mellor. She had been an unusual case. She had been well brought up too. He remembered how he had first come across her. How her existence had been so shocking. It had been around six months since he had first met her, in that godforsaken freezing squat. He would never forget those addicts and their existence. It was by far the most depressing and harrowing place he had ever visited.

He wondered whether Tracey was even alive …

Nine

Tracey

December 2003

Six months earlier

Going under the radar was something at which Tracey Mellor was usually skilled. She had managed to avoid any health professional since becoming pregnant, but that day, an agonising ear infection forced her to seek medical aid.

It was unfortunate that she was asked to remove her oversized duffle coat and roll up her left sleeve. The doctor turned away from her to pick up the blood pressure meter, and for a moment she considered refusing this perfectly reasonable non-invasive procedure. But this would surely raise his suspicions. Her time was up. She took a deep breath as she did as he asked.

Such a malnourished and frail figure, the give-away large bump instantly persuaded him to ask, "How many weeks do you think you are?"

"I'm not sure." Tracey frowned. She knew to say little, but this was the truth.

She looked down at her trainers, not noticing how worn out they were. The waves of shame hit her as the doctor unwrapped the monitoring machine. Now the accusations would begin. But surprisingly none came. What a relief that he made no reference to the faded track marks. The sores and scars on her legs and feet were fresher, but thankfully they were safely hidden under her tracksuit bottoms.

The nomadic and criminal existence she had led of late did her no favours. She regretted selling herself to fuel her addiction, but she had had no choice. She could fall further still, and she knew that she may end up incarcerated. Hurt, she realised that the people she surrounded herself with were not her friends at all, and had just been using her. She had to get away from Fenton with some urgency. Certainly before the police discovered her connections.

It hadn't been a good weekend. The news that a school boy had fatally overdosed had sent her into a panicked state. She hadn't been high up in the chain and was being stitched up. It wasn't fair. She had only been an intermediary. She felt her baby kick. The single reminder that she was a human being. It was time to try and accept the rehabilitation offer. This time she would make a massive attempt to keep all the appointments with the drugs worker. She would have to change over to methadone scripts. That would ensure she could keep the baby.

She put her duffle coat back on quickly and absentmindedly played with a strand of cotton that was coming loose from a button on the cuff. If she fled the surgery now, it would be empty-handed. With her ear causing her such excruciating pain, this would, she considered, be short-sighted and foolish. Besides, she was lonely and had instantly warmed to this doctor's gentle and seemingly non-judgmental attitude towards her. Suddenly she felt quite emotional.

These days there were few people who acted considerately towards her. It had taken her many years to realise the obvious. Everyone had their own agenda and couldn't be trusted. She stared down at her trainers again to avoid the doctor's concerned gaze.

Still, at least there was the benefit of being in a warm building. She raised her head to absorb her surroundings. The mahogany desk scattered with papers. The modern frame encasing a photograph of two grinning children. The Victorian coving reminding her of the house she had grown up in. The cream dado rail dividing up two unappealing shades of green. The smell of instant coffee and the bright mug engraved with "Ibiza". As the doctor searched her records on the computer, Tracey knew that she was avoiding the reality of the situation. That she was probably far closer to her due date than she realised. Finally, she had been found out.

"There are no records here of any antenatal appointments," the doctor said, now searching her blank expression for answers. Tracey queried whether she should make something up. Perhaps she should lie and say she had been registered with another practice in this interim period. She concluded that silence was the best response.

"Well, I can take a guess from your position that you are full term." He frowned as he swung his chair to position himself directly in front of her and stared at her swollen stomach. Tracey found herself reminding him as to why she was here and eventually, he picked up his otoscope to probe her ear.

He was in no rush to conclude the examination. The presentation of this pregnant patient was shocking. It was obvious that she was addicted to illegal substances and he forgot about his coffee going cold as he tried repeatedly to engage her. He explained sympathetically that he had discovered that her ear was infected and attempted to ask her how she was looking after herself.

Skilled at fabricating the truth, Tracey rapidly concocted a vague tale about how she had had a difficult couple of weeks and had split up with her boyfriend, but everything was sorted out now and she would get in touch with the midwives soon. She even asked him to write down a phone number for whom she should call.

The GP nodded and Tracey took this to mean that he believed her. She estimated that he was in his early sixties. Warmly dressed for this winter day, he wouldn't, she assumed, know anything about what it was like to try and survive on the streets. Surely now she would be given the prescription and she could leave. She knew he meant well, but the questioning had been invasive.

But the alarmed doctor still did not appear to be in a rush. He swung his chair round to face his computer screen again and spent several minutes in silence. The scant medical history evident before him was more than concerning.

What happened next took Tracey by genuine surprise. He reached for his phone and asked for assistance from the practice nurse. She caught what sounded like a secret code. Feeling let down, Tracey heard the disquieting words, "Send for an ambulance, please."

Seconds later, a nurse and a male practice manager entered the room without knocking. All she had wanted was antibiotics and she felt disheartened and trapped. Desperate to go back to sleep she pleaded with them just to allow her to go home. She just didn't have the energy for all this hanging about in a hospital waiting room. She argued too that she was not about to go into labour imminently.

But the medical staff were firm. Horrified, the middle-aged practice manager stared the patient up and down. What a pitiful sight. Her gaunt cheeks, open sores and matted hair spoke volumes. Overruling her wishes, they all insisted that she must attend the antenatal department that day in order for the staff to check her and the unborn baby.

Once in the ambulance though, she realised, again to her surprise, that she was enjoying the attention. Everyone was kind towards her and hid their disapproval well. She was told she wouldn't have to wait long and chatted away to the student nurse whose job it was to accompany Tracey to ensure she didn't flee.

The radiographer acted as if she didn't know anything about the new patient being pushed to the front of the list. The give-away track marks were observed in silence, as Tracey hesitantly rolled up her tee shirt for the scan. As always, priding herself on the professional rules of conduct, the radiographer only made polite remarks prior to the examination beginning. When it was concluded, she handed the photograph of the fully developed foetus to the clearly lonely and malnourished patient.

Tracey was curious to know the sex of the child and was informed that she was carrying a baby girl. But by now the low mood had set in, the exhaustion and cravings intensifying. Instead of studying the black and white image carefully, she instantly tucked it into her coat pocket.

With the confirmation that she was around eight months pregnant, there was still no real sense of excitement. The familiar loneliness swept through her, as it had for these past ten years. Her feelings had been dulled a long time ago.

The radiographer seemed pleasant too and Tracey instantly opened up, telling her that her mother had died of cancer when she was a teenager. She told her that her name had been Eleanor. She hadn't thought of baby names before but she decided on one now – Ellie. The radiographer led her out of the room, commenting insincerely that it was a lovely choice.

The outpatients antenatal department was busy, yet Tracey found herself instantly given a side room where, of course, there was a barrage of searching questions and concerned looks from midwives. She realised why she was being chaperoned everywhere. No one trusted her. In a strange way, though, she was sorry when all the assessments were concluded. At least people cared about her here. There would be a follow-up appointment, she was told, in five days' time, but for the time being, she was free to go.

Exhausted, she picked up her antibiotics from the hospital outpatients pharmacy and took a bus back to the squat. She had only lived there for a month or so and was grateful for security. The abandoned terraced house in the Barnham Hill Estate was better than living on the streets, and an acquaintance had managed to change the locks.

Glad to be back, she closed the bedroom door and fell asleep, only to be woken two hours later by the inevitable intrusion of the police, threatening to break the door down if it wasn't opened. They searched the property and arrested one of the inhabitants for breaching his bail conditions. The questioning of the others made Tracey feel anxious. It wouldn't be long before it was her turn.

A man in his late thirties now arrived at the property. He wasn't naturally good looking, Tracey contemplated, but he had a certain sex appeal about him. He targeted her straight away, asking to speak to her privately. Tracey led him to the kitchen as he introduced himself as David Lindley, and explained that he was a social worker who happened to be on duty that day. Well spoken, he didn't take off his thick navy puffer coat, and commented on the bitterly cold premises. Tracey pointed out that there was no central heating in the place and that she intended moving on as soon as she had the baby.

The years had not been good to Tracey. She was so damaged by her experiences that she couldn't seem to read people at all. David had been gentle in his approach, and she warmed to him, particularly as he didn't seem fazed by the fact that she lived in a squat. She hoped that he could help her find alternative accommodation in time for the birth.

But Tracey was in her own world. A simplistic one, where, if she could be rescued, then everything would be good again. She was still in the mindset of that fourteen-year-old girl, before her life crashed around her. Almost childlike, she lacked any insight into her lifestyle and her situation. With no responsibilities to others, no ties, no demands on her time, she had spiralled, long ago, into seeing herself as a blameless victim.

David's perspective was very different. It was hardly a straightforward matter of moving her to new accommodation. He had become experienced and skilled at masking his feelings. His upbringing couldn't have been more different from what he was faced with at that moment. His own father was a landlord of both residential and commercial properties and always feared the intrusion of squatters. Of course he judged her. What she and her associates were doing was illegal.

The way they had trashed the place revolted him and he just wanted to get out of there as quickly as possible. It was really a form-filling exercise, purely so he could "tick the boxes". Official-looking letters lay unopened in the hall. Predictably, the conditions of the bedrooms and bathroom were revolting. In the kitchen, he noticed part of the fridge door seal was hanging off. He saved himself the trouble of opening it.

He followed the police into the lounge, dreading what would face him. Other than two battered mock-leather couches, there was no other furniture. Possessions were stuffed into plastic bags. Debris including drugs paraphernalia was evident. He noted, too, a slug trail on the carpet near the fireplace. A dishevelled older man sat staring in a trance-like state. A thin woman, possibly in her late teens, got up to leave the room. It was hard to place her age, and she was anxious as to what was going on, but was unable to articulate herself.

It was a deeply depressing sight, and David observed silently as the police began interrogating everyone. He felt sad too that Tracey was unable to tell him who these individuals were. He looked at his watch. He had been here long enough. Seven minutes was all it had taken him to decide that Tracey would not be keeping the baby.

He had to get out of this godforsaken place, and suggested to the police officers that they take Tracey back to his offices to interview her. It was only a seven to ten minute drive away, he pleaded with them. He did not give an explanation as to why he was refusing to take her in his own car. He didn't feel he would be safe alone with her.

But Tracey wasn't at all keen. It had been a long day for her and she hah had enough with all the questioning.

"I've been up all night with a bad ear infection. I need to go back to sleep," she told him firmly, assuming he would understand. "I will pop down to your place later," she promised David, smiling at him in an attempt to win him over.

Her complete lack of awareness of the seriousness of the situation bemused the officers, who looked at each other, raising their eyesbrows. But David was adamant, and Tracey was persuaded that there was a real appeal in the promise of a warm reception room, a hot drink and a sandwich.

Back at Fenton Childcare Services, a rather stressed David found a free interview room and left his new client to rest there while he attempted to work out what to do with her. At eight months gestation, Tracey could technically go into labour at any time and if this happened whilst in the squat, there would be serious implications for the department. He had to cover his back. He didn't think Bill would be able to guide him, but he knew he would have to discuss this latest case with him, merely as a protocol exercise.

It had crossed David's mind in the car back to the office that Tracey may well go on the run now she had been exposed. There was no next of kin down on the hospital forms and he was aware that patients could present at a different hospital using an alias. This case was going to take up a lot of his time, David could tell.

Having picked this referral up whilst he was on duty, he would be forced to keep it too.

Seeing Siobhan on the stairwell, he gestured to her impatiently to end her personal call. She wasn't too happy about this interruption and complained that she had been in the middle of enquiring about when it would be a good time to visit a puppy! Now she told David that she was worried the owners would think she wasn't committed and needed to call them back and explain. David was unimpressed and told her forcibly, "Forget your dog, I have a heavily pregnant druggie to sort out!"

Always in the mood for an exciting drama, she reverted back to work mode and followed him into the interview room. When David returned from making an urgent phone call to the child protection midwife, he discovered his colleague and Tracey chatting easily, almost like friends. Whilst Siobhan wanted to impress David with her interpersonal skills, she knew what to look for. She was in search of more background information on this extremely damaged vulnerable mother to be.

An emergency like this usually involved a team effort. Yotunde offered to go to Asda and pick up a sandwich and a drink for her, but getting the petty cash paperwork signed off by Bill took too long and by the time she returned with the items, Tracey had folded her arms on the table and appeared to be sleeping.

"Her mother died when she was fourteen, she's alone and in a right mess," Siobhan whispered, for once quite sympathetic. She motioned that she would stay with her as long as necessary.

This released David to discuss the case with Bill. Naturally, he wasn't in his office, but he was shortly found taking yet another smoking break. Informing his manager didn't take long and David volunteered to take charge of the case himself. He did so reluctantly but he was motivated by the suspicion that Bill would mishandle it. Or worse still, wouldn't allocate it quickly enough. He didn't consider this case to be particularly difficult, as long as it was dealt with quickly and firmly.

Prioritising this as an emergency case, within a week, three out of the four pre-birth assessment sessions had been completed. It had been difficult to keep Tracey on track though, as she tended to veer off the subject of her lifestyle, preferring to talk about her family background. It turned out that Tracey's maternal grandmother had arrived on Kindertransport and had been placed with a non-Jewish family. David looked puzzled. He had no idea what Tracey was talking about. He made a joke about how history hadn't been his thing at school and asked her to explain in more detail.

Over another hot drink and a sandwich, Tracey explained that her grandmother and great aunt had escaped from Berlin but had been placed separately from each other. They never knew what happened to their parents, but assumed they had been murdered by the Nazis. Her grandmother decided never to tell anyone she was Jewish for fear that antisemitism would happen again and she brought her own children up having nothing to do with the Jewish community. There were no Jewish symbols in their home, and Tracey's mother was not given a Jewish burial.

This was all very interesting, David thought, and Tracey had an endearing way about her. But the baby was due any day and this was a diversion tactic. Nothing would alter the fact in his mind that the outcome of the assessment would still be negative.

As with many clients that David dealt with, Tracey didn't attend the final assessment session. When he finally got hold of her, she was unable to offer any acceptable explanation for her absence. It didn't make any difference. David had all the information he needed. His notes weren't back from the typing pool yet and therefore it hadn't been put before Bill to sign off. But the outcome was clear and time was of the essence.

A week after first meeting his new client, David visited the squat for what he hoped would be the last time. For safety, he took Siobhan with him. A ploy was crafted, to arrive at 9am, to hopefully catch Tracey at home. The two social workers were well prepared and had the night before persuaded Bill to release £5 from his precious Section 17 fund!

Thankfully Tracey answered the door, and they promised her breakfast on the way back to the office via the drive through McDonald's. The ploy worked. Their client needed little persuading to get in the back seat of David's car. It would only be a short meeting, they promised, relieved not to have to linger in that deeply depressing squat.

Tracey had very much enjoyed the attention she had been receiving from them both. But because Siobhan was called away on various duty emergencies, he found himself having to face Tracey alone.

He took no pleasure in what he had to say. His new client was at times engaging, and he had enjoyed listening to her rather witty remarks. He respected, too, the fact that she seemed to have the ability to laugh at her circumstances. He was sure that if it hadn't been for her drug addiction, none of this would be happening. He imagined how things would end and at that point, he felt for her.

He pulled up a chair and took a deep breath. As delicately as he could put it, he advised his client that the pre-birth assessment outcome was negative and that her baby would be removed from her care at birth. There would be a caveat, he continued. There would be some flexibility around the timing, he told her. If Tracey wanted to care for the child whilst she remained in hospital overnight, this could be arranged, but she would need to be supervised by the nursing station at all times.

Tracey sat perfectly still. The only comment she made was to enquire politely if she could use the toilets. David led the way and waited outside in the corridor, just in case she tried to flee the building.

Locking herself in the cubicle, Tracey stared hard at herself in the tarnished mirror above the sink. This was devastating news that she was half-expecting, but the tears never came. She was used to feeling humiliated; perhaps this was why she was numb.

Always in her thoughts, she recalled how her beloved mother would remark how beautiful she was at every opportunity. What was reflected back shocked her somewhat. She was unrecognisable from the teenage girl in her school photographs. She was frail and looked older than her twenty-nine years. Her once thick long blond hair was now matted and thinning. Her cheekbones were pronounced, her skin tone was an unhealthy pallor.

Desperation and realisation hit her again and again. She was totally alone and it felt all too much. The addiction, the abusive relationships, the drug dealing, the prostitution. The net had closed in on her, overwhelming her. She felt her foetus kicking gently but instead of enjoying the sensation, she panicked. Where was she supposed to flee to now? It was all too much aggravation for her to deal with, and this current squat was totally unsuitable for an adult let alone a newborn. With a heavy heart, she knew that fighting to keep her baby girl and find alternative accommodation would be pointless. She needed to accept the facts.

With only one realistic option available to her, she made a decision. She would sign any papers that the social worker put in front of her and would relinquish her baby for adoption. She surely had some pride left, and would try and walk out of hospital with her head held high, knowing that she had given her baby a better start in life. This wasn't a planned pregnancy, and she didn't know who the father was. It was a terrible situation, and the sooner it was resolved the better.

Meanwhile, David was on guard to expect an unpleasant scene, and had been considering whether to call upon back-up staff for support. On their return from the toilets, he positioned himself nearest the interview room door, and kept it wide open. Furthermore, he kept his left hand hovering near the emergency buzzer, located under the table.

Instead, a civilised conversation followed. Tracey appeared to be relieved. She was not going to challenge the negative assessment outcome. She told him that she was sorry for wasting his time. That he had been right. She needed to do a lot of work on herself and things would be different in the future.

David tried not to show his relief at this passive reaction. Anticipating all options, he had in his briefcase the relevant form and showed her where to sign. As she borrowed his biro, she asked him for one favour. She begged him to find her somewhere else to live.

But as Tracey was now relinquishing her baby at birth, her lack of suitable housing wasn't technically his problem to address. However, he had grown fond of his new client and felt it wouldn't hurt him to give her some telephone numbers for housing associations and such like. "Just wait here," he said, "I have a new student social worker. She can perhaps make some phone calls for you. The drug service will help you as well." It was a small price to pay for the fact that there wouldn't be a child protection case conference and an imminent court case to prepare for.

But when he returned, Tracey had gone. She had left the paperwork duly completed on the table and he scanned it quickly. On the last page she had signed her name, printed and dated it. David felt quite elated with such a speedy and satisfactory outcome.

He didn't look outside for her and bounded upstairs to his office. Extremely pleased, he explained the ropes to Natasha, his keen new student. A relinquished baby was a relatively easy case for her to co-work, he told her confidently. He advised her to fax the paperwork to the fostering and adoption team, and prepared her for the next steps. "In good time, there will be a matching panel meeting to prepare for, which will just be about dotting the i's and crossing the t's," he said over confidently.

He told her, too, that there would be the adoption ceremony in the courts for them to attend. He discreetly flirted with Natasha, repeating many times that he would be there at all times to supervise her. Yotunde observed disapprovingly as he tried to impress the striking woman at least fifteen years his junior.

When Siobhan returned from a home visit, David immediately shared the good news with her too. Neither of them appeared concerned as to Tracey's and the unborn baby's immediate welfare. Siobhan told David that Tracey had, "started to get on my nerves, constantly whinging on about her mother's death." For maximum impact, David announced, "Those druggies, always the same, blaming someone else." He thanked Siobhan for her assistance that morning, and they congratulated each other on achieving a really positive outcome.

Meanwhile Yotunde had been taking in the conversation around her and was distinctly unimpressed. "Aren't you going to find her a hostel where there will be staff on call when she goes into labour?" she queried, alarmed.

David had, in all the drama, not properly thought through this problem, but was unwilling to lose face in front of his new student and directed Natasha to start this process. Yotunde scowled at him, clearly disgusted with his conduct. At any time soon, a vulnerable destitute woman's life and that of her unborn baby could be at stake. She now raised her voice at David, telling him that he should not be allowing his client to be alone in such unsuitable conditions when her waters burst.

"Lighten up, for God's sake!" he told Yotunde despairingly. He wanted to take control again, and added for good measure, "The baby isn't even due for weeks!"

But the damage was done, and to laugh at a client's utter misery and misfortune was deeply unacceptable. Yotunde wasn't shy to hide her repulsion. "Sorry to be such a killjoy," she said, "but Tracey still has to keep her word ..."

Ten

January 2004

With hindsight, David realised Yotunde was correct. He refused to admit it, but he had been foolish to believe that he could rely on Tracey. Her signature on the relinquishing papers hardly amounted to a legally-enforceable document. It was, however, a strong indication that his client would probably accept that the unborn child would be placed for adoption, thus avoiding a protracted court case. But, as always, he knew to take the necessary steps to cover his back.

There were now daily email exchanges between himself and Santosh, the child protection lead midwife at North Fenton General Hospital. A planning meeting was held and using a recent mug shot, the police released a flier to the other maternity hospitals and district childcare teams in the surrounding areas. It was a sad fact that Tracey wouldn't be the first to attempt to create an alias and in doing so, slip through the net.

On hearing the news that her patient had presented at the hospital in the early stages of labour, Santosh gathered her team around her.

She updated them again as to Tracey's vulnerability and suggested to the staff that they offer to care for the newborn child at the nursing station as an interim measure before it was placed officially into the care system. If the new mother wished to keep the child with her, she advised strongly that the curtains be kept open at all times. If this scenario was to happen, Santosh required staff to bleep her straight away. An urgent working agreement would need to be drafted and signed in these circumstances.

A skilled nurse, Santosh was still under no illusions as to the difficulties she was about to face. "If necessary, we will have to request that the police initiate an emergency protection order," she instructed.

No matter how many similar situations she had been involved in, it was never easy to be involved in the separation of a mother and a newborn.

Despite the extensive briefing, the team were shocked as they came face to face with their new patient. Looking exceptionally frail and unkempt, Tracey's pale pallor was accentuated by the unforgiving bright lights of the delivery suite. The shapeless blue and white patterned hospital gown gaped at the shoulder, hinting at her protruding bones.

Out of earshot, the whispered comments and raised eyebrows made their way through the corridor and into the staff room.

"It took me twenty minutes to find a decent vein in her arms. Most of them have collapsed."

"I could see some fresher bruising on one of her feet. She will be injecting in there."

"She's very lonely. I feel sorry for her."

"That poor foetus. It's going be withdrawing for weeks."

It wasn't until the child was born, on 22nd January at 9.50am, that Tracey realised that she had been rash in signing the adoption relinquishing forms. She assumed, though, that it wouldn't be too late. Her beautiful baby girl hadn't been planned, but would be a link to her late mother. She was overjoyed that the name she had come up with suited her so well. It had a softness to it. What a welcome tonic Ellie made. The tending midwife looked on, taking care to show her how to support the baby's neck. It wasn't her role to judge or discourage the bonding.

Maximising the attention, Tracey welcomed a midwife who entered the birthing suite, her hands full of neatly folded tiny clothing items. She dressed Ellie, swiftly putting a nappy on, followed by a faded babygro. She said she would be back in a few minutes with tea and toast. Tracey lay back in the bed feeling exhausted. As she rested, a plan began to form. It was simple. She would stay here, in the hospital, until David found them both somewhere to live! There must be a free bed somewhere and David had indeed sounded earnest. He had to honour the promise that he would assist her.

As her mobile phone was out of credit, she requested a pen and paper. There were items she would need and she could give the list to David. She would tell the staff to call him and ask him to visit her straight away.

Feeling elated, she confided in the friendly midwife who had helped keep her spirits up during the delivery.

"I don't know what I was thinking!" she announced joyfully. "I would never give her up for adoption. I am keeping her." She was indeed proud of herself and added, "I love my daughter to bits."

"I'm going to get my senior to talk to you," the nurse replied. She was softly spoken, but her message was unwelcome and unexpected.

Stunned, the patient watched the nurse silently as she seemed intent on pressing digits into her bleeper. She then gently took Ellie from Tracey's arms.

"I'm just going to give your baby a check over," she told her. "I will need to concentrate now."

Starting to panic, Tracey propped herself up and, as forcefully as she could, asked the nurse to call David. She apologised that she didn't know his surname but explained that he worked in Fenton Childcare Services. She explained that he had been so helpful, and she was confident that he would sort things out for her and Ellie.

But her thoughts were interrupted as yet another midwife entered the room, introducing herself.

"I won't hurt her. We just need somewhere to live." She was pleading, but no one responded. The two nurses had their backs to her and were focused only on undertaking the statutory newborn baby health checks.

Breaking the awful silence, Santosh now strode in, carrying a modern tan briefcase. Self-assured, she tended to dominate the conversation. Tracey watched with an increasing fear as the swing door opened and closed. There were now too many people in the room. She had been enjoying an intimate bonding session with her daughter. Now these precious moments had been ruined.

Tracey became convinced people were talking about her outside the room. She could even hear a burst of laughter down the corridor. Feeling ashamed, she wished she could take Ellie and leave. But her legs felt so weak, she wasn't sure she would even be able to climb off the bed. Ashamed and crying, she turned her face towards the wall.

It was left to Santosh to spell out the situation tactfully. Ellie would be placed with foster carers. The pre-birth assessment was negative and nothing since then had indicated anything had changed. As Tracey processed the message, she felt the familiar flat mood returning. She was crushed. Those few minutes had been so intensely powerful. Her happiest in years. Dreaming of what could have been, but that's all it was.

Ellie was less than half an hour old. Her mother could only lie there as the staff cleaned her up, taking away the bloodied sheets. They handed her daughter back to her, but she began to cry. One of the midwives left the room and returned with a bottle of formula milk. Santosh explained gently that due to Tracey's drug addiction, she should not attempt to breastfeed. But Tracey wasn't in the mood to be dictated to any longer.

"You are all the same. Judging me. You think I am stupid," Tracey muttered in a low voice.

Half expecting Ellie to be dragged from her battered arms, she was now impressed at the reaction from the medical staff. There was nothing but dedication and genuine concern towards their charges.

One midwife grabbed a hand towel and dabbed it in soapy water. "Here, let me wipe your face. You will feel better once you are freshened up," she said, starting before Tracey had a chance to reply.

"We are here to help our patients. It's not our job to judge anyone," Santosh said, moving a chair and sitting down next to her. Another nurse sat on the other side of her. It was evident that their patient was vulnerable and alone. Trying to pacify her, the nurse impulsively stroked her hand as she spoke.

"Haven't you got lovely long fingers?"

"Yes, my mum also had long fingers. I would massage them when she was dying."

She took any opportunity she could to talk about her traumatic loss and the words spilled out naturally.

"I was thirteen when she got ovarian cancer, and fourteen when she died. I used to tuck her in every night in the hospital."

She glanced around, making eye contact with each member of staff as she spoke. No one interrupted her as she continued, "None of my family want anything to do with me. My life is hell and I need my mum." Her audience nodded supportively. They didn't seem in a rush and allowed her the space to open up. "I've moved about so many times, my stuff was stolen. Now I've lost my favourite photo of her."

Crying visibly, Tracey found it comforting to see them all nodding simultaneously. There were no condescending tones, only decent people who appeared to care about her. She tried to focus on what Santosh was saying. She was suggesting an urgent referral to a drugs rehabilitation programme.

"This would give you somewhere to live for six months," Santosh offered, trying to be practical. She handed out a tissue as she added gently, "That's a goal to work towards."

But Tracey had been down this route before. Five years ago, she had been an inpatient for a month, before being asked to leave for breaching the rules. Such was the systematic cycle of abuse, she now had no confidence to make positive long-term changes.

One of the midwives mentioned bereavement counselling too and they all agreed with her. Recognising the brightness in their faces, she didn't want to be any more of a disappointment to them. So Tracey smiled and promised them she would definitely make enquiries.

On that seemingly positive note, Santosh made her excuses and left the room to telephone David. He informed her that a court hearing was booked for 10am the following morning, and he was confident that the judge would award the local authority, parental responsibility. In the interim, Ellie was at risk of significant harm and the hospital had to manage this. Together, they quickly drew up an agreement which set out steps to ensure immediate protection for the newborn child, whilst her mother cared for her on the ward.

Going back into the delivery suite with the hastily handwritten document, Santosh presented it to Tracey, advising her to read it carefully. Shattered from the labour, she was past caring. She was given a pen and duly signed where instructed.

No one wanted a scene, and perhaps it was for the best that she didn't fully recognise the requirements of her. The instructions made harsh reading.

"The curtains are to remain open around my bedside. Ellie has to be visible to staff at all times.

I will leave Ellie at the nursing station when I need the bathroom or wish to leave the ward.

Providing I am medically fit, I will discharge myself after a maximum period of three days. Ellie will be left with medical staff.

Any indication of drug use will terminate the agreement immediately."

A burly porter now arrived, pushing a wheelchair, and the midwives popped in to say their goodbyes. They took turns to embrace their patient and were generous with their messages of encouragement for the future.

Glad not to have to walk, Tracey gladly sat down and was pushed into the lift, her sleeping child snug in her arms. One of the midwifes escorted her to the fourth floor, making a good attempt at light conversation. By now, Tracey had guessed everyone was taking precautions against her fleeing the hospital. But there was nothing she could do. If she wanted to stay with Ellie, albeit temporarily, she would have to put up with it.

Minutes later, they all arrived in the busy postnatal ward. As she was wheeled down the corridor, she instantly noticed several private rooms. Only one of them was occupied. She was desperate to be on her own. Especially after living in that godforsaken squat. But her heart sank when the porter turned into a four-bedded ward. Even worse, he stopped at the first bed, positioned directly under the nursing station's window. She sighed. Literally no one trusted her.

The short period that Tracey stayed on the ward was an extremely distressing one. None of the other three patients even smiled in her direction. She was convinced that they all knew her status and she was right. The short-sleeved hospital gown exposed the laceration of track marks running down both of her arms. She tried hard to ignore the cravings, but she was increasingly in need of a fix. Apart from Santosh, there were no other visitors. All she had was Ellie and she had to brace herself for the inevitable separation from her.

Watching the new mothers chatting to each other only made the feeling of loss more acute. But there was worse to come, as she hadn't factored in visiting time. Just before 2pm, a member of staff wedged open the double doors. Tracey tried to avert her eyes, but, whichever way she looked, she couldn't avoid the steady stream of noisy siblings, elated partners and proud grandparents, carrying helium balloons or carefully arranged bouquets or the inevitable last-minute garage flowers!

The ward was now full of people, talking excitedly and taking photographs. An elderly gentleman approached Tracey, asking her politely if he could borrow the chair next to her bed. She nodded to him and watched as a younger man now walked across, interrupting him.

"Dad, don't do that. Here, I'll lift it."

The respect, the love, the excitement for a new life. A celebration. She was attending a party to which she hadn't been invited.

With four hours of this hell to endure she pulled the dreary curtains round her bed. But now she could hear footsteps and spotted a pair of ugly black shoes peeking out from under the fabric.

Yanking them back open, one of the nurses whispered, "Love, I know it's hard for you but the agreement says you need to keep the curtains open when the baby is with you."

The following morning, Tracey looked at the large clock above the nursing station. She planned to leave by 1pm at the latest! She didn't want to bump into any enthusiastic visitors who arrived early. Following her standard routine, she wheeled Ellie to the nursing station, requested more paper knickers, and informed the nurse that she needed the bathroom.

Taking the only items of clothing she had worn when she had arrived at the hospital, she planned to take a shower, and locked the door behind her.

The hot water felt so good but when she looked down, she was dismayed to see the continued blood loss trailing into the plug hole. She had hoped that by now this would have eased, but it was just as heavy as the previous day. She would have to request another packet of sanitary pads. The two that they gave her at a time would clearly not suffice.

Her awful existence was overwhelming, threatening to send her to the usual place. The huge dark holes on each side of the narrow path. The lack of mental energy to walk one step at a time. Alone. She had learnt strategies, and for now, she needed to break up the mammoth task ahead of her. The first thing to do was to get dressed, and she ripped open the hospital plastic bag that contained her possessions. She had brought no change of underwear, slippers or deodorant. There had been no one to help her plan for her hospital admission. No one that cared enough.

The thin hospital towels she had been given felt rough against her battered vagina. She wished she had been better prepared as she struggled to dry her feet on the wet shower room floor. Her right hand shook very slightly as she put on paper knickers, packing them with sheets of toilet paper. Her maternity jeans were a better fit now and she tightened the expandable waistline several notches. There was no mirror in which to examine her stomach but she could tell that her long-sleeved cotton top felt more comfortable.

Her milk had come in and her breasts were so full they were painful. Her bra was far too small and she had no choice but to put on the dirty socks from the day before. A fresh gush of blood rushed from her body as she bent down to zip her boots. Thankfully there were plenty of packets of sanitary towels in the bathroom cupboard to replace the sodden tissues. She needed another shower and to her horror she noted her jeans were now stained. How humiliating. Why had no one told her about the after birth effects? This whole process was taking too long. She needed to be out of here.

The small matter of getting showered and dressed had been an ordeal in itself. There was nothing she could do about her hand trembling. The side effects were taking hold. She wasn't sure if the ward was stifling, or if she was sweating from needing a fix. Probably both. She tied her coat sleeves round her waist and unlocked the door.

The next thing was to gather her few possessions. Her phone charger and mobile were all in the bag. Anxious, she searched her zipped pocket for loose coinage to pay for the bus fare. She counted out the rolled notes, and bound them again tightly using a hair bobble. A hundred and ten pounds. It was all intact.

Dealing Class A drugs would be near impossible now the school boy had died. Rumour had it that the police had issued various arrest warrants on the Barnham Hill Estate. Things were dire and she knew it was a matter of time before she would end up before the magistrates. It would probably be moved to the Crown Court this time. As usual she took one day at a time and allocated herself eighty pounds for the heroin and cocaine. Today wasn't the day to suffer the hellish cravings. Life was back to its normal dysfunctional cycle and she hated herself for being so weak.

The sorrow felt immense as she approached the nursing station and, apologising, she handed the student nurse the blood-stained towels. Her voice was timid as she requested as many sanitary pads as the ward could spare. She wished the staff would put their arms around her. Guide her to a private room and give her some clean pyjamas. She would take another shower and slide into the sheets whilst they sat by her bed chatting about films perhaps. Places they had visited on holiday. Anything. She just longed for company. Then they would turn off the light, tuck her in and let her sleep. All the while they would be watching over Ellie.

Instead she waited for the said items to be brought to her, grateful no questions were being asked.

It felt surreal to be a mother, as she bent down to the crib and gently picked her daughter up. At that very point everything felt so natural. She was in awe of her angelic features, the deep brown eyes, her soft plump little cheeks, her tightly pursed lips. She cradled the child, cherishing her being, stroking her hair, inhaling her fresh smell. Then reality hit her again and hot tears flowed freely.

With the staff absorbed in their paperwork, it was just the two of them for the last time. There would be no separation of love from her acute grieving. In the same way there had been no let-up in her own bereavement, this loss would only serve to trigger a deeper depression from which she would never recover either. It was all just too agonising.

After she had gently placed Ellie back in her cot, she stood uncomfortably in front of the desk waiting for them to notice her.

"I'm leaving now, have you my social worker's details?"

She didn't wait for an answer and continued to explain that she had given Ellie a bottle an hour earlier, at exactly midday, and had changed her afterwards.

One of the nurses immediately pressed on her bleeper, and they both got up quickly and walked round to the other side of the nursing station. One gently placed a hand on Tracey's arm.

"You know you are allowed to stay for another two nights," she told her, as her colleague wheeled the cot in, and she guided the patient to a private office.

"Would you like me to take a photograph of you with Ellie?" the midwife offered, trying to maintain eye contact.

Tracey nodded, managing a tight smile, and stood posing with Ellie for the camera. The hopelessness of it all, the humiliation. It was too much. She had to get out of there.

"I will make sure that your social worker sends you a copy, love." The midwife didn't mean to sound patronising, but Tracey could not help feeling that this was really a little service that they offered everyone in her position. There was nothing truly spontaneous about it.

"Is there anyone you want to call to collect you?" she asked kindly.

"You shouldn't go home on your own," the other nurse added.

Tracey shook her head, struggling to speak. How could she tell her the truth? There was no home. There was nothing. Just a box room in a filthy freezing squat, with overflowing carrier bags that had probably been rummaged through. In fact she didn't even have a proper bed. It was just a mattress on the floor. She didn't even know if she still had this, having been away from it for the last two days.

"How will you get home?" the nurse enquired, genuinely sounding concerned.

Did she really want to know? The isolation was hitting her in the face, huge waves smashing into her. These questions were just making everything worse. They were refusing to leave it alone.

"I will walk or get a bus. It's not far." Tracey avoided her gaze, staring instead at the large elastic belt that accentuated the woman's wide hips. Why did they have to wear a belt anyway? It wasn't holding up a skirt or trousers. It was something of a relief to be able to distract herself from what was a truly devastating situation even if only for a few moments.

She was instantly brought back to reality.

"You will need to wait a little while," the nurse's tone was firm now, "just until Santosh sees you. She's responded to the bleep and is on her way to the ward."

Tracey checked her phone. It was now 1.30pm.

"No. I have to go now."

"I have been looking for you." The student interrupted the awkward moment, handing her two large carrier bags. "I've put extra supplies in," she said, trying to be helpful. "I've got you small boxes of cereal and orange juice cartons too."

"Thank you."

"I know it's a bit heavy but when someone gets you, they can carry them for you." The student glanced at her colleagues but they shook their heads slightly, willing her to end this dialogue.

The staff had been so kind and had treated her like a human being, but shortly this would end and she would be on her own again. She could feel the blood oozing from her and she needed to return to the toilets. But this would have to wait until she was off the maternity ward.

There was one thing she had planned to do. To hold Ellie one last time. To kiss her and tell her that she would always be desperately loved and missed. Every single minute of every day. But it was all too much.

Instead, she abruptly turned and walked quickly towards the

ward exit. She heard her name being called but no one could do anything more to help her. Life felt even harder right now. Many of her acquaintances had already left this world. Not for the first time, she prayed that it wouldn't be long before her own miserable existence ended and she could be finally reunited with her mother.

If she had turned round, she may have seen several of the nurses wiping away their own tears. But their distress was only for Ellie. They had seen this all before and knew exactly what lay ahead of her in recovering from foetal drug addiction.

Eleven

Ellie

THE KEEN STUDENT WAS GIVEN THE RESPONSIBILITY of caring for the sleeping child until one of the nurses informed her that some special visitors had arrived. David, Ellie's social worker, had telephoned the ward and explained some of the background information. He had told the nursing staff eagerly that the people arriving were not bog standard foster carers. Melissa and Dan Baum had accepted an offer to be enrolled in Fenton's pilot fostering-to-adopt project. The details of the trial scheme weren't really relevant at that particular moment. To all intents and purposes, this childless couple were about to meet their baby daughter.

On hearing this news, the student midwife placed Ellie carefully in her cot and almost ran to the entrance to the ward to introduce herself. She pressed the entry buzzer and welcomed them. The smell of the woman's perfume hit her instantly and she couldn't resist looking them up and down! In her unflattering uniform, and the obligatory flat black shoes, the trainee felt instantly dowdy standing next to this well-dressed couple.

The prospective adopters had a certain air to them. Slightly stocky, Dan wore chinos and a checked blue shirt which complimented his olive skin. Holding his hand was an elated striking woman, his wife of almost ten years. The nurse couldn't tear her eyes away from her, taking in her attire. Petite, slim and youthful-looking, she smiled constantly, and was instantly engaging. With her slim fit jeans tucked into knee-high tan leather boots, she clearly took care of her appearance. She pulled a small suitcase behind her.

It was impossible not to note the sharp contrast to the bedraggled broken figure that had abruptly walked out of the very same double doors some four hours earlier. There had been real empathy for Tracey but this was all replaced now with such positive energy as the nurse guided them to meet Ellie.

The nurse thoughtfully pulled the curtains round the cubicle as Melissa impatiently flung her coat and handbag on the stripped bed – the same bed that Ellie's birth mother had miserably vacated hours earlier. Dan tenderly picked her up, adhering to advice from the nurse, as to how to hold her safely. It was an intimate and emotive moment, the two of them ecstatic as they cradled the infant together.

The Baums were instantly likeable, and the student was quite taken with them. She offered to make them a drink, but they were obviously besotted and just about managed to shake their heads in response.

"We have waited four years on the adoption lists," Dan told her as he took out his camera from its case.

Through her tears Melissa added, "We have our baby daughter now. We don't need anything else."

Sitting in the armchair, Melissa posed happily for photographs. Her long glossy hair fell over her face as she gazed overjoyed at Ellie in her arms. No one would have been able to tell that neither of them had had much sleep that night. The long-awaited phone call had come at 5pm the previous afternoon, their adoption link worker excitedly informing them that the child had been born and that they should be ready to head to Fenton District Maternity Hospital once the birth mother had left the ward. The details of the arrangement seemed on paper to be straightforward. They were told that Tracey would have a maximum of three days with the child, but it could be anytime within this timeframe that they would be called upon.

The last two weeks had been exceptionally tense and, just in case, the Baums had kept the potentially thrilling development secret from all their family and friends. They had learnt much about Tracey Mellor in that time period and had met once with David Lindley, her allocated social worker. He had been adamant that there were no family members to assess as potential carers and that the infant would definitely be placed into local authority care.

The impending birth was all Melissa and Dan had talked about during this period of waiting. Time went painfully slowly, both of them naturally anxious. Simultaneously, as the due date approached, David had given Tracey the absolute minimum in terms of support. Now the assessment had been concluded, he hadn't needed to try hard to engage her anymore. He found her to be childish, and his position had shifted somewhat. He was more concerned with the unborn baby and now conducted himself in an aloof and judgemental manner.

He moved his efforts, becoming readily available to the potential adopters, trying his best to reassure them. He gave them his mobile phone number, offering that they should phone him at any time if they needed him! He enjoyed cultivating this highly unprofessional friendship, thinking nothing of it.

David had forwarded the proforma requesting potential foster carers willing to adopt the unborn child. Interestingly, he had then been made aware of a significant fact. Jewish babies apparently rarely came up for fostering and adoption. In the rare cases that children needed to be placed, family members usually came forward. In this regard, he totally understood why this delightful couple hadn't been successful in being matched previously.

Meanwhile behind the scenes Melissa and Dan were struggling to get through this fraught period. Feeding off each other's insecurities, they were relieved to have work to focus on during the day. They were also full of apprehension about whether this fostering-to-adopt project was for them. The rows escalated. What would happen if they had to give the child back to the birth parents? They would never cope with this scenario. The project just wasn't feasible, Dan had argued. It was too much of a gamble. But they both acknowledged the hard and undisputable fact that they were desperate and needed to take this risk.

Finally, they heard the news they had been praying for. The baby had been born. With the adrenalin surging, they had the suitcase packed and their phones fully charged, ready to drop everything and travel together to the hospital. Their mood lifted instantly and finally they felt it safe to start informing their respective families of their wonderful news. All they were now waiting for was David to call them to say that Tracey had left the hospital.

They were here now and without a doubt it was the happiest day of their lives. They were being introduced to their baby girl. But Dan's anxiety hadn't dissipated. Whilst also euphoric, he found himself quite nervous. He found it useful to keep himself occupied, so he busied himself opening the carry-on case. The student looked on, again shocked at the dissimilarity between the two mothers. Tracey hadn't brought in any clothing items. There had been no preparation at all.

The suitcase was filled with brand new clothing. Melissa and Dan told the student that they had felt superstitious about unwrapping anything until it had been final, but the only exception had been to wash several babygros to rid them of the chemicals. They had been meticulous, ticking off items from their checklist. Dan located the muslin cloths depicting animal prints and handed one to Melissa. Ellie now opened her eyes and began to cry. This prompted the student to excuse herself to bring a bottle of formula milk. She was also caught up in the moment and she offered to stay to help with the feeding process, rather proud of herself. This was a particularly special day on the maternity ward. One she doubted she would see repeated in some time.

The prospective adopters thanked her. They had had lots of experience with their baby nephews and nieces, but a newborn was different. They had taken to the young nurse, who seemed so earnest. As they waited for her to return with the milk, Dan and Melissa took it in turns to pose with Ellie for their camera. They opened the curtains to get more light in, and it wasn't long before one of the other visitors on the ward came across to them, offering to take a picture of the three of them together.

The other new parents had taken an interest in the developments in bay one. Although wrapped up with their own additions to their families, they had whispered what little details they had assumed to each other. Word had got out to their extended families too. Everyone shared the same opinions about Ellie's birth mother.

In that long morning that Tracey had suffered in that same cubicle, no one had uttered a single word to her. They had purposely glanced away when she looked in their direction. Directly after lunch, she left the ward and suddenly she was the topic of conversation. Especially when one of the midwives removed Tracey's coat from the wardrobe. One of the visitors commented that they had observed a distraught-looking woman getting into the lift. She had been alone. Several of the new parents approached the nursing station concerned for the baby's welfare, and tried asking the midwives what was going on!

It was still visiting time when this glamorous couple had burst into the room looking ecstatic and impatient. It had been disappointing when the student nurse had pulled the curtains round the cubicle in question. It had been impossible to hear the conversation, but something was clearly going on.

Unable to hold back any longer, the young mother whose bed was directly opposite where Tracey had slept now walked across the room to offer her congratulations. Another now ventured, "I saw all the track marks. The poor baby's mum is a proper druggie!"

But Melissa and Dan were educated and sensitive people. They had also participated in the adoption training days and knew better than to engage with them about Tracey. Instead, they changed the subject back to Ellie and what a beautiful child she was. They had the sense to know that everything they had been told about Ellie's birth mother had to stay strictly confidential.

David had finished his day, and was on his way to the maternity unit. He didn't give Tracey much thought as he navigated the rush-hour traffic. He didn't even attempt to ring her to see if she was alright. He was only focused on Ellie and her new carers. He warmed to both of them, noting again how striking Melissa was, was her soft features, her natural make up, her wide smile and perfectly shaped whitened teeth. There were no words for the joy he read on their faces. This delightful fashionable couple in their middle thirties were just his type!

It was nice for once to be treated well by professionals. He took a seat and accepted an offer of a cup of coffee from the student nurse. She was in no rush to leave and volunteered to stay past her shift. He witnessed the Baum extended family now arriving in dribs and drabs, all hugging and kissing each other. He was introduced to Dan and Melissa's parents, smartly dressed, carrying a tasteful floral arrangement. Dan's sister arrived too, having left work early, bringing with her a large bag stuffed with baby gifts.

Shortly afterwards, Melissa's two sisters arrived, brimming over with excitement. With visiting hours now over, they took over a waiting room, using every spare chair they could find. Someone had purchased a large selection of sandwiches from Marks and Spencer. Ripping a packet open, Dan noted that David seemed to be quietly observing the obvious closeness of the two families interacting.

David offered an explanation. "In my line of work, I don't see enough supportive families!"

Offering David something to eat, Dan explained, "For some reason there is always food at a Jewish event and this one is proving no different!"

It was clear that Melissa and Dan hadn't just brought with them their own unique brand of love and laughter. They had brought, the immeasurable feeling of relief. For this childless couple, the rollercoaster years of fertility treatment had taken their toll. Today was a new beginning and it didn't get more heartening than this.

David was in no rush to go back to his bedsit and spend the evening alone watching the television. Instead, he chatted to Dan, learning that they had lost a stillborn boy at eight months gestation. The Jewish adoption issue was raised again. Everyone in the family knew that it was extremely rare for a Jewish baby to need a foster or adoptive placement. Everyone knew that this meant that it would be unlikely that they would be placed with a child. They had openly disclosed that this had been a desperate measure, and they had only agreed to the fostering-to-adopt scheme as an absolute last resort. They realised that they would have to start looking at inter-country adoption.

Crossing boundaries, David found himself assuring Dan straight away. He told him rather forcibly, "You don't need to worry! There is no chance on this earth that Tracey is getting this baby back!"

There was the obligatory paperwork to complete but David didn't want to ruin their special day by getting them to focus on that just now. He decided to wait until later to deal with the cumbersome bureaucracy.

Santosh now visited the ward and asked for a word with David privately. Once in the office, she shut the door and expressed concern that he should check up on Tracey and whether she had got back to the squat safely. He looked at her directly as he blatantly lied. He didn't feel this was any of Santosh's business but wanted rid of her questioning, so he told her he had chatted to Tracey on the telephone and confirmed that all was well. He prided himself on the fact that he could fob anyone off.

The truth was that he did not care at all for Tracey. He deemed her to be a disgrace, a selfish and weak individual who dwelled on the past. He was sorry her mother had died, but he imagined that she still had a loving father and sister. Which was more than most of his clients. Choosing to distance herself from her family wasn't clever when she was clearly so vulnerable. Like him, Tracey had been lucky to enjoy a grammar school education. Now, at best, he considered her a scrounger on the state.

As the due date became more imminent, he had become verbose in his incessant complaining to his colleagues. It was all very well, he would announce, that Tracey presented as a pleasant character on the surface, but the impact of her excessive drug use inflicted daily on her unborn baby hadn't occurred to her.

David made no secret of the fact that he had enjoyed a sheltered childhood. Before embracing a career in social work, he had never come across any Class A drug users. He couldn't relate to them at all. It was something alien to his middle class private school upbringing. He felt he had much more in common with Melissa and Dan and had enjoyed spending time supporting them over the past fortnight, becoming very fond of them. They had wonderful people skills and coping mechanisms. They were organised and fully prepared on a practical basis to take on a newborn.

What an extreme contrast they posed to Tracey Mellor, the immature birth mother who had proved that she was only able to think of her own needs. Furthermore, David couldn't fathom why Ellie's mother chose to mix with homeless individuals when he was sure that somewhere she had a loving family. It was unfortunate for Tracey that she had been allocated such a bigoted social worker to undertake the pre-birth assessment. She had been taken in by his superficial kindness initially, but there was little depth to him and certainly only selective empathy towards any of his clients.

David relaxed in the hospital armchair, observing the prospective adopters, and felt very comfortable in their company. He allowed himself to be fully absorbed into their inner circle. The Baums' private party, which he was entitled to attend. It made him feel less alone. It was good that Tracey had left the maternity unit a day earlier than he had anticipated. Less aggravation in keeping Ellie safe. Events had moved on and he felt rather smug. This was all going very well thanks to him. From now on, Tracey would be irrelevant to him.

The consultant paediatrician and his team now arrived. Santosh and David joined the meeting with the Baums in a private room behind the nursing station. The medical team professionals advised the prospective adopters that it would be a matter of days before Ellie's tiny body would start to withdraw from the cocaine and heroin exposure. This may manifest itself in potential epileptic fits, but this would hopefully calm down once the withdrawal was complete. During this potential period of instability, they were advised that Ellie may be transferred across the corridor, to the High Dependency Unit. They were told too that it would take several weeks, if not longer, before she would be discharged to their care.

None of this information came as a shock to them. Melissa was a pharmacist and they had both been warned in the adoption assessment of the risks of taking a baby who had been exposed to excessive amounts of drugs or alcohol in the womb. They had done their own independent research too. They knew that in some rare cases, seizures could become so severe that a child might become brain-damaged. They were worried sick, of course, about this potentially devastating scenario. But with their large extended family and relevant professionals on hand to support them, all they could do was to hope and pray that Ellie's symptoms would be mild and short-lived.

Twelve

THAT SAME EVENING, IT WAS PAST 8PM when David finally returned from the hospital. His girlfriend, Gina, ignored him, twisting her face as she turned her back on him. He made no attempt to engage with her. What was the point? With the children already asleep, he made himself a cheese toastie and ate it whilst watching the football.

He refused to give in to her silent treatment. The children on his caseload relied upon him. He thrived on the interaction with their carers, and would lose this if he progressed up the ladder to management. The last six months had been hard. The obsession with Natasha, his ex-social work student, had left him feeling humiliated, but had highlighted to him just how much he had stopped respecting Gina. He knew he was leaving a trail of errors in his life, and he questioned whether leaving the family home would be one of them. It was crucial that he kept himself busy in order that he didn't have to face his own circumstances any more than necessary.

The day's events at the hospital provided him with exactly the right kind of diversion. Melissa and Dan and their extended families seemed just his type. They had been ready at a moment's notice to step into Tracey's shoes and they were prepared to co-operate with any demands placed on them by all the professionals concerned. David prided himself on the fact that he was utterly dedicated to his cases, and he vowed to go over and above what was required of him to ensure the Baums were supported.

Over the next few weeks, Melissa and Dan certainly were grateful for David's support. Within four days of her birth, Ellie began the horrifying process of cocaine and heroin withdrawal. For her foster carers the frequent fits she now endured on a daily basis were distressing to watch. But supported by their respective families, they maintained their positive outlook and knew that this deterioration was only going to be temporary.

A newborn baby, who was being cared for round the clock by the High Dependency Unit and devoted carers, certainly did not require anything but regular phone calls to the ward at that stage. But the lost and totally misguided David chose to provide a heavy social work presence. Every few days or so, after work, he would find himself driving in the opposite direction from his home in the east suburbs of Fenton towards the town centre. There was the rush-hour traffic to contend with, then the struggle to find a car park space. But nothing was too much trouble for him.

For the next two weeks, he entered the ward on the sole pretext of being concerned for Ellie. His toxic home environment hardly beckoned him in the evenings, and it was during this period that he built the foundations of what he thought would be a lasting friendship between the Baums and himself.

Thankfully, by the end of February, Ellie had recovered and was settled into a routine in her new home. In this whole period, David had heard nothing from Tracey. He checked, and he wasn't surprised that the six-week deadline for her to register Ellie's birth had indeed lapsed. He took this as a sure sign that Tracey had disappeared permanently, and he went to Fenton Town Hall to undertake the relevant paperwork willingly.

With his personal life in crisis, David's work ethic had completely lost its direction. Like everyone else on Area Team Three, he never received regular supervision sessions from Bill, which should have looked in detail at the progress of his caseload. But being left to his own devices at this time was positively dangerous. With his darkened mood, he began caring less about his general workload.

Everyone had noticed how their colleague appeared to favour dealing with this particular case. On being challenged by Yotunde in particular, David would describe in great detail how wonderful

Melissa and Dan were. How embracing they were towards him. How they made him feel valued as a social worker. A rare event! He would justify what he coined his "platinum level service" too, by telling the other social workers all about the issue of being Jewish and childless. By the time he had finished explaining the cultural problems, they could appreciate why David had chosen to spend his time helping them, but privately they shared concerns.

Yotunde was more vocal than the others. She would argue with him that he shouldn't pick and choose which client to help. She entered Bill's office and slammed the door behind her. This was wrong. David had never suffered in life, she told Bill. What did he really understand about people who struggled to put food on the table for their children? Many of their clients had been brought up in the care system themselves. She warned Bill that she felt that David had crossed professional boundaries to such an extent that he should be removed from Ellie's case.

But as usual, Bill sounded uninterested and showed her the door. Minutes later, he passed David whilst on his way out of the room to enjoy a cigarette break. He told him curtly, "A supervision session is well overdue." David nodded, but they never did diarise a slot.

Over the next few months, there was relatively little to do on Ellie's case. There were, though, the first of three Looked After Children review meetings to co-ordinate with the allocated health visitor. As statutory requirements meant this must be chaired by an independent reviewing officer, to check that the care plan was being met.

All these types of meetings were usually held at the foster home. In this case, it would have made perfect sense for both him and the newly-allocated reviewing officer to travel together to the meeting, as they only worked a mile and a half from each other. But with the financial gain of bumping up their monthly mileage claims, they had decided to travel the thirty-mile round trip in separate cars.

At the very first gathering, Ellie was reported by her carers to be a little anxious, but this was to be expected after being exposed to drugs in the womb. In the Looked After Children minutes, it stated that it would be difficult to establish if there was any long-term emotional damage until Ellie began formal education.

Sounding convinced that the only outcome would be an adoption order, David updated the meeting that there would be no contact sessions with Ellie's mother. The child had no siblings. Furthermore, there was no information provided as to the birth father or grandparents. Indeed, Ellie was too young for nursery provision, so there was very little else left to discuss. The reviewing officer was so busy enjoying being in such pleasant surroundings that she didn't challenge what the arrogant social worker had to say. Instead she relaxed on a tan leather recliner whilst eyeing up the lounge. She then commented inappropriately, "I wish I lived in such a nice house!"

David cringed as he took in her dated attire. Social workers were not known for their haute couture but this was farcical. The frames of her glasses were too small for her face. The long grey hair did her no favours. Her amply filled voluminous skirt fell below her knee. The white flesh. Her swollen feet oozed out of her wide-straped sandals. The unpolished toenails.

The unsightly reviewing officer personified the type who David felt were attracted to work in social care. Melissa raised her eyes at him, bemused. They could both take a guess what the other was thinking. This so-called professional was a misfit, lingering too long and taking up everyone's precious time.

The Looked After Children review meetings were tiresome and far too frequent for David's liking. To his disappointment, it was always the same officer that attended. She appeared to draw them out for the sake of it. After all, everything was going smoothly and there was very little of relevance to discuss. She seemed overly concerned about when David would be able to give the Baums their copy of Ellie's life story work. She wasn't to know that he hadn't even made a start on it, and began nagging him to get it done.

But David hadn't given this any thought or priority. He had his own agenda. He wanted to be on his own with the Baums. He continued to undertake more than the required statutory home visits to check on Ellie. Never acknowledging his double standards, he too would linger in their kitchen, readily accepting their offer to make him lunch.

It wasn't just the tasteful décor and the relaxed atmosphere that attracted him. He would observe how Melissa and Dan's little family was evolving. It was plain to see that they had put their traumatic experience behind them and were counting off the days until the judge would rubber-stamp their adoption hearing application. There would be the celebration hearing scheduled for a month after this. Everything was so exciting for them and David was happy about his crucial part in it all.

The life story project was proving to be impossible, even in its most basic form. The reason for this was that, instead of trying to contact Tracey when she had left Ellie at the hospital, he had let this lapse. Only recently had he tried ringing her. And he had discovered that her mobile number was unobtainable. He found, too, the thought of visiting that squat again to be both unnecessary and depressing. As judgemental as ever, David assumed that Tracey would have moved on from there, and no one would know or even care where she had gone.

At the time of the pre-birth assessment, undertaken in December 2003, she had confided in him that she did not know who the father of the child was. At the time, he had wondered whether Tracey was a sex worker, but had felt it was none of his business and had not delved further. He had been only too happy to get the forms submitted and signed off by useless Bill well before the estimated due date.

It wasn't like David to make quite so many errors on one fairly straightforward case. He knew the reason why. For around the same time, his obsession with Natasha had escalated. He had been afraid that the one and only time they had sex they had both been drunk, and his performance was inadequate. He thought that she may be used to a twenty-one-year old who could keep going all night. He had hardly slept worrying that he could lose her as a result. And shortly afterwards, he had been proved correct!

Providing life story work at this stage was near impossible. Four months on, he had forgotten about the shoddy rushed assessment he had undertaken on Tracey. Any half-decent social work manager would have refused to sign it off, but Bill never properly read paperwork in any event. This error was now coming back to haunt him. He didn't want to let Ellie and her prospective adopters down. It would have been a basic fundamental requirement to ask Tracey for next of kin details. He knew full well that she had both a father and an older sister from whom she was estranged.

He doubted that Tracey's family had even known she was pregnant. But in normal circumstances he would not have needed her permission to contact her family. After all, it was standard procedure to see whether they would want to be put forward as potential carers before adoption plans were sought. He knew his mind was all over the place. He had placed several babies before with adopters, but usually the family support worker would undertake the life story work task. Social workers often found assisting a child in the care system with his or her background information to be the easy part of the job. Everyone understood that creating a child-friendly booklet was crucial in helping them forge an identity in later life.

But in Ellie's case, it was more than the fact that Area Team Three's family support worker was off on long-term sick leave. There was no one to fill in the gaping holes of Tracey's life. As a last resort, Yotunde helpfully tried to suggest that he search the Fenton social care database for any other children in care with the same surname that could be a relation of hers. He wasn't surprised to find that this route led to a dead end too. He recalled what Melissa and Dan, and indeed Ellie's own fostering link worker, had told him: very few Jewish children ever entered the care system.

He was finding this task utterly impossible, and was only able to scrape together a message that Ellie could read in her teens. A single page, explaining in child-sensitive terms about the problems Tracey had in the years leading up to when she fell pregnant. It talked about her drug use, her chaotic lifestyle, and lack of family support.

He managed to fill the page out as best he could, talking about how much Tracey mourned her late mother. He couldn't write about heroin, homelessness or the insecurity of living in a freezing squat. It just wasn't appropriate. So there was nothing else for it but to soften the message by saying how much she was loved and missed.

When he was done, he read through the final paragraph and

reconsidered his choice of emotive wording. He deleted the word missed. He didn't want Ellie looking for her birth mother in years to come. Instead, David wrote that Tracey had been honest and he praised her for making the sensible decision to relinquish her then-unborn baby for adoption. He knew, though, that this wasn't good enough, and that the reviewing officer wouldn't let up until she was satisfied. So David turned to Wayne for assistance on this particular aspect of social work practice. After all, his colleague often bragged that he was a specialist on life story work!

But Wayne had noticed that, of late, he had often found himself providing an emotional crutch for David. He, like David, was lonely, and threw himself into his work. He relished any opportunities in which to interact with his colleagues and got stuck in.

"So give me the photograph of Ellie's mum," Wayne said to David as he read the scant document.

"Er. I lost it." David looked uncomfortable.

"Well, call up the client and get another one."

"The line is dead." David shrugged his shoulders. "I've no clue where she lives now!"

"You utter moron. This is going to be impossible." Wayne's enthusiasm was waning.

"I don't suppose you have any photos of Ellie's birth family either? Grandparents for instance?"

David shook his head, not even willing to admit that he had failed in this particular respect.

Wayne didn't mask his frustration. He hated letting children down, and David's deteriorating standard of practice was infuriating him.

"You are pathetic! So what hospital was she born in?"

On receiving the relevant facts, Wayne googled Fenton General Hospital and cut and pasted a photograph of it onto a new word document. He then typed "I was born here" at the bottom of the picture, changing the font colour from black to purple.

But even for Wayne, producing something meaningful was impossible on this occasion. Instead, he focused on symbols of hope. He printed and cut out a large red heart which nicely filled up half a page. An image of a rainbow worked well too. Smiley faces, ducks and birds now bordered the odd sentence that he managed to put together.

It still didn't mask the fact that the book was scant and superficial.

Impressing himself at his creativity, Wayne took down from the noticeboard the photo from last year's Christmas meal of himself and David. He cut the photograph in half, eliminating himself from the image, and sellotaped it to a fresh page. But it looked too tacky and he abandoned this idea.

"So what's the message you want to put?"

"Best of luck Ellie?" David shrugged his shoulders again as he began eating a tuna sandwich. He tried to move the conversation along and told Wayne he was sick of the budget cuts and it wasn't his problem that their family support worker hadn't been replaced in a whole year. Undertaking life story work was not, his responsibility, he complained in his unbecoming bitter tone. He had received no training in it, and in any event, he was trying to save children's lives. It just wasn't essential to his job remit.

But Wayne wasn't interested in excuses. "Have you no imagination, David? It sounds more like a bog standard good luck greeting card."

Not waiting for an answer, Wayne typed a more meaningful farewell. He talked about Ellie's wonderful future ahead. How it had been a pleasure being involved with her adoption.

"Now, get it from the printer and read what I have put." Wayne loved dictating instructions. "I think you will agree that it sounds much more personal! Now sign it."

For the final touches, Wayne had selected all the text and enlarged the font to a mighty size sixteen. He then told David to ask the staff in the typing room to laminate each page. It wouldn't do for the book to be torn in years to come. And the finished product would be far more substantial-looking, if nothing else.

What had been done simply met basic requirements. It had been good of Wayne to help him out, and it was obvious that he had enjoyed his little arts and crafts session. It was unlikely that there would be any further Looked After Children reviews to be held, as the impending court hearing was so soon. So David felt lucky in this respect. He certainly didn't want the reviewing officer requesting to see this shoddy piece of work that wasn't worth the paper it was written on.

The very next day, David cancelled a home visit to another of his clients, a single parent of twins, suffering from diagnosed post-natal depression. Ignoring her pleas for help, he promised her he would rearrange to visit soon. Instead the blasé social worker made an impromptu arrangement to grab a coffee in Melissa's favourite store, the eclectic independent bookshop that doubled up as a café on Mosforth High Street. David felt very much at home in this rather affluent neighbourhood. It reminded him of the area that he had grown up in and he felt a warm sense of security.

For once, it felt like he had a "normal" job, as he gave the young waiter his order. David's grammar school friends had mostly gravitated to London and many were successful, working in the city. Their big bonuses had lately made him feel resentful, as he deleted emails from Fenton Social Care directorate, stating that social work salaries would be frozen again. He was sick of it all. This was now the fifth year of cuts!

But for now, he put to one side his bitterness. After all, how many of his old friends could say that they changed children's outcomes for the better? He watched with pride how radiant Melissa looked, as she lifted Ellie out of her pram into a highchair. It was obvious how she cherished undertaking even the most mundane tasks of raising her baby. He nodded sympathetically when she explained that they needed her income and therefore she had made the difficult decision to return, albeit part-time, at the end of the year.

As David handed her the plain black ring binder he felt quite embarrassed. He hoped she wouldn't be associating with other adopters, who would surely have received a more meaningful book from their allocated social worker. His wasn't even decorated with the child's name! He watched Melissa's face as it registered her disappointment when she turned over the first page. Immediately she pointed out kindly that there was a mistake. Ellie's date of birth had been written incorrectly!

As cheerful as ever, she still invited him for dinner two nights later. He arrived early, handing Dan a cheap bottle of white wine. He had felt honoured to receive the invitation, and some homemade food would be a welcome change from his usual pot noodles or sandwiches.

Over the meal, the conversation turned quickly towards the impending adoption party plans. What type of food to serve as canapés was discussed. And there was a disagreement between them about whether the food needed to be kosher.

David found the minutiae of the conversation to be quite fascinating. There was so much to organise. All the gazebos had to be erected and trestle tables and chairs had to be hired. Around eighty friends and family were expected.

Their celebration was understated. There would be casual dress and definitely no speeches were planned. They were just happy to be a family finally. David had been most impressed that instead of gifts, guests were advised that charity donations would be appreciated.

As the evening progressed, and over a second bottle of wine, the subject turned to David's crisis. Melissa and Dan knew that things hadn't worked out for Gina and himself and that he was now living alone. But now he let slip about his affair with his twenty-one-year-old social work student. How this had merely been a game to Natasha, and that he felt shown up. How his recklessness had cost him his children. That he was struggling to cope with life generally.

He couldn't remember the last time he had truly laughed out loud. All his friends now had children that occupied their free time, and he didn't fit in anymore. Slightly drunk, he offloaded on his clients, justifying it to himself that they were more like good friends. Besides, he told himself, he had put himself out for them in the early days when Ellie was a newborn!

Melissa and Dan showed themselves to be good listeners. With the floodgates opened, David shared more and more. How furious he was that his parents hadn't offered to pay for a solicitor. That they knew he didn't have a good income or significant savings to fall back on. And all that wasted rent having to live in a bedsit in Fenton's run down town centre. He bragged that his parents had an investment property portfolio and complained that it was so unjust that he was having to suffer.

The worst thing was when he disclosed how he hadn't seen his two young boys for a month. Oddly, he didn't feel ashamed that he had made no formal attempts to assert his rights in this regard. Dan and Melissa looked at each other, confused. Bizarrely, he offered in response that he had signposted many a client to the Citizens Advice Bureau but couldn't face queuing up himself. He had an answer to every problem. Perhaps, he told them, taking official legal steps would fuel Gina into poisoning the kids into saying they didn't want to see him. And he felt that this catalyst may send him over the edge.

Clearly seeing that David was distressed, his audience proved to be good listeners. Furthermore, they had solid advice for him. Dan suggested that he could have a word with his older brother who had worked as a solicitor based in Mosforth High Street. He would hopefully do Dan a favour and help David try and fight to see his children. But David explained that he had no way of paying legal fees.

With the Baums every problem seemed to have a solution, and Dan promised to speak to his brother, and try and clarify whether David would be entitled to legal aid representation. David was touched that they cared so much. Feeling so lonely, he offered more background information. He told them that his parents had sided with Gina and repeated how they refused to offer to assist him financially. He then went a step further. He told them how his team was led by a dysfunctional manager who he described as "an inadequate freak!" As the effects of the wine took hold, he couldn't seem to shut up.

This was a wholly inappropriate way for any social worker to conduct themselves, but David knew that immediately after the adoption celebration, he would need to close the case. And this was only two weeks away. Melissa and Dan pointed this fact out too. They were kind enough to say that they had been extremely fortunate to have had such a dedicated worker in him and they promised to try and support him.

It had been such a pleasant evening and David had enjoyed all the attention. There was a warm glow about him. It was probably the effects of the wine. Any inappropriate sexual feelings he might have entertained towards Melissa were somewhat tempered by her parting advice to him.

"Don't be late for the adoption hearing, David. And smarten yourself up a little!" she teased.

But, then, as he climbed into his burgundy twelve-year-old Ford Focus, he realised it was scarcely a passion wagon!

Thirteen

Sunday 18th July 2004

This was the second weekend in a row that David had spent entirely on his own. With plenty of spare time, and on Melissa's advice, he had sourced a white shirt in his size, from his local Marie Curie. He had been pleased with his find, as it still had the package crease lines in it. He had located, too, an expensive silk tie from years ago – a Christmas gift from an aunt, stuffed in an old suit pocket. It would have to do for Ellie's adoption court hearing. What with continuing to pay half the mortgage, and the rent on the studio flat, he had to monitor his expenditure.

He tried on the suit but it hung off him. Why were so few people reaching out to him? It seemed only Melissa and Dan cared. He was certainly struggling to adapt to living alone. His signature thick hair needed cutting for the adoption party. He was practically the guest of honour and it wouldn't do to look shabby.

The antidepressants were starting to work, and he was pleased that he had managed to make himself an omelette for lunch. It made a change from sandwiches. But the evening stretched ahead of him as usual. He studied again the rather unusual homemade invitation to Ellie's long-awaited adoption party. It had been sitting in pride of place on his window ledge. Anyone who put themselves forward for the fostering-to-adopt scheme was taking a brave gamble, and he respected Melissa and Dan for it. In the nature of his work, he often came across amazing dedicated foster carers and he felt an immense feeling of satisfaction in this particular case.

It was only 5pm, and he couldn't get ready for bed yet. There was no one he felt he particularly wanted to speak to. Certainly he didn't want to see old friends. It was easier with Wayne. He had nothing to prove to him, and he now looked forward to catching up with him the following morning. Perhaps he would invite him out for a curry next Saturday night to mark his birthday.

But first, there was his workload to address. His Sunday night routine was unchanged from the days when he lived at home. The only difference was that then he would wait until his children were in bed before catching up on his work. He couldn't face trying to call his boys, knowing that Gina would tell him that they didn't want to speak to him. Instead he turned on his computer and watched the bold print marking a sign of at least twenty fresh emails. How they flooded through. He was used to the onslaught. Carers didn't need to wait until Monday morning to email him that placements were breaking down. And out-of-hours social workers would send across urgent updates as they came in, which were at any time of day or night.

He scrolled down, selecting which ones to open up first. He ignored the cases that bored him. The cases he had held for years, where for one reason or another, no progress was ever made. He would read those another day.

Instead, he worked on a case involving an eleven-year-old boy with learning difficulties. He had been found caring for his two younger siblings whilst their mother had gone on a date. The case was in the court arena, and he needed to finish his statement. This deadline had been looming all week, but he had chosen instead to have lunch with Melissa. He still didn't regret making that round trip to Mosforth, eating unnecessarily into three hours of precious work time. His infatuation with her was pointless, he knew this. It wasn't that he wanted to have sex with her. Well, maybe! But it was more that he felt she was so genuine, so happy, giving and loyal. He hoped she would always be in his life, offering the hand of friendship.

He tried to take a grip of his feelings and forced himself instead to get back to his work. He needed to grasp the facts on a file that Bill had forced on him a week earlier. It made unpleasant reading. Fourteen-year-old Ebunoluwa (known as Ebun) had been found starving, having been smuggled into the UK in the back of a lorry. Terrified, he was isolated and the authorities had placed him in a residential home on a temporary basis.

This case would be far too problematic, not to mention time-consuming. The teenager would need somewhere permanent to live. He had to be enrolled in a school and would need specialist trauma counselling. David knew he was out of his depth. He knew nothing about Nigerian culture and Ebun's identity. How exactly was he supposed to arrange for him to see his family?

He felt no guilt for doing absolutely nothing for Ebun for over a week. Instead, he decided to force his case back onto Bill. Ignorant of the world, he would argue that Yotunde was from a similar cultural background and therefore would be more suited to assist him.

He knew exactly what he would be facing the following morning. He pictured Siobhan, his gym-gear-clad drab colleague, sitting digesting her muesli breakfast mix. The remnantswould be left in her Tupperware box all day. He found her habits to be revolting and took offence at how ineffectual and immature she was. Even Bill had told her off for researching puppies during work hours, but she seemed to perceive this as an observational comment, not an intended criticism.

His mind wandered to the cases in the past that had meant something to him. The sixteen-year-old boy he had successfully talked down from a bridge would stay with him forever. He had dealt with the whole matter quickly and had most definitely been impressed with his own leadership skills. It was the one of the few times that Gina had shown an interest.

He would never forget the devastating case of Lena either, a twenty-eight-year-old single mother from Poland who was fatally injured in a car crash. Her six-year-old daughter Emilia had been discovered, physically unhurt. David had been on duty that morning and had rushed to Accident and Emergency, to find the child inconsolable and the nursing staff in tears as they struggled to pacify her.

He had been proud of his decision to stay with the little girl all day and to assist with the arrangements. It had been a natural choice to wait for her grandparents' flight that same evening. He was determined to avoid placing Emilia with emergency foster carers. It would take days until the formal assessments could be undertaken on the extended family. The system was flawed and this wouldn't be in her best interests. He had been a passionate social worker in those days and he thought outside the box to achieve results.

So somehow he managed to persuade the police to hand over Lena's keys and had driven with Emilia to the airport to meet her grandparents' flight. This way, he could check them over whilst he dropped them off. He had spoken to both of them on the phone at length and was satisfied that they enjoyed a close relationship. A brief chat during the car journey back to her home would have to suffice in these extenuating circumstances. He could return the following day to conduct the viability assessment, and would just predate the notes. Bill certainly wouldn't be double checking and would only be too happy to sign it off and get the file closed.

Ignoring procedures could have cost him his job, but all he was thinking of was little Emilia and her mother. He had chosen social work because he had wanted to make a difference. And that day, a deeply traumatised girl needed to sleep in her own bed, cared for by her loving grandparents. He was not prepared to make her life any worse by subjecting the bereaved family to a paperwork exercise.

By the time he arrived home it was nearly midnight. He had tried to explain, but Gina had been furious with him and told him to make sure he got paid for the extra hours. Years on, he often thought of Emilia. That haunting image of her, in her school uniform, sobbing hysterically in a nurse's arms. He had witnessed the most horrendous things in his job, but this had been the hardest to watch. He estimated that she would be around thirteen now. He wondered if she still lived with her grandparents and whether she was OK.

These past few months had hardened him and he hardly recognised who he had become. He was selective about whom he assisted and could offer no insight into why he was in self-destruct mode. He looked around his sparse bedsit in disbelief. He shouldn't be here. He should be at home with his children, creating a family life for them. His friends had always commented how caring he was, but he knew this wasn't really true anymore.

Several hours of intense work and the attempts of self-analysis had worn him out. It was 9pm, and he had had enough of his day. He put Ebun's file back into his briefcase and decided to get ready for bed. He was about to close his computer down, when he saw that several new emails had dropped into his in-box. Others were clearly working out of hours too! One was marked, "High importance re: Tracey Mellor."

What the hell was this about? He instantly froze, trying to rationalise his bad vibes. Was this an overreaction perhaps? After all, he acknowledged that his own mental health was unstable. But to receive any communication so late on in the adoption process was certainly concerning. It had been a whole five months since Ellie's birth, and there had been no word from Tracey in this entire time.

Perhaps Tracey was requesting a recent photograph of Ellie. Of course, this wouldn't be a problem, and he would provide this as a goodwill gesture. He hoped she wouldn't remember the one of her, looking frail and sad, holding Ellie in her bruised arms. He clearly recalled receiving two copies several weeks after her birth. A compliment slip, signed by a student midwife, had stated the images had been taken just before Tracey had left the hospital, relinquishing Ellie.

At the time, David knew he should have forwarded these to his client, but dealing with more urgent tasks had been his priority. He never did get round to it. Now it was too late, as they had been mislaid amongst the mounds of files, precariously stacked up on every spare surface of his desk. He guessed that they had slipped into the wrong client file by mistake. He was sure they would turn up at some point, but for now, he would have to deny ever receiving the photographs.

It was his own fault. He recalled how many times the team had received the directive from senior management instructing them to put all confidential files away in locked filing cabinets at night. Everyone chose to ignore this, laughing at the ridiculous concept that the cleaning staff actually lingered long enough to snoop.

Perhaps there was another reason why this solicitors' firm was contacting him. She must be passing on Tracey's details so that she could engage in the "letterbox" process. The exchange of yearly update letters between adopters and birth parents couldn't happen without a forwarding address. That, too, would be acceptable. He was sure, that Melissa and Dan would co-operate with this. They had always struck him as extremely accommodating and easy-going.

The light of the day was starting to fade, and David felt his neck stiffen up. He realised that he had been staring at the screen for some time now. Without noticing, his right hand was covering his mouth. Of course, he had noticed that the email had been sent from a solicitor from a well-established family law firm based in the town centre. It wasn't a large firm, and he had crossed the senior partner in court on several occasions. A passive aggressive character, Adreen Wood was well known across the Fenton Area Teams for taking on Childcare Services.

This was no good. He had to fight the negative vibes. He had worked out, by process of elimination, where he had made some errors in this case. It was in the early days, and seeing as Tracey was a severe drug addict, he judged her as someone who wouldn't be the type to make a formal complaint. He would sort out getting copies of the lost photographs somehow. And if not, he would have to meet the woman at a one-off goodbye session and take the pictures then. It would be a pain to arrange. She probably wouldn't even turn up. But this was his own fault. He had to be more organised in the future.

None of these thoughts made any sense. Why would a solicitor be writing about something so minor? Something was wrong. His right hand hovered over the mouse for several more moments before he finally clicked on it.

Fourteen

There was only a brief cover note, requesting he read the attached documents. Within seconds, he had grasped the gist of it. He was an experienced child protection social worker with over twelve years under his belt. He could hazard a guess what this was all about. Tracey had made significant progress and wanted her baby back with her. The well-meaning solicitor, Adreen Wood, had the wrong agenda. Her law firm were trouble.

His anxiety quickly turned to anger. He knew how the Adreens of the world operated. He had met enough childcare legal advisors in his time. He imagined that she too was a hardened advocate. He could visualise her positioned opposite Tracey in one of the prison interview rooms. She would be well-dressed, probably wearing a black fitted polyester trouser suit. Her shiny hair would be tied back in a pony tail, her makeup subtle. She would nod at the right moments, leaning forward to show interest. She would be experienced at multitasking, listening carefully whilst jotting down notes using a fountain pen.

It was all about the billing. Like many others, she wouldn't be in a rush to conclude the interview. She would be lapping up every sentence uttered by anyone instructing them. In the event that nothing added up, where their back story didn't make sense, they would remain silent. A moral standing was not required of them. It was quite simply none of their business.

In David's experience, all childcare legal representatives viewed everything from their client's perspective. They were paid to represent their clients and that was the end of it. With their huge legal fees fully covered by the tax payer, there would be no financial risks. It was a win-win for them. Easy money. Cynical, he couldn't imagine any of them awake at night, worrying about vulnerable children being returned to their abusive caregivers.

He found himself perspiring and opened a window to get some air. He was sick to death of lawyers and barristers encouraging his clients to fight the system. It wasn't fair on the children he tried to protect. Delaying court cases meant delaying decisions for permanency, and this, was against his beliefs. Children needed to know where they were going to be living. He tended to keep his views to himself for obvious reasons. It was his opinion that parents and caregivers should be given a single chance. If they messed things up, they should do the right thing and walk away.

But he did have to acknowledge, albeit resentfully, that clients were capable of change if they wanted to. Four months being incarcerated was a long time and help was available in the prison system. Crucially, it wasn't quite too late for Tracey to fight for her daughter. Clearly her circumstances had changed significantly and he found himself hunched over the computer despairing.

How could this be? David was shocked. The last he had heard, Tracey had been charged with drug-dealing shortly after Ellie had been born. He had been informed by her probation worker that she was facing a long custodial sentence. He had been horrified to hear that a school child had died as a result of taking illegal substances and that Tracey and her "friends" had been directly involved in this tragic accident.

He knew that in theory he should send Tracey copies of the Looked After Children reviews. But in the circumstances, he was disgusted with her. Whilst it wasn't his place, he didn't feel she deserved to know how Ellie was progressing. He had contributed towards the criminal justice system's request for background information and had received the sentencing outcome. In view of this, he had assumed the path was clear for Melissa and Dan to apply to the court for the adoption order.

This remarkable development was totally unexpected. The legal letter spelt out that Tracey had completed a four-months long drug detoxification programme, and Adreen had attached the certificate as evidence. Another attachment contained a report from the staff supervising the Harlton Wells exhibit at the Royal Horticultural Society flower show. Tracey was apparently a keen participant in the project and was due to attend the show on day release at the end of the month. They were all hoping for another silver medal. The report ended by saying that Tracey was a popular member of the team!

He skimmed each document, horrified. There was so much detail and he felt light-headed with what he was learning. More worrying than the gardening were the twice weekly appointments with her allocated volunteer mentor. By now, David had guessed that someone within the prison system had empowered Tracey. From his clear memory of such a severely damaged woman, he very much doubted that she would have been in a position to make so many positive changes on her own. Now he realised what had happened. This mentor was the backbone of her plea.

He imagined this random "do-gooder" poring over the *Guardian* newspaper every morning. Her little hobby, "helping the under-privileged", was purely to improve her own self-worth, giving herself something different to talk about at dinner parties. She was most probably a bored housewife.

Having been through private schooling himself, he was familiar with what he perceived to be the type. The wealthy parents of friends who tried to fake concern for the underclasses. They may even do a little fundraiser black tie dinner for a worthy charity, and be pictured for the local papers. Perhaps they would be competing against each other to be their child's school governor. But was it all about their status? He was sure that none of them had a clue how it felt to queue up in the rain for the food bank. To have the bailiffs at the door. To have no support system. In Ellie's case, to foster a newborn baby suffering from drug withdrawal symptoms.

David wasn't an intelligent man. He couldn't see just how similar he was to his vision of the mentor. He was a product of his middle class upbringing and, in some respects, he had inherited his father's aloof right-wing mentality. As always, he was deeply judgemental. He felt he knew Tracey better than the mentor and the other professionals who were trying to help her. In his eyes, nothing Tracey could do would be enough. She wasn't fit to parent and that was the end of the matter. All this had achieved was to raise a troubled woman's hopes, and surely that was morally wrong?

The best argument was saved until last. It was Adreen's saving grace. A killer. The letter stated that there was now a vacancy in HMP Harlton Wells mother-and-baby unit.

This was extremely unfortunate timing. He had always been aware of a national shortage of places for mothers wanting to care for their babies in prison. Predictably, via her solicitor, Tracey was requesting a reassessment to care for Ellie in there.

This was ridiculous. Ellie was already placed with prospective adopters. She was settled and thriving. In any event, there were strict rules about mother-and-baby units. Surely they wouldn't take Tracey. But then he quickly reminded himself that she had never demonstrated any violent tendencies and was now, according to these reports, drug-free.

His mind raced as he did the maths. He knew that children had to leave the unit once they reached eighteen months. If Tracey was due to be released in ten months, Ellie would be a year and a half old by then. With the after-care team responsible for finding suitable housing for them upon release, it was impossible to fault what was a comprehensive appeal on behalf of Tracey. Adreen Wood was no fool. She had anticipated every hurdle and sounded capable of finding solutions.

He swore out loud repeatedly, horrified at the likely ramifications for Melissa and Dan. He was acutely aware that, in all this extensive correspondence, there hadn't been one single mention of what was best for baby Ellie. The letter appeared to be saying it was a forgone assumption, that a child was best placed with biological parents.

He thought back to six months earlier. When he had assessed Tracey during her latter stages of pregnancy, she hadn't been remotely interested in co-operating with social care. That day he had told her the negative outcome was clear in his mind. She had chosen to leave the offices when he had asked her specifically to wait while he located some housing association phone numbers.

Perhaps it was about gaining suitable housing once released

from prison, he thought bitterly. A simple but effective tactic that could work if the child was returned to her care. Tracey had struck him as a friendly type on each occasion she had met him. She had probably made friends with other inmates with young children. Perhaps some of them were living in the mother-and-baby unit. He imagined that it was probably less institutionalised and more cheerful.

His empathy lay only with Melissa and Dan. The timing of this bombshell could not have been worse for them. From the moment David had met them, he had treated them as Ellie's adopters. He had prided himself that it had been a wonderful match, and they couldn't have done a better job nursing her through the drugs detoxification process.

It wouldn't just be their own lives that would be shattered. What about the immense distress to their extended family too? Her four grandparents who doted on her. The small army of aunts, uncles and cousins, who saw Ellie frequently and utterly adored her.

His body felt heavy as he got up from the chair and picked up the adoption party invitation again. It was due to be held the same night as the adoption hearing in two weeks' time. There was also a reception in the synagogue to which the entire community was invited the following Saturday morning. Now this would have to be cancelled. At best, everything would be delayed. But at worst … he didn't know how they were ever supposed to cope with this unimaginable heartache.

For some strange reason, he had invested serious energy into "helping" Melissa and Dan. They had a large supportive family and had barely needed him. It had been good to have him as a sounding board in the early weeks when Ellie was being weaned off the drugs, but they had certainly not needed him since. They were genuine kind people and had seen how much he had been struggling emotionally and tried to help him. It was probably payback for all the encouragement they had received from him, but David didn't see it at all this way. He was lonely and viewed them as extremely close lifelong friends.

What now? The extended family would turn to him for immediate answers. This was a horrific nightmare. They would rely on him and would expect one hundred per cent reassurance that Ellie would not be taken from them. But based on this letter, and the evidence so far demonstrated, how exactly could he give them any?

David was again consumed by his own losses and bad decision-making processes. He had no faith in himself anymore. Without his own children in his life, he questioned whether he would ever recover and become a loving father once more. In the meantime, he knew he wasn't the right person to remain on the case. He couldn't help himself and it was clear that he couldn't help the Baums.

Six months previously, he had had no choice. Decisions had to be taken before his heavily pregnant client went into labour. He had been of the opinion that the assessment was a total waste of resources from the very beginning. The matter had been concluded nicely too, because there were no relatives that Tracey was able to identify to assist her, or her unborn child.

If there had been a relative, this would have complicated things somewhat. Sometimes a family member came forward to be assessed as a potential carer, but in this particular case, Tracey had informed him that, once close, her father and sister couldn't cope with her criminal lifestyle and had ceased contact some years earlier. David at the time had taken her word for it but he realised now that he should have found out for himself what her family's view was. He should have insisted on her providing a next of kin. Instead he had faxed an urgent referral to the newly set up foster-to-adopt service. Yet another gross mistake that could cost him his job.

This was an absolute crisis. He drank several shots of neat vodka as he pondered more on the errors made. All of these mistakes had been made around the same time that he had been obsessed with Natasha, his social work student. It had all been going well and they had both enjoyed a close working relationship. He had always loved being a practice teacher and flirting with the young students. But that disastrous sex after the Christmas meal out had ruined everything for him. He had tried to forget, too, the humiliation when Natasha had made a formal complaint to her university lecturer. He had quickly deleted the insulting email informing him that the placement had been abruptly terminated. His mind certainly had not been on the job at that time.

He hadn't meant to, but he knew he had been judgemental as usual. The most fundamental error, he realised now, had been not securing an interim care order for Ellie. Instead, he had got Tracey to sign a voluntary Section 20 arrangement whereby the client and Fenton Local Authority would share parental responsibility. This plan had made sense at the time and he certainly hadn't had any guidance from Bill to say otherwise.

To be fair, thought David, he had written to Tracey several times after the birth, but there had been no response. Another more dedicated social worker would have made the effort to go round and knock on the door of the squat. This would have been the usual procedure in these circumstances. Instead, he had purposely sent the letters unrecorded in the post, hoping she would never receive them.

It certainly appeared that way, as six weeks after the birth, David received the confirmation he had been expecting. No birth family member had registered Ellie's birth. In accordance with social work procedures, he had visited the town hall himself to deal with the formalities. Yet another task to do, but he didn't complain. After all, this was another strong indication that Tracey had walked away.

On his way home, he had hesitantly parked outside the squat. There was the matter of requiring his client's signature on the formal relinquishing papers. He had been relieved to discover the property vacant, the front door boarded up. As Tracey was now officially described as of "no fixed abode", he considered his involvement with her to be concluded.

Weeks later he recalled receiving the news he had been expecting from Tracey's probation officer. Tracey had pleaded guilty and had been remanded into custody following the drug-related crime, whereby a fifteen-year-old school boy had died of an overdose. David hadn't masked his disgust and voiced out loud his sympathy for the deceased child and his grieving family. His colleagues had agreed with him. Furthermore, he showed no interest in the court developments involving his client, and there had been no statutory requirement of him to attend the Crown Court.

As time went on, David was contacted again to update him that Tracey had been transferred to HMP Harlton Wells. He had updated his files with this new information and left it at that. This was, according to his mindset, the end of the matter. Ellie was now officially abandoned. There were the usual steps to approve the adoption plan, and he had encountered no issues at any stage.

In time, he had been thrilled to tell his new friends that they were free to apply for the official adoption order.

Who could ever have predicted this present scenario? In all the years he had practised as a social worker, he had never come across such a damaged client who had turned their life round within such a short period. In the child protection arena, most social work mistakes can't be rectified. It was playing with people's lives.

He berated himself again and again. Why had he been so preoccupied that he hadn't even taken legal advice from his own local authority solicitors? It wouldn't have cost him anything personally. He knew the answer. Because he thought he knew best. If he had focused on his job and not his attractive social work student, he would have been advised to put the case in front of a judge. By now, a care order would be all the security he had needed.

He poured himself another shot of vodka. What the hell had he done? He was as bad as Bill. Worse. Everything could have been avoidable, if only he had followed basic social work guidelines six months earlier. It would have been too late for Tracey to reappear on the scene.

He lay on his bed drunk, trying desperately to think of a way out of this crisis. His head whirled round, the same issues. And then, in the early hours, it came to him …

Fifteen

The Coward Opts Out

Monday 19th July 2004

The morning couldn't come soon enough for David. Hyper-anxious, he arrived in the office at 9am. A full fifteen minutes after the official start time, but he was still the first in! He realised that he was in no fit state to undertake any home visits that day and banged out several emails explaining that he was unwell and needed to rearrange meetings for another day. He also made a quick telephone call to one of his clients, the young single mother struggling with post-natal depression. Lacking all empathy, he cut her short as she tried to offload. It had been a trying weekend for her, but David couldn't find the energy to listen. He told her he had an emergency and would call her at the end of the week to reschedule.

He put the phone down feeling slightly guilty. He was exhausted and had driven to work having consumed half a bottle of vodka in the early hours. All he could do today was to deal with the Ellie crisis. Once it was hopefully resolved, he planned to head straight back to his bedsit and get some well-earned sleep. The sooner he implemented his strategy the better for all concerned.

Having cleared his day, he dropped Ebun's file on Yotunde's

chair, a common practice in local authority social work offices. The peculiar etiquette involving reallocation and swaps tended to be a casual matter. Another day, perhaps later in the week, he made a mental note to explain to Bill that he couldn't take on Ebun's complexities just now. He didn't have any real empathy for this traumatised starving teenager discovered by border control hiding between boxes in the back of a lorry, no doubt absolutely desperate for support.

It was a well-known fact within the team that Bill had a shocking memory. As an afterthought, he decided to play on this and felt it would probably be safer to deny ever being allocated Ebun's case in the first place. Over the years David had become very skilled at justifying his own actions. There was nothing wrong with how he conducted himself. Ebun simply deserved a social worker with more time to assist him. He had no idea whether Yotunde even had space in her caseload, but either way, he was determined this matter wouldn't be dumped back on him.

It was frustrating to wait for his useless manager to turn up. Indeed his stomach felt tight as he printed off Adreen's email and the relevant attachments. He noted several faxes that were stacked up from the weekend, emergencies that needed attention. He ignored them. It was as much as he could stand just to try and deal with the potential catastrophe over Ellie. In any event, Wayne would arrive at any moment and it was his unofficial job to sort out the duty referrals.

The phones started ringing out. The calls would be from healthcare professionals or teachers, throwing at him such difficult challenges and expecting him to come up with magical solutions. This was the reality of a frontline team and he was sick of feeling needed. Not for the first time of late, he lifted the receiver off the hook. All the while he nervously kept watching the door, praying that his manager would arrive soon.

It was gone 9.15am when Bill arrived, his brown short-sleeved striped polyester shirt already showing signs of escaped sweat.

"We have a massive disaster!" David announced, pouncing on him without offering any pleasantries. He followed Bill into his office and silently handed him the relevant materials for him to peruse.

An exhausted David slumped into the blue moulded plastic chair. He stared at his dishevelled manager mutely. It was like watching someone in slow motion. The reading glasses had to be located. Then he had to get his biro out of his drawer. Finally, he began reading the paperwork. David sighed quietly in exasperation as he waited. He knew exactly why Bill had been elevated to team leader. The rumours about the affair with spinster Norma Cresswell, the previous director, were probably accurate!

The truth was that Bill was slightly put out. He was in the habit of making himself a coffee. Once he had finished, he would then head outside to the designated area for a cigarette. That morning though, he realised he was going to have to delay his usual routine. David and Wayne were his most experienced workers and despite the very nature of child protection work, they tended to have a relatively calm disposition. Obviously something was very badly wrong.

It was strange that Bill's attention was more focused than usual. The team had pinpointed the change after the explosion of negative verbal feedback from last month's Ofsted inspection. Ever since, Bill had shown far more interest in what was going on. He would probably go back to his old ways, but for now, he was taking too long to read the crucial information. He was also irritating David with all his questions!

"It's the relinquished baby, surely you remember?" David answered him, loudly sighing this time. "The druggie mother I found living in a freezing cold squat in December." He spoke clearly, but was in a rush to explain. "Drug dealer, no antenatal care, heroin, cocaine, you name it." He paused only to take a breath. "The filthy squat, Bill!" he repeated for good measure.

"Oh yes, of course."

Of late, Bill often struggled to recall clients' details. He didn't know if this was due to the fact that he was exceptionally uninterested in the work, or whether this was the beginnings of early-onset dementia. He tried consoling himself that David was talking about events six months ago. He couldn't be expected to recall all of the cases. There were so many. He hoped that things would get easier for him once he implemented the mandatory monthly supervision timetable for his staff. He had reassured the Ofsted inspectors that this would be a positive way forward. It would be an excellent way of keeping up to date, and he hoped that he wouldn't be sacked for gross incompetence in the meantime!

He was aware, though, that he allowed all his staff to speak to him with a general air of disrespect. David continued to hurl the facts of Ellie's case at him.

David recognised in Bill the familiar signs that he too lived alone and perhaps struggled to care for himself. The dirty reading glasses and nicotine-stained teeth were a giveaway. It wasn't a pleasant thought that he now fell into the same category as his manager, verging on dishevelled.

But his manager's enthusiasm took him by surprise. His voice was elevated somewhat. "Wow ... What a transformation ... Good on Tracey!" he interjected every so often as he continued to read.

Standing up suddenly, David butted in forcefully, "Over my dead body is she getting that baby back!"

"On what grounds?" Bill leant back in his chair and stared at him. Placing his hands behind his head, he was unaware of the sweat marks. He was curious about what David had to say. What dramatic behaviour. He didn't care for such an overbearing presence. This wasn't like the David he knew at all.

"Well, Ellie has been very sick." David launched into his appeal. "The Baums took it in turns to sleep by her bedside whilst she was in the high dependency unit for two whole weeks." He expected Bill to nod, but there was nothing. He couldn't read his thoughts at all. For good measure, he added, "She is their life and there are special circumstances too as Ellie is of Jewish heritage."

It was with passion that David described the background. He explained concisely that there was a national shortage of Jewish children cominge up for adoption. That Melissa and Dan had suffered a stillbirth, and had already been down the line of IVF. Bill appeared to be listening intently as David stated his case. "They have already waited four years on the adoption approval list. They will be unlikely to be placed with another child again."

He found himself pleading, "This will be a tragedy for them, and certainly isn't in Ellie's best interests."

But Bill's response was clear. "Look," he said, rereading the documents as he spoke, "she's the child's mother and she has clearly done everything she can to address her problems. So get out to the prison and reassess her!"

It was with some shock that Bill saw how closed-minded and unprofessional David was sounding. None of this was new to him, for Yotunde and Wayne had separately raised concerns that David had become too emotionally attached to the prospective adopters. He should have listened to them. He realised that he had relied upon his juniors to make decisions for him. He had been too detached. That jobsworth Ofsted inspection duo had harangued him for two long days, so he didn't need any additional stress. David wasn't the only one stressed. Every morning he waited for the predictable outcome to arrive. Then he would be finished.

It was true, David was seemingly unbalanced lately, but he would address this instantly. He now interrupted him in full flow. "Let's book in a date for a formal supervision session," he said, trying to equal him in vigour.

"This is supervision!" David shrugged, adding, "I have no time for this!"

Bill was used to feeling bullied by his juniors. It was pathetic that he had to make such a stand against David. He sat up tall and announced firmly, "Should Tracey be deemed fit to care for Ellie, you will need to make immediate plans for them both to be reunited!"

Misinterpreting what Bill was saying, David felt exasperated that a team leader could have such a simplistic thought process. What a gaping hole in his child development knowledge. This was extremely worrying. In this regard, David felt it necessary to state what he felt was obvious.

There was no debate to be had with this idiot. These were the facts. Ellie would not be returning to her birth mother's care. Not now, not ever! He had always been an indefatigable arguer. Tracey Mellor was in a secure facility where she was supported by her mentor and other staff members. She didn't need to worry about providing enough money for food for herself. It would only become clear upon her release whether she could indeed sustain long-term change. Independent living may present many challenges to her and she may regress into drug use.

"You must remember, Bill," he was pleading with him now, "why do you think she's serving a sentence?"

But his manager shook his head slightly, looking vacant. He willed David to go on.

David explained that Tracey had been one of a gang of drug dealers who had preyed on naïve school children outside Barnham Hill comprehensive school. A fifteen-year-old boy had died from a Class A overdose just before Christmas 2003. A month or so after giving birth to Ellie, she was arrested and pleaded guilty to the crime. Both she and her three associates had all received long custodial sentences.

"But the report says she has shown remorse," Bill interrupted now. "I suppose everyone is entitled to make mistakes," he offered.

David was incensed. Why did he have to be saddled with the most ineffectual social work manager in the borough? Usually it suited him to be left alone to run cases as he wished, but today, he needed him.

This wasn't going too well. His manager was a robot. This case had probably made the papers. Most probably there would have been a large photograph of the grieving family, giving a statement to the press outside the courtroom. A child had lost his life. Why didn't this register with him?

But Bill took a stand. "I am sure that Melissa and what's his name have done an excellent job in difficult circumstances," he acknowledged reasonably. "But that's what the fostering-to-adopt scheme is geared up for."

It was with some pride that he stood up to David. "people are desperate for babies and everyone who enters this programme accepts that there is a significant element of risk!" he announced vehemently.

David despaired. On this point he had to agree. But this was a whole different set of circumstances. Being Jewish, the odds had been stacked against the Baums ever adopting, and this appeared to be their only chance of becoming parents.

"Have you ever been desperate, Bill?" David turned on

his manager but he refused to acknowledge this invasive and inappropriate question. "Have you?" David demanded of him again.

His team leader was riled by this last insinuating comment. His private life was his business and this felt wrong on every level. This social worker was his junior. He ran the team and if he continued down this path, he would do well to remind him of this.

"I can't tell them that they may lose Ellie!" David blurted out, almost shouting. "Get someone else to take over!"

"What?" David's childish outburst was so unlike him, Bill thought. He never normally shirked from his responsibilities. He was a strong team player and took on cases that other colleagues couldn't manage.

"I'm not joking. Take me off the case now!" he demanded, adding forcefully, "You can swap me with one from Siobhan's delightful collection!" He anticipated that his colleague would complain bitterly. But her caseload wasn't as high, and after all, this was a crisis, and would have to be prioritised immediately.

Bill had always felt unfortunate to manage such an overbearing group of social workers. He was constantly being dictated to and patronised or plain ignored by them. And let's face it, he didn't particularly care either way whether David came off the case or not. He personally wouldn't be losing any sleep over it.

Refusing to get up, he called Siobhan to join them in his office. It was cramped with three people and the handover was brief. Siobhan didn't take long to decide which of her clients to get rid of. She told David that he could have the Smith family with the greatest of pleasure. "It's always nice to be greeted by the older kid," she laughed, "he hangs out of the window shouting expletives at you!"

Everyone knew about the dreadful Smith family dynamics. Their paternal great-grandparents had been in the care system, and now they represented four generations on the at risk register, approximately seventeen of them at last count. Their reputation was known to every professional in the building. This wasn't a fair swap.

David recognised that managing the Smith family group would entail a lot more work than a simple reassessment of Tracey. But he needed Siobhan's skills in manipulating assessments to achieve the desired outcomes. She wasn't afraid to take risks and she was planning to leave the social work profession anyway, as soon as she could.

It would be relatively easy to handle Siobhan, as he guessed that she had a crush on him. In her, David recognised the same judgemental middle class mentality. He offered to take her to McDonald's for breakfast and have a chat there. He had been too proud to admit his errors in front of Bill, but he realised he was going to have to tell her the truth. Oblivious as ever to confidentiality issues, David began offloading as they waited in the queue to be served, explaining the process as he saw it.

David had more patience for Siobhan, and answered her questions as they flowed. He could see that she was enjoying the attention he paid her and was impressed that she grasped the facts of the case fairly quickly.

"I can see exactly where you are coming from, David," she enthused. "That's why you picked me for the job! And Carmel!" They both sighed loudly. They were united in how disgusted they were that Bill had allowed her to continue on long-term sick leave for over a year.

"I bumped into her in Boots at the weekend," Siobhan said, "All she said was she was a bit depressed. Aren't we all?"

They both laughed loudly. They were comfortable in each other's company, Siobhan quietly wishing that David would notice her. Truly notice her.

"You know I will be sensitive when I speak to Melissa and Dan." she said, her face falling as they both focused on the dreadful crisis again. "This is so sad, and I know they will be shattered."

She stole a look at her colleague. It struck her that he looked pale and tired that morning. His thick brown hair was looking untidy. He was an attractive man and she loved him in her own way. She wanted to look after him but she didn't know how to approach this awkward situation. She knew all about Natasha, Gina and the sorry mess he had created, but she was too polite to ask him. Why didn't he make more effort to see his own children? Why didn't he go through the court process? It wasn't her style to challenge him.

They were just friends and it was safer to talk about work-related issues.

"You know yourself, I can only manipulate the updated assessment on her to such an extent," Siobhan quietly informed her clearly agitated colleague. "Tracey is the child's birth mother!"

"I know ... I know." He sounded despondent, but his tone lifted somewhat when he heard that she would contact the Baums and make an appointment to tell them in person what had happened. "Try and reassure them," David told her. "Melissa and Dan are about to host their adoption celebrations. This isn't fair on them."

But Siobhan had a better plan. She told him that she wouldn't inform the Baums that David had messed up with the court procedures at this time, but she wanted David to come with her. "Why are you such a coward?" She gently flirted with him. "We can joint work this case if you need support."

"Absolutely not. Just tell them I am ill!"

"As if they will believe that old story. This will add to their panic. When will you grow up and face your fears?"

David looked around, hoping no one was listening to his colleague berating him. He put up with it though, as she was the only one in the team that could potentially resolve this to his advantage.

It was time to disclose the real reason why he had to come off the case. How he had relaxed his professional boundaries, not only with Melissa and Dan, but the extended family too. He had been touched and grateful for all the meals Melissa and Dan had given him and they were all close friends.

Siobhan shook her head, not hiding her disappointment. She had thought he would have had more sense than to behave in this manner. This was the kind of thing you learned on your first day on a university placement. David was supposed to be in a trusted position as a trainer of social work students. What a joke he was.

He would have been more careful, he tried explaining to his appalled colleague, had he anticipated this shocking development at the final hour.

There was little sympathy from Siobhan. "It's always the same with you, David," she said patronisingly. "Don't get me wrong. I am very fond of you, but you try to befriend your clients."

She instantly realised she sounded harsh, and softened her attitude accordingly. "I know you are having a really hard time at the moment, but now look what's happened!"

David was aware that his irresponsible conduct would reflect badly on Siobhan's reputation. But there simply wasn't the time to dwell on this further. There was work to do.

"I will call the Baums tonight, but I want to make the appointment to visit Tracey first."

David's tense features relaxed somewhat as he mouthed a silent thank you.

"I can probably do an updated report in a couple of sessions," Siobhan said, adding, "It shouldn't be too difficult to manipulate the assessment. I should be able to swing it."

The two colleagues sat two feet from each other. She wasn't a worldly person, and didn't seem to hold political views, preferring to talk about television programmes. But they had bounced case resolutions off each other for years. Siobhan could be equally unprofessional, having been taught well by David. He liked the fact that she was always only interested in the children and their wellbeing and she wasn't afraid of a challenge.

Ignoring the fact that they were conducting a case discussion in a public place, they continued.

"So brief me from the beginning, will you?" Siobhan said. "I can't be arsed reading the file."

David pulled his chair closer and leaned forward. He began summarising the key points. That in early December, he had received a referral from Tracey's GP, worried that the woman was clearly a drug addict and was hiding her pregnancy. "Remember her, Siobhan?" he asked her hopefully. "You chatted to her in the office interview room when I was worried she would do a runner!" Why did no one remember Tracey? It wasn't that long ago. David offered more information: "The smack head! She was a mess."

There had been so many clients since then coming through the door, and Siobhan looked blankly at him as she took another sip of her milkshake. David's tone remained hopeful as he continued to describe Tracey in more detail.

Siobhan interrupted him mid-flow. "Ah, the posh druggie. Spoke really nicely. Matted hair. Really polite, kept talking about her mother dying when she was a teenager?"

"Yes, yes, that's her!" he leant forward eagerly, unconsciously playing with his bottom lip with his fingers. But Siobhan didn't share his enthusiasm.

"Well, I still want to hear what Tracey has to say for herself first!" she said. "I reckon she has her future all planned out, all that moral support in prison!"

Both social workers were fully aware that Ellie's case may well end up in a contested hearing. But the worst nightmare of all would be if the judge went against Siobhan's recommendation, and ordered that Tracey be reunited with her child. What would they be able to do then? They would have to instruct their own local authority solicitor to appeal this decision. But if this were the case, would they even have the legal grounds to begin this costly process?

Outside McDonald's, Siobhan spontaneously reached up to hug her colleague. At five foot two inches, she was much shorter than he was. He responded positively to the embrace and for a moment she wondered if the feeling was mutual. Helping him out to manipulate Tracey's assessment would serve to bring them even closer, and finally, he would hopefully realise just how much he needed her!

Sixteen

Monday 19th July 2004

The very nature of child protection work usually entails undertaking assessments at breakneck speed. Whilst Ellie wasn't at risk of imminent harm, there were other factors and Siobhan began setting the wheels in motion. She did this in sympathy with Melissa and Dan, recognising that, once they were informed of the news, they would find the stress and uncertainty unbearable.

The first step was for her to book a two-hour prison visit, to meet with Tracey. This process was riddled with bureaucracy and took her far too long. The difficulty was added to as David stood over her desk, mouthing at regular intervals instructions such as, "Just get rid of her!"

At first Siobhan lapped up the attention, pacifying David in her belief that the crisis would resolve itself within the next day or so.

In the three years she had worked alongside David, she had never seen him so agitated. He had always guided her, and he and Wayne, were her unofficial managers. It was clear to Siobhan that David's home set-up had sent him into this depression. He used to be so lively and upbeat. He seemed quieter these days. Quite unreachable. And she was sure he was drinking far too much.

She had guessed that he didn't find her sexually attractive, but that didn't stop her from wanting to make him happy. When the call ended, she had swung her chair round to him and had told him that she had no intention of ripping a settled baby out of the Baums' arms. He had smiled albeit nervously back at her. It was all he had wanted to hear.

Her next task was to google HMP Harlton Wells to work out her route. It would, she estimated, take around an hour and a half to get there. She wondered whether it would be possible to make two separate trips, which would bump up her monthly mileage claim nicely! But it wouldn't be fair to delay the assessment outcome for the Baums. So unfortunately she concluded that everything would have to be wrapped up in the single visit.

She now concentrated on her strategy for the interview. She would often feel quite tense before important meetings. Her student placements had been in the probation settings, and she could have done with a manager to guide her these last three years. She found it useful to prepare her questions in advance. On this occasion, she decided to engage Tracey first on a neutral topic to break the ice. The HMP Royal Horticultural Gardening show garden was probably a good opener. It was always good to start on a positive note.

The recollection of when she had first met heavily pregnant Tracey, before Christmas 2003, came to mind as she skimmed the case notes. At that time, she had been called upon by David to try and keep his new client safe in the interview room, whilst he had informed their manager of the serious child protection risks. David had been correctly worried that Tracey may go underground once she knew that social workers were on her back.

How lonely this troubled woman had been – it had been easy to engage her. The fact that she was well spoken gave away the fact that she had probably come from a middle-class background. She had been happy to tell Siobhan about life before her mother had passed away. At the age of eleven, her parents had been thrilled when she won a scholarship to attend the top private girls' school, a fair distance from her home in Woodfield.

All had been going well, but suddenly ... the new normal. Thirteen months of taking two buses after school to the cancer hospital in the city centre. Forcing herself to be strong. To be optimistic.

It had been she who had consoled her broken father and older sister in the waiting room. Breaking the silence that told it all, on the car journeys back home. Baking the cakes and decorating the front door with colourful welcome home posters, only to have their beloved mother home for a couple of days at a time. The warmth of the palliative care nurses wrapping their arms around her and her sister. The coma and the traumatising wait for it all to end.

David had written that his client had been composed as she had recounted how her wonderful mother had left her, her emotions dulled by years of drug abuse. It had been recorded in the weeks after the funeral that she had felt no reason to hold it together anymore. It had been impossible to focus on her GCSE course work and she made a choice to put her energies into a relationship. Her new boyfriend was a troubled young man who experimented with drugs. It was a welcome chance to escape her pain and so the downward spiral began.

Initially the school tried to support Tracey, but they eventually lost patience and expelled her, causing her father and older sister more heartache.

Reading through the notes of that day, Siobhan found the story captivating. Siobhan remembered how she had found Tracey to be immature and living in the past. Everything was clearer now. She had spent a good hour listening and had made the right noises. All the while, her colleagues had worked together. Yotunde had gone out to pick up some hot food for their hungry client whilst she had kept her talking. David, meanwhile, had been preoccupied, taking the important steps to ensure the unborn child would be protected.

How different Siobhan perceived the situation to be now. At the time, she couldn't recall any pleading for help with drugs rehabilitation. Just the acceptance from this highly-vulnerable young woman that this was how life was now. All this trouble today was unnecessarily taking up valuable time when there was other urgent work to get through.

The preparation for the questioning was taking time, and Siobhan needed a fresh angle. With some cynicism, she jotted down some notes. Where were the friends of her late mother? What interest did her extended family take? She still had a father and Tracey hadn't said whether he had ever been abusive towards her or if they were ever close.

It was clear that the pre-birth assessment was flawed, and

would have been ripped apart by any judge, had this matter been put before the court. But circumstances were totally different now. A five-month-old baby was at the heart of this case. Tracey had walked away and hadn't taken independent legal advice. All this wanting to be reassessed was a whim, just more evidence of self-centred behaviour.

Ever since she left the one-day-old Ellie in the maternity unit, critical time had lapsed without a word from her mother. Everyone involved had been far more concerned about the lasting damage that may have happened as a result of the excessive drug exposure in pregnancy. Reaching out to Tracey had always been low down on David's to-do list.

The more she read the documents, the more she came to the same conclusion as her colleague. This drastic transformation had all come about too late. It was unfair on Ellie who had bonded with her prospective adopters.

This would be the first experience of her attempting to manipulate an assessment to such an extent. She felt it necessary to liaise with David to try and gain a more in-depth understanding of the issues. Siobhan wanted to please him. For him to see her in another light. And naturally, she lapped up the attention she received.

She took notes as David began his tirade. He was sure that Tracey's solicitor would have advised her client to enquire about Ellie's welfare during the interviews with any social worker. Of particular importance to David was that Siobhan should refuse to allow Tracey's mentor be in the interview room.

"This interfering do-gooder has caused this bloody nightmare!" he ranted.

Siobhan found herself nodding in full agreement.

After a full briefing, Siobhan now felt more confident about her ability to deal with this matter. She would focus on the negative influences and avoid, say, whether the mother-and-baby unit would be able to offer support. Instead she would guide Tracey to discuss what steps she planned to keep herself and Ellie safe once she was released from prison. She anticipated that Tracey would have limited insight into these crucial subjects.

David was becoming out of control, even by Siobhan's low standards. She decided it was best to keep quiet when he began directing her not to speak with any professional about Tracey's progress in the prison. She knew full well that she needed to seek the guidance of the manager of the mother-and-baby unit for example. She nodded, but ignored David when he insisted that the unit would have a distorted view of how Tracy would be a competent mother. He went on and on, telling her that engaging all these people would be a waste of time.

"Tell the manager of the unit to give away the bed!" David directed, sounding frantic. He kept his telephone off the hook in case he was interrupted and now began googling how many mother-and-baby units there were in the country. He was transfixed on his computer screen like his life depended on it, reading out the relevant sections for Siobhan's benefit.

It appeared that there were only six units across Britain, holding sixty-four places. He announced that the process to apply could be long and complex and said that he found it strange that Adreen Wood seemed so convinced that a bed could be offered so quickly.

"That druggie doesn't deserve to be a mother, for God's sake!" David had his guard down and he wasn't holding back!

"Right, Siobhan!" He paused briefly before continuing, "You need to delve into Tracey's past and find someone who knows more. We really need to look for a violent incident involving her."

He knew he sounded hard and detached. Even cruel. This was all Gina's fault for poisoning his young children against him. This new side to him, a hateful streak, was all her doing.

"If you don't find anything, you are going to have to make something up!" With this, he clapped his hands together, pleased to have come up with such a brainwave. Unashamed, he ignored Siobhan's mouth dropping wide open. "If you are questioned on it under oath, you will have to say it is hearsay third party information and that the source is anonymous!"

Satisfied that he had the answer to swing the assessment to negative, David's mood lifted somewhat.

"They will never take Tracey in the unit if she has a history of violence," he told her, excited that he had thought outside of the box and had come up with a foolproof solution.

Siobhan shook her head and sighed. But instead of doing the right thing and challenging David's unscrupulous practice, she told him to go across the car park to Asda and pick up some lunch for them both. She wasn't remotely hungry after the breakfast at McDonald's, but David needed distracting. His persistent lectures were starting to get tiresome.

With that few minutes of respite, she gathered her thoughts. It was clear that her position as a social worker was compromised. Her alliances were obviously with Melissa and Dan, but her colleague was being so forceful. She thought that if David was so driven for the result he wanted, he should have just kept Ellie's case! This would have made the best sense, especially if he was indeed so skilled at manipulating assessments. He was asking her to lie. This wasn't fair.

The earliest visiting slot at HMP Harlton Wells was offered for the following day. Allowing for security checks, this would entail her being out of the office all day. Siobhan purposely selected the Tuesday one o'clock visit slot. This would usefully entitle her to claim the £7 lunch allowance. As an added luxury, she decided not to fill in the whereabouts diary in order that she could enjoy a well-earned lie-in before setting off in good time.

The major drawback to this sorry business was, of course, breaking the news of Tracey's appeal for a reassessment. Siobhan wondered how on earth she was going to inform Melissa and Dan. She didn't want a face-to-face meeting for the simple reason that they would only want to know whether Ellie would necessarily be returned to her birth mother at any point. There was no way she could reassure them at this stage.

To facilitate matters and avoid direct contact, Siobhan decided to delay telling them until that evening. She could call them from home. Hopefully they would both be available and would be able to support each other on hearing about this unthinkable development.

She lived at home with her parents, and talked about the case incessantly with them over dinner. Afterwards, she could delay relaying the dreaded news no longer. She brought upstairs a glass of orange cordial and positioned it on her bedside table. It was likely to be a difficult call. She asked her parents not to disturb her, and closed the door.

She spread her notes on the bed and moved her Paddington Bear and several other cuddly toys that were in her way. There was no space for these and her files too. Stress like this was no good for her health. She made herself comfortable and decided just to get it over with and dial the landline without any further delay.

Melissa answered. Siobhan apologised for the lateness of the call and, using her gentlest tone, she introduced herself as Ellie's new social worker. She made sure to establish that they were both able to listen to the conversation.

In the first instance, she needed to explain David's position. It was simpler to say that he had fallen ill. She couldn't give details, of course, since it was a confidential matter! She felt guilty about telling them a lie, but she could think of no easier way of managing the scenario. Their response was of concern and reinforced the positive impression David had always given of this delightful-sounding couple.

It made it all the more difficult, of course, to give them the unpredicted and unwelcome news of Tracey's demand to be reassessed. Hesitating for a moment, Siobhan then told them that it was necessary for Fenton Childcare Services to provide a formal statement to the family courts. That there had been an unfortunate development and that this would mean an inevitable delay with the adoption hearing.

The pleading began straight away. The adoption celebration party they had organised to follow the hearing could absolutely not be cancelled at such short notice. Why had this been sprung on them now? Then there was an ominous silence, as the shocking news sank in.

Feeling nervous, Siobhan had to continue talking, trying to reassure them that she totally sympathised. She told them too that she was dealing with this matter as a top priority. She explained that she had made an appointment to see Tracey the following day and would be reporting back to them as soon as possible.

The questions were hurtled at her, but she tried to answer them calmly. She explained that she would need to speak to prison officers and there was her team leader to consult with too. She explained that there may even be a second assessment session to organise, and in this event, it was up to the prison booking system clerk to allocate a slot. In other words, further delays were inevitable. It would not be possible, she repeated, to give immediate feedback after meeting with Tracey the next day.

Every single word uttered was driving these innocent parents to be into deeper despair, their world crashing around them whilst they could only sit and wait. Siobhan felt deeply sorry for them as she continued to explain the process of reassessment.

"I can't listen to this!" Melissa blurted out. "I feel sick!"

She demanded that Siobhan tell her the truth, adding that David had been fine when he had seen them the previous week. "It sounds like he can't face us!" she said as she broke down.

Siobhan was silent for a moment whilst she decided how best to respond.

Melissa then began shouting that they would be instructing their own solicitor. She yelled, "No one will be taking our baby away from us!"

Dan now grabbed the receiver, his voice so raised that Siobhan moved her mobile to arm's length.

"We know all about David's personal problems but this is an emergency." His words were measured. "No drug-dealing convict is taking our baby from us. Get him on the phone now. He has to help us!" he railed.

Siobhan knew from David that he had given out both his personal mobile number and his work one. They had discussed this matter in the office, and in anticipation of this likely reaction, he had told Siobhan that he would not be answering any calls from Melissa and Dan that evening. Obviously, they would be understandably distraught.

Dan demanded the email address of Siobhan's manager to make a formal complaint. He added that he would be contacting his local MP too.

The sound of hysterical shouting could be clearly heard in the background before the phone was slammed down on her.

It was with some relief to Siobhan that the dreaded phone

call was terminated. It was her view that the Baums were clearly people who tended to get what they wanted out of life. Siobhan didn't blame them, but like all her colleagues, she found it so time-consuming to have to deal with the many complaints raised against her on such a regular basis. This was more about David in any event. She began writing the notes of the conversation up, feeling rather hurt by the sheer unwanted aggression. None of this was her doing. Her mobile phone rang. Predictably it was David.

"They don't believe me about your being unwell!" she told him, not bothering to say hello. She told him firmly that it had been a mistake on her part to agree to swap the Smith children with this one.

"I'm entitled to be ill!" he told her. "They don't have my medical records. How would they know the truth?" he wittered on. "What exactly did you tell them about me?"

"It's always about you, isn't it, David?"

"I'm quite depressed at the moment. You know that."

"You could have waited until they adopted the child formally before becoming best mates."

"No offence, but you have no idea what it is like to have your own children turned against you," David sounded bitter and sad. "I haven't seen them in ages."

Siobhan was touched by the sound of his distress. From the moment she had started working at Fenton Childcare Services, she had been drawn to him. She had naturally never made a move, knowing that he had a long-term partner. She had even met Gina once.

Even when David had left his family home, she always felt that he would never give her a passing thought. She saw herself as dowdy and unsophisticated. She also knew the kind of woman he was sexually attracted to. Natasha, the social work student, had been fashionable and reeked sex appeal. But she had left David's life too, laughing at him no doubt to her fellow students on her university course.

She listened to him, filling up with resentment. Before she had been drawn into this horrendous crisis with Ellie and her potential adopters, she had never noticed something. It was so obvious now.

David was weak. He had even resorted to insulting her with his reference to her having no children of her own. She turned it back on him.

"Perhaps you should not have relied solely on Tracey agreeing to relinquish her baby voluntarily." Siobhan went on the attack. There was silence. She knew she was right about this aspect.

"If you had gone down the court route, it would probably be too late for her to be reassessed," she added assertively. "I am sorry, but this absolute screw-up is down to you!"

His silence was telling and with that she told him she was tired and was going to end the call.

In anticipation of another fitful night's sleep, David mixed himself a vodka and tonic and drank three double shots in fairly swift succession. Finally it did the trick and he relaxed. He wrote himself a note to remember to replace the near-empty bottle the following day. He vowed to stop this excessive drinking once the situation with Ellie was resolved positively. Hopefully Siobhan would give him good news the following afternoon. He would call her on her way back from the prison. She would be done, he estimated, by 3pm at the latest. Less than twenty-four hours until this was over.

He checked that both his phones were safely switched off. Before taking a shower, he glanced nervously outside. For a horrible moment he imagined that the Baums were entering the building, working out which intercom to press. Thankfully there was no name against his flat number. This was absurd. He worried he was losing his mind but perhaps it was the effect of the stress and that he had hardly eaten all day.

It had, he realised now, been a one-way friendship for some months now. He had been more than happy to receive such kind hospitality from them. They didn't know his address and had given him the adoption invitation in person. No social workers in their right mind were listed in the phone book. The Baums only knew he lived in one of the newly built flats in the centre of Fenton. He thought things through, trying to be practical. His surname was a common one. Surely they wouldn't travel from Mosforth now. It was already 10pm.

Then he recalled something. Some weeks ago, he had enjoyed dinner at the Baums'. He had taken the train there as he wanted to drink. Afterwards he had accepted a lift home from Dan. He had been grateful and had nipped out of the car at the traffic lights. Thankfully Dan had driven straight off.

It was with some trepidation that he switched his work phone on. Seven missed calls in succession. Half a dozen texts. Polite but begging him to respond urgently. He quickly turned it off. There was no point in booting up his computer either. He knew what would be waiting for him.

There was nothing else in his power that he could do to help his good friends at this stage. He simply had to wait it out.

Seventeen

Nature v Nurture

TUESDAY 20TH JULY 2004

PROBATION-TRAINED SIOBHAN HAD BEEN TO ENOUGH prisons in her time and knew what to expect. She dutifully handed the security officer her trainers, and stood on a box with her mouth wide open whilst he undertook the standard drugs-smuggling checks on visitors and professionals alike.

None of the above was an issue, but after the long journey, she needed the toilet. She felt slightly claustrophobic when the door was locked from the outside, and it felt humiliating to have to call out when she was ready to leave!

Finally, she was led to a small interview room and instructed to sit with her back against the wall, facing the door. The prison officer showed her the panic button and told her to shout out if he was needed.

Shortly afterwards, the same guard brought in a slim healthy-looking woman. Standing before her, Tracey was barely recognisable. The formerly emaciated-looking client seemed younger now. The once-matted dull blond thinning hair was no longer tied messily into a bobble. It seemed thicker now, framing her attractive features. Her brown eyes, no longer sunken, were bright, and her cheek bones no longer protruded. The multitude of old bruises evident on her arms and hands were the only visible indication of the previous drug-fuelled lifestyle.

An impressed Siobhan smiled at her, saying that she looked

well. She reminded her that they had met before Christmas, at her offices, but Tracey appeared to have only a vague recollection of this meeting. She apologised and said that that part of her life was something she wanted to put behind her.

As predicted by David, Tracey immediately asked after her daughter. She expressed deep regret for exposing her to drugs in the womb. These were just empty words to Siobhan, and she felt under no obligation to respond directly. Instead, Ellie's new social worker offered superficial conversation as she glanced at her carefully created notes. She wasn't going to be diverted from her own agenda, or drawn into empty platitudes.

With the extensive briefing and preparation she had done for this meeting, she was ready to challenge Tracey on the reality of what would happen once she was released into the community. On this point, she felt relatively confident that Tracey would have little or no insight into how to manage with no regular income or support networks to fall back upon.

But Tracey had been preparing too. She had spent nearly five long months incarcerated thinking things through. She had taken up every opportunity offered. This included many hours of trauma therapy, not to mention the three times a week mentoring sessions.

Indeed, Tracey's face lit up as she gave Siobhan the update on her family. She had been lucky to have a strong bond with her mentor who felt like a friend. In the sessions, she had taken up a suggestion to write to her estranged sister and father. In the letters that followed, she apologised for all the distress she had caused them over the years. Her father had, allegedly, been thrilled to hear that she had dealt with her demons. Her sister had held back at the beginning, and it had taken some time for her to trust her again.

Things had moved on considerably since then, and she looked forward to seeing her family at the visitors' centre once a week. The sessions were only for two hours but it was better than nothing. They were speaking on the telephone too. It was a start to what Tracey hoped would be a solid relationship once more. She anticipated, too, that they would support her and Ellie upon her release, which was estimated to be around May 2005.

This was most unexpected and alarming news. The pre-birth assessment had failed to mention any extended family. Siobhan thought that if they had been at all interested, surely they would have enquired as to how Ellie was progressing and asked to see her. Again there was great big gaps in David's management of the case.

She explained that, as part of the reassessment of her ability to care for Ellie, it would be her role to check out these facts, but Tracey was co-operative and was forthcoming with providing both her father and older sister's contact details.

With the very nature of child protection social work so unpredictable, Siobhan could not now fathom why David had thought it would be such an easy task to "get rid of her!" His behaviour was quite irrational and obsessional these days. He had taken advantage of the fact that she wasn't a particularly strong character, and she realised that she had been foolish to allow herself to be guided by him.

Putting her own obsession with David to one side, Siobhan refocused on the vital task in hand. Her carefully crafted questioning was slanted towards only the negative aspects of caring for a child. Siobhan pointed out that, as a single parent, Tracey may find it hard in terms of finance and isolation factors. However, again Tracey surprised her by demonstrating an insight into these potential hurdles. She sounded self-assured as she informed Siobhan that she planned to engage with the council Sure Start team and that she hoped to make new friends.

She wasn't sure where she would be relocated, but she planned to enrol on a personal training course beginning in September 2005. Furthermore, Tracey mentioned in passing that her mentor had checked out the potentially problematic issue of having a criminal record, and apparently this fact would not hinder her application. Ellie would also be old enough to qualify for the college's free crèche places.

The issue of poor peer group influence was discussed, and Tracey said that she would be looking to move a safe distance from her drug associates on the Barnham Hill Estate upon her release in ten months' time. In the meantime, she understood that Ellie's care would be supervised under the wings of the relevant local authority childcare team. Most clients resented social workers involving themselves in their private lives, but it was different with Tracey. She seemed to want the support. In fact, overall, she appeared willing to do anything to prove she had changed her ways.

David had been correct on only one aspect so far, for it was obvious that the so-called "interfering mentor" had put in her hours with Tracey. For every problem, there were viable solutions.

This reassessment was not going according to plan. Feeling somewhat desperate, Siobhan now tried appealing to Tracey's good nature. It was highly unprofessional of her, but it was worth a shot.

She talked quietly to avoid anyone hearing the full gist of it. She chose her words carefully and explained that Ellie had been placed with a Jewish couple who had been desperate to have children. There was plenty of time left that she could use wisely with Tracey before concluding the interview and she continued down her avenue of emotional persuasion. She launched into details about how her colleague David had been struck by how beautifully they cared for Ellie and how they loved her so much.

With Tracey seemingly showing interest in what was being said, Siobhan felt safe to continue what felt like a final plea. It was totally improper to conduct herself in this manner, but the previous evening's phone call to Melissa and Dan still resonated with her – that unforgettable, terrible sound of two good people terrified that they would lose Ellie. It was cruel that they were forced to suffer such unbearable torment.

It wouldn't only be Ellie's carers waiting desperately for good news. David would be too. The multiple errors that had occurred whilst he had held this case were unusual. She had always believed him to be such a capable worker. In social work practice, there was no excuse for errors such as these. Siobhan felt for certain that David would be instantly suspended and possibly sacked. But she loved him, or so she thought, and had to try and support him. She had never met the Baums, but her loyalty was with them. She had to get Tracey to back down and move on with her life.

Siobhan needed to be careful not to disclose Ellie's carers' surnames for security purposes, but she shared what other social workers may have felt was confidential and irrelevant information. For instance she explained that they had waited on the adoption register for four long years and that they were beside themselves. How they cared for Ellie round the clock during the period that she spent in the high dependency unit detoxifying from the drugs. That Ellie had strong attachments to them and was the centre of their world. She even went into detail about how all their relatives doted on her too.

When her appeal had finished though, Tracey appeared to have little time for the thinly-veiled message Siobhan was trying to get across. Her only concession was that, if they wanted to send Ellie birthday cards and presents, for example, that that would be acceptable. She would, of course, be happy to thank them for looking after Ellie so well. On that final point, Siobhan could hardly make eye contact, and temporarily distracted herself by making notes on her thick pad of A4 lined paper.

The meeting came to a natural end, and Siobhan found herself torn. It irritated her that Tracey assumed that it was a done deal and that she would be reunited with Ellie and moving to the mother-and-baby prison unit. But on so many other levels, she had to admit to feeling significant respect for what she had to say.

Tracey Mellor was an extremely self-centred woman in Siobhan's eyes. But no one could argue, against the fact that she had climbed her mountain. Being selfish wouldn't necessarily make her a bad mother – certainly not bad enough. How much her past would inhibit her ability to parent was still relatively unknown. There was an additional issue to consider. Ellie's exposure to drugs in the womb was excessive, and she knew that, sadly, she may develop behaviour issues. This would only be identified once she reached school age. But due to this factor alone, there would be the question of whether Ellie would require above-average parenting in order to thrive.

It was hard to take an objective stand. Perhaps a different social worker would take the view that Tracey's insensitive attitude towards the carers for her daughter was understandable. The bottom line was that Tracey was Ellie's birth mother and, therefore, could be as ruthless as she wanted in her efforts to fight to have her returned to her care.

The case was not clear-cut. To take a cherished child out of a settled environment and place her in a prison setting needed carefully weighing up. Tracey wasn't a tried and tested mother who had made the wrong decision and had made amends. Ellie had no older siblings, whom Siobhan could assess to see whether they were achieving their potential.

Despite all the relevant factors, Siobhan realised that if it ended up being brought into the court arena, within days a judge may well award Tracey interim custody, and would have harsh criticism for Fenton Childcare Services too! And this certainly included David. And without doubt, her good name would also be dragged into this dreadful mess.

There would be telephone calls to make, to Tracey's mentor, and to the probation service after care team for example, to clarify various things that Tracey had said. But even before this would happen, Siobhan knew that there would be little reason to book in a second assessment session at this stage. Rather flatly, she informed Tracey that she would write to her with the outcome and terminated the interview with a tight smile.

There was one last thing she needed to do before she set off on the motorway back to Fenton. From the privacy of her car, she waited for Tracey's father to pick up the receiver. His position was most critical to the reassessment outcome.

Predictably, there was solid evidence that Tracey had made positive changes in her life. Mr Mellor sounded perfectly amiable and was saying all the right things too. He had received a letter from Tracey several months ago, and this had been the first time he had learnt of his grandchild's birth. He couldn't understand why he hadn't been notified by the department at the time of the birth. Siobhan fell silent when he calmly expressed dissatisfaction with Fenton Childcare Services. Of course, he was perfectly within his rights to make a formal complaint, but she wasn't going to point this out to him! David was in enough trouble.

She tried explaining that from her understanding, Tracey had given no next of kin details. Ellie's grandfather didn't sound angry, just confused and upset. He politely told her that it would have been easy to find out where he lived, as he had never moved from the house Tracey had grown up in.

Ellie's grandfather reported suffering from multiple health

problems himself, and explained that even if he had been approached, he would not have been in a position to be assessed as a potential carer for his granddaughter.

Siobhan put the phone down, promising to be in touch with him very soon. This problem was weighing her down. Every single element of this mammoth blunder had Bill's name written on it too, as he had signed off the pre-birth assessment.

She drove off, imagining the unpleasant scenario when the barrage of complaints would eventually reach the "silent assassin". David was being obnoxious and she prayed that he would take full responsibility. She wanted to please him but that didn't go to the extent of having her good name dragged down with him. Why had she been so stupid as to agree to swap the Smith children for this? He had made it all seem so straightforward. Foolproof.

It was safer, she felt, not to discuss anything at all with David until the following morning. When the predictable calls came, she refused to pick up. He had no right to harass her. She would speak to him when she was ready.

It wasn't just Bill who was a liability. Yotunde and Wayne had been complaining recently about David to her too. They had told him to his face but he hadn't listened. They had advised him to take some time out. To get signed off by his doctor. Everyone else did it. Why couldn't he accept that he wasn't fit to practice at the moment? Now it was too late and he would be struck off the social work register. And with this, there would be no sick pay to soften the blow.

Feeling under pressure, Siobhan didn't much enjoy her late lunch which she ate at a Motorway Service Station. On a matter of principle, though, she ensured she spent up to the £7 allowance to claim back from the petty cash. She didn't delay filling in the mileage claim form either, going to the trouble of adding extra miles here and there. The money all added up and there had to be some perks to this godforsaken job. Wayne had trained her well in this regard, and she had been told to say she got lost if ever there was a query.

The journey home seemed to take forever and she was consumed by this highly problematic case. In three whole years in Fenton

Childcare Services, she had managed somehow to avoid being the subject of a disciplinary procedure. But her time had come. The "silent assassin" would be waiting for her.

As regards David, if he wasn't suspended immediately, he would, most probably, go off on long-term sick leave. She knew that he loved being at work and needed the interaction and stimulation of it all. She also knew how low his mood was currently and how he masked his true emotions. But this time he would be left with no other option. She would miss him, but she resented how she would be left alone to shoulder the blame. Your fingertips touched the file cover, it was yours. That was how it worked in a child protection team.

Back at home, she felt so stressed that she cancelled her aerobics class and fell back on her bed to try and recover. She didn't keep up with politics but knew enough from her colleagues that the Labour government, like Conservative before them, refused to invest in the social care staffing crisis. Her meagre salary was an insult, however, there was nothing she could do about that, but there was something that she could do about the toxic bullying culture.

Like so many others who had made the mistake of choosing a career in social work, she knew she had to take the time to work out her exit strategy.

The familiarity of the room she had slept in her entire life gave her comfort. Having turned thirty this year, she worried that she would always be here. The pastel dotted wallpaper looked childish. Her GCSE level charcoal-art coursework still hung in the same place next to a faded WHAM poster. Primary school class photographs were still in their frames. Even when it came to university she had opted to study social work just a bus ride away!

Her mind raced to the shocking outcome of her prison visit. At least Tracey had had the courage and confidence to address her difficulties and to step out of her comfort zone. It could not have been easy to come off the drugs. To be incarcerated. All in all, perhaps she should be given a chance to be a parent to Ellie.

But at the same time, the Baums were the innocent party. They did not deserve to have had their hopes raised. Effectively, they were her parents, and now she would be snatched from them. It was not their fault that David had been so incompetent at seemingly every opportunity.

She came down for supper and shared her dilemma with her parents. She always valued their opinions, and sometimes she ended up adopting their views too, despite the fact that her mother worked in a bank, and her father was an electrician. They loved hearing the stories, but this one was something else! They had been waiting for her news and were keen to hear the nitty gritty.

There was no point in turning her work phone back on. She had nothing to say that anyone wanted to hear. David could also wait until the morning. She imagined him, sitting alone panicking in his studio flat that he so often mocked. At this stage in the assessment it would only feed his anxiety.

The following day Siobhan dragged herself out of bed, predicting an onslaught of questions from David. She hadn't slept well with all the worry but she would have to fight the exhaustion. Her first refuge was McDonalds. A breakfast meeting venue no less! She felt she needed some degree of protection when David inevitably went berserk. As additional defence and distraction she persuaded Wayne to join them.

David was not averse to this on the condition that Wayne paid the bill. It was a sign of how lonely Wayne's life was that he actually agreed to this.

Desperate to have Siobhan's account of the prison visit, David started even as they queued for their breakfast.

"So the druggie was no good then?" It wasn't really a question to which he needed an answer. He would never forget the squat she lived in. The people living there. The filth. The hopelessness. He was assured in his mind that Tracey was an utter waste of time.

Siobhan's answer surprised him. "I am sorry but the matter is more complicated than that," she told him, trying her best to sound assertive. She gestured towards the other customers who were within earshot of them, adding, "I am not going to discuss it right now!"

Surely this was a sick joke on her part. He didn't need this dialogue to be drawn out. It was not some kind of little party game. But Siobhan looked serious.

When they had sat down she launched into her summary of her

meeting with Tracey. He kept rudely interrupting her, saying that he couldn't care less about what programmes she had completed in prison. He stated firmly that the damage had been done to Ellie and she would be adopted by the Baums and that would be the end of it.

"I'm sorry, but I cannot agree with you there," Siobhan said quietly.

"What the hell is wrong with you?" David raised his voice slightly, gesturing wildly with his hands. "I trusted you to get rid of her. You said you would do it!"

Siobhan instructed her colleague to lower his voice. She knew he was on the edge but this was about a case decision, not him. He tried pleading with her, telling her that the Baums were his very close friends, and that they were decent and kind and wonderful parents. At the end of his little lecture, he directed her to have compassion.

"Well, I told you to keep the case." Siobhan was holding her own. All three colleagues were often over-familiar with one another and this was a typical example of how matters often escalated between them.

"What's the decision then, Siobhan?" Wayne had now joined the conversation. Having paid for the meal, he felt entitled to do so. But she ignored the question and kept the focus on David.

"I will do many things for you and I value your friendship," she said quietly. "But I am absolutely not prepared to lie under oath. And this is what this case will come to." She purposely avoided looking at either of her two colleagues as she told them that Tracey had changed in every possible way.

This wasn't sounding good. David needed to choose his words carefully at this point. He was acutely aware that he seemed to damage everything that he touched these days. Siobhan had been right and he should have kept hold of Ellie's case and faced the Baums. What was this idiot social worker doing messing things up even further? If she dared let him down, he would never bother with her again.

There had been a reason why he hadn't asked Wayne to take on Ellie's case. He stood up to David and may not have done what he had asked. But Siobhan? It was obvious that she had a crush on him, but she wasn't his type. She was weak, immature and naïve. They had worked together for three full years, and in this time, she had leant on him for advice countless times. In the absence of a decent manager, she had looked up to Wayne and him, and this was how she repaid his kindness! Now that Siobhan had officially become Ellie's social worker he had no formal influence at all on the case.

"And how do you think Melissa and Dan will take the news?" David asked. "You haven't thought of that, have you?"

Siobhan thought it sensible not to respond and shrugged her shoulders slightly.

Wayne knew all about this nightmare case, having had David phone him for over an hour the previous night. He felt entitled to express his own view and interrupted, volunteering his own opinion. "I am not convinced you have reached the correct conclusion here, Siobhan," he offered, gently.

David was happy that Wayne had sided with him for once. This act gave him more confidence to launch into a tirade against Siobhan's lapse of judgement, her irrational decision. He told her that the child would become institutionalised. That she was thriving where she was. He wondered just how many times he would have to state the obvious. It felt like he was talking to a brick wall.

Unbeknown to Siobhan, there had been a new development the previous evening. David now shared the news with his two colleagues. He had received a text message from Dan's sister. It just contained the facts. Dan had spent the night on a hospital trolley, having, amongst others, ECG tests, and Melissa had been so distressed that she had had to be sedated. The family were rallying round to care for Ellie. That was it. He didn't even want to read into what this effectively meant. Was this a heart attack scare? There was nothing that David felt he could reply that felt appropriate. So it felt safer for him to turn his phones off again.

"I know for a fact that Dan's brother is a solicitor in a firm in Lower Croft High Street," David suddenly blurted out. He was running out of cards, but played his last one here. He continued, "I bet he will get involved and there will be complaints made against us both."

If Siobhan looked detached, she was just trying to be strong. She said nothing, staring at her food.

Wayne chipped in again, directing his conversation at David, telling him to stop bullying Siobhan. But he too had strong opinions.

"Tracey is probably all talk, Siobhan," Wayne offered in a kindly tone. "David is right. It's only been five months. Anyone can turn themselves around in prison."

Siobhan tended to be influenced by Wayne's viewpoint. It had been a wise move bringing him. He was usually an excellent practitioner, and was only ever interested in the welfare of the children.

"The Children Act," Wayne continued, "is crystal clear. What is in the child's best interests is paramount," he quoted. He stopped to take a breath, then continued, "This isn't clear-cut, as in the short term, it's not in her interests to move from a loving home to a prison mother-and-baby unit for months on end."

There were additional factors to the dilemma that Siobhan and David had not thought of. Wayne raised the subject of what would happen if Tracey was charged with further offences during her incarceration period. And what would happen to Ellie in this unlikely set of circumstances? All children in the mother-and-baby unit had to move out once they reached eighteen months old. Would Ellie have to go back into the local authority care in that event?

David leant forward, impressed with Wayne's sharp arguments. He nodded enthusiastically as he listened to him. Tracey had hidden her pregnancy, and if she did fall back into her old ways, no one would know if Ellie would be at risk of significant harm.

Wayne had touched on something relevant here. David added that Fenton Childcare Services would probably close the file, deeming Tracey suitable to parent without a court order supervising her. David reinforced this for Siobhan's benefit.

"The baby needs to stay exactly where she is," Wayne said. "It is obvious that's the right decision for her. In fact, for everyone." He had sympathy for Tracey too, acknowledging that it would be hard for her to manage upon her release, and he felt that the additional pressures of caring for a child may set her up to fail.

But Siobhan took a firm stand. She told them both what had happened when she spoke to Tracey's father, and that it would be likely that a barrage of complaints letters would pour in. She feared that Adreen Wood would instruct a barrister, and the whole court process would delay permanency for Ellie. It wouldn't be David that would be cross-examined, as he would probably be off either on long-term sick leave, or suspended. No, it would be her, and she couldn't justify the action they both wanted her to take.

Siobhan was focused as she announced, "Once I have finished my assessment investigations, I will need to sort out how best to proceed with the introductions."

David stared at her, shaking his head in disbelief. Just for the avoidance of any doubt on his part, Siobhan reinforced what she was trying to get across. "So Ellie can start the bonding process with her mother."

As an experienced social worker, David knew that clients were capable of talking a good game. This was just cheap talk. That's all it was with Ellie's mother. But his naïve colleague had been seduced and manipulated by Tracey's slick performance.

David felt somewhat ashamed of himself. He knew he would rely heavily on his inept manager to overlook the implications of his actions. But surely, even Bill, would suspend him over this mishandling of the case. This horrendous outcome for Ellie, Melissa and Dan and their entire family was down to him. From the text message he had received the previous night, they had already fallen apart. And at this stage, they still believed that they would be keeping Ellie but that the adoption order would be delayed. They would have had no valid reason to think differently. How many times had David promised them that the child would never be returning to her mother? How were they supposed to recover from this nightmare ordeal that was about to happen?

With that, he pushed the plastic tray away and stormed out of McDonald's, leaving his untouched packet of French fries and a milkshake for Siobhan to consume.

Eighteen

Wayne's Unexpected Visitor

THE BLAZING ROW HAD PUT SIOBHAN OFF her food too. Wayne knew full well that his colleague found David very attractive. He knew too that the feeling wasn't mutual. He suggested that they bring back David's untouched milkshake for her to give him as a peace offering. Close to tears, he took her arm gently as they walked the short distance across the car park, back to their building.

Comfortable with confrontations, he calmly explained that the argument had purely been work-related. However, he readily acknowledged that David had overstepped the mark. His tone had been too forceful and most definitely controlling. Siobhan told Wayne that she was annoyed with him as well, for making a judgement without meeting Tracey and seeing for himself how she had addressed her difficulties.

Wayne wasn't going to apologise. Extremely opinionated, he often made sweeping statements without knowing the full facts. However, he offered to speak to David and tell him to make things right between them. But they both agreed that this conversation should wait at least a couple of days.

Siobhan was a people pleaser by nature, and shared that she was dreading the onslaught of complaints. They both predicted that someone representing Melissa and Dan would be demanding to hold an urgent meeting with senior management. Perhaps their MP would be in touch. She didn't blame any of the parties and cursed David yet again for lumbering her with his errors.

In an effort to lighten her anxious mood, Wayne suggested that they both place bets on who would be waiting for her in reception.

Tracey's father or sister perhaps. Surely not the interfering mentor they had both heard David rant about! It may be a member of Ellie's extended family. Perhaps all the involved parties! For once, Wayne was thankful that this utter crisis was nothing to do with him and he could afford to be so dismissive.

His banter worked and Siobhan's eyes lit up as they both looked through the glass door to the waiting area. There was only one person in reception. A thin woman had her back turned to them and was reading the notices on the wall. Breathing an exaggerated sigh of relief, they were about to turn their backs and head upstairs, when the receptionist raised her eyes from the novel she was reading. Catching Wayne's eye, she muttered, "Her over there!" Gesturing to the client in a dismissive manner, she rudely added, "Says she's waiting for you!"

Wayne chose not to reply. He had challenged that particular member of staff before, and it hadn't made any difference. He was minded to add this incident to his next whistle-blowing report. He would be careful how to word the matter and be vague. It would make this his third anonymous letter addressed to the "silent assassin". The bulk of the complaint usually focused on Bill's dangerous management style. Each piece of correspondence was drafted with extreme care, changing the font and style of writing. He had written to the director of Fenton Local Authority too, using the external postal system to avoid recognition.

The two colleagues parted, and hesitantly Siobhan climbed the stairs and walked down the corridor, bracing herself for what she may face when she arrived at her desk and opened up her emails. Coupled with that, she had David sitting within three feet of her to contend with. With Wayne now preoccupied, she felt alone. Bill would only show a superficial interest in the Ellie crisis; she knew this fact for certain. Just how many times had her manager picked up his biro and signed off her own case reports without even reading her conclusions? Now he was in trouble too. The repercussions in this particular case were huge. He couldn't just shrug her off, eager to get back to his beloved smoking hut. She willed herself to force him to show an interest. To resolve this untenable situation.

Meanwhile downstairs, Wayne ignored the receptionist as he

walked past her, the glass protection screening her from potential intimidation. She, like Bill and many others in the building, got away with treating clients with disdain. But there was no more time to dwell on this, as he was shocked to discover that it was Saira that was waiting for him. He knew it was a rare occurrence for Mr Leigh to allow his abused wife out of the house. And here she was visiting him of her own free will. Wayne anxiously looked around him. Surely her husband was in the toilets or was lurking round the back of the building.

But Saira confirmed that she had arrived alone. There had clearly been some sort of incident, for her left wrist had been carefully bandaged up with a gauze and tape. Her badly swollen hands had received medical attention too. A mobile phone was sticking out of her jeans pocket. An indication of positive progress. Perhaps Mark Leigh had been critically injured and was in a coma! Better still, he had a vision of the body lying in a mortuary! All wishful thinking on Wayne's part.

He knew though these were only pipe dreams. Ushering her into an interview room, he waited until they had sat down before asking, "what's happened to you?"

"My boys. How are they?"

"They are doing better." He purposely didn't give any more details as he needed to ascertain what had happened and keep her focused.

"My husband always blamed me after you took Kyle and Brandon away from us. I found out yesterday that he was planning to torch me alive!"

Wayne fell silent. After all, he had fought a court case against Mark Leigh and had always known exactly what type of brute he was. He took a deep breath and moved a chair to sit closer to her.

Saira's tone was flat as she recounted what had been an everyday occurrence for her since they lost their custody fight. "He would lock me in the house when he went out for hours at a time. He used to tell me it was for my own safety."

Wayne allowed her space to talk.

"I'm such an idiot, I believed him," she said sadly, expecting him to nod.

"He became obsessed with taking revenge on you." This was the first time she had opened up since he had been allocated the case a year earlier. "He was so controlled about everything. He hardly ever lost his temper with me."

Wayne stayed silent, for she was trying to normalise this abusive behaviour.

Leigh had apparently been recently spending time in the children's bedroom and had fixed a padlock to the outside of their door. It raised her suspicions but his response had been to mind her own business. On several occasions she had seen him coming into the house with bin bags and dumping them in their room. She knew something wasn't right, but she didn't dare ask again.

Then, yesterday, she got her opportunity to find out. Mark had left the house at 10am, but had left the key to the padlock by his bedside table by mistake. She noted where the item had been left to ensure she put it back at exactly the right angle. He was usually back around 4pm, so she had time to try and work out what he had been doing in there. "I saw instantly that something was different. All the clothing and bedding had been shoved into the bottom of the wardrobe."

Her eyes were fixed on the floor as she recounted that she instantly knew something was amiss. "And there it was. Underneath the huge pile, twigs, firelighters, matches, a large bolt, rope and a knife." Saira now glanced up at Wayne but was unable to hold her gaze, her large brown eyes welling up.

Unable to control her emotions any longer, she broke down as she revived another memory. Leigh had screamed at her recently, when she had thrown out the free newspaper, and had made her retrieve it from the dustbin. She paused, clearly traumatised by the events and years of abuse. "Now I know why he was spending so long in there. He had used them to build his fire logs. He was going to set me on fire in our children's bedroom!"

For once Wayne found himself speechless.

"I knew I had to leave immediately. I grabbed the thickest pair of socks I could find and ran downstairs."

Now rocking slightly in the chair, Saira continued. "Most of the windows are double glazed but I knew the kitchen one would be my best chance of escaping. I had to find something to break the glass."

She went on. "He would never let me open the windows, and kept all the keys to them hidden from me." She glanced at Wayne momentarily then stared again at the floor. "I now realise that he lied to me the whole time. He said it was safer so we wouldn't be burgled." Saira stopped for a second and took a deep breath before continuing. "I grabbed the broken chair leg from the lounge."

Wayne nodded. He knew which broken chair she was referring to. The same one that had lain in the corner of the lounge when he first visited. He had probably thrown it at her or the children in the past.

"I put the socks over my hands, and smashed the glass," she declared, adding, "I got rid of as much as I could. I lifted myself onto the sink and climbed out."

With that, Saira held up both her arms, but Wayne didn't need any proof.

"I was in agony with all the shards of glass in my wrists."

He shook his head sympathetically as he listened.

"I fell on my knees and I could feel the blood running down my legs. I managed somehow to pick myself up and ran round the corner to the hardware shop on the parade."

He gently interrupted, telling her to take her time.

"I ran in, begged the owner to call the police. To help me!"

In the past, Wayne had been unable to reach out to Saira, but right now he felt immensely proud of her. He tried to reassure her that she was safe now.

Saira explained that the owner of the shop took her through to the back, locked the door and called the emergency services.

"I was in A and E for ages as they had to get the shards of glass out of my wrist." She pointed to the bandages as if to prove she was telling the truth. She divulged too that a specially trained domestic violence police officer stayed with her all the time and took a statement. It was a relief for her to learn that the police had broken in and taken photographs of the evidence before Leigh returned from his errands.

It struck Wayne how Mark Leigh had robbed her of a right to a family life, and had ripped apart every shred of her self-confidence.

It was clear that she was in shock that the police had protected her. Leigh had always made her believe that the authorities would never take her seriously and that it was her fault she had lost the children. She relayed how a support officer had even driven her to a refuge the previous night, and had returned earlier that morning to update her on the latest developments.

That same morning, Saira had learned that Leigh had been charged and was currently in custody. There were no plans for a bail application. Unusually, he had informed his duty solicitor that he was planning to plead guilty to the charges of false imprisonment and intent to commit murder.

"So where is this refuge? Is it local?" Wayne interjected. Much as he liked Saira, he couldn't be with her all day as she relayed all the details. "Have you got any family you can stay with?" he inquired, trying not to sound impatient. Already a plan was forming and time was of the essence.

Saira explained that her family were traditional Muslims and had been disappointed when she became involved with a white man. They had met him once and told her that she was making a terrible mistake and he was a bully. They hadn't disowned her, but told her to come back when she was rid of him.

She wished now she had listened to her relatives. They had been right. Looking back it was so clear what had happened. She had been gaslighted. Leigh hadn't even allowed her to have any say when choosing names for their children. She would have loved to have called them traditional Asian names.

She had made such progress in a day. From the refuge, she had contacted her brother, and he had immediately invited her to stay with him and his family. She told Wayne that she was currently staying in a refuge outside of the town centre. There was CCTV monitoring the property and she felt safer there than with family. It would only be temporary until she gained more confidence and could make plans.

Wayne hadn't received any domestic violence training, and his knowledge was limited. He suggested that now she knew what would be happening with Leigh, perhaps she could move. But still Saira was fearful whether Leigh would be released on bail at some point. If this was to happen, she had been advised that she would have to move instantly to another safe house, some distance away from the Barnham Hill Estate.

For the first time since he took Brandon and Kyle's case on, she was acting on advice. Wayne was impressed. He learnt that the police were due in court that morning requesting an interim injunction to assist her. Furthermore, she was demonstrating some insight into the difficulties ahead. She would need legal advice regarding a divorce, and would have to become independent for the first time in many years.

There was so much for her to do. There was a separate bank account to open, and she needed to sort out her benefits. The hostel workers had lent her clothes but she needed to go home to pick up her belongings and this task was currently too traumatic for her to endure.

She thanked Wayne for listening and expressed her gratitude that so many people had tried to help her. She took out the mobile phone and pointed to a button on it. All she needed to do was press on it, and police would assist her immediately.

What progress Saira had made in the space of a day! But sadly, it had taken this distressing discovery for her finally to realise just how dangerous Leigh was. She hadn't been proactive in the past, and the children had been badly neglected, but her bravery now needed to be acknowledged.

"I should have done it sooner," she said, reading his thoughts. Her shoulders sank as she proclaimed, "I have made such a mess of all our lives."

"Well, you have escaped now," he told her gently. He smiled as he told her, "I will help you to see your boys. You know they talk about you and miss you." As Wayne spoke, he watched Saira's eyes fill up with tears again. Passing her a box of tissues, he explained that he needed to check out what was happening with the police directly and had to make phone calls to the foster carers and speak to his manager. He informed her that he may be upstairs for a while.

"When I come down, I can bring you the number of the imam at the local mosque," he told her.

She nodded gratefully.

It was unusually quiet when he walked back into his room.

Absorbed in the new development, he got straight to work. His email box was full of new messages, all relating to Saira. Several were from the police domestic violence team, informing him of the news he now already knew. He had been too busy sitting in McDonald's, involving himself in Ellie's case, to attend to them! He read each one and methodically typed a short reply where necessary. It wasn't that he didn't believe Saira, but he needed to hear it from the professionals now involved in this case.

Unsurprisingly, she had not been exaggerating. There was communication directly from the Crown Prosecution Service spelling out that even if she were to drop her charges, they would still proceed with prosecuting Mark Leigh. There were photographs too of the chilling evidence that Saira had discovered hidden at the bottom of the wardrobe.

But for Wayne, there was more alarming news. Mr Leigh had disclosed during the police questioning that he had initially planned to lure Wayne to the property too, but this plan had become too complex to engineer, and therefore he had decided to focus his efforts on just killing his wife.

"Are there grounds for a lengthy sentence?" Wayne typed his reply, feeling light-headed with it all. He prayed he would receive an instant response! He needed to get back to Saira – his priority was to get her reunited with her boys, ideally after they finished school today. Wayne cancelled a statutory visit to another child in care that afternoon, then rang Kyle and Brandon's foster carers, Ian and Brenda. A year had been an extremely long time for them, particularly as there had been no contact whatsoever with their mother. They asked about her daily and were clearly worried for her welfare.

The phone discussion with Ian went well. Wayne updated him on the dramatic developments, thankful to have such understanding and experienced individuals looking after Kyle and Brandon.

With the support of their foster carers, a plan was emerging for that very same afternoon. In order not to get the boys' hopes up, they would only be told what was happening once Wayne gave the go-ahead that they were both on their way. This strategy made the best sense, as Saira had not been reliable for whatever reason in the past.

In the event that the reunion went well, Wayne asked whether Ian and Brenda would consider having Saira visit her children in their own home. Supervised contact in a centre was far from ideal and he would love a relaxed natural setting for them all to benefit from.

Within this question lay another potential worry. He knew well enough that statistically many victims return to their abusers. Saira had suffered many years of an unhappy marriage, but this had been her life as she knew it. Today she was willing to accept the offer of counselling, but could she sustain positive change or would she give in to Leigh's apologies? In that unlikely scenario, the safety of the foster placement would be jeopardised.

"I wouldn't worry about that." Ian laughed. "I will tear out Leigh's throat if he comes anywhere near us!" But something in his tone made Wayne think that he wasn't joking.

Wayne would need to give careful thought another time about whether the boys could still be placed for adoption. It hadn't been easy to find a match for them and the farm couple that he had found had probably been snatched up. He had little faith in the criminal justice system. He hoped Leigh would receive a long sentence, but even if he did, at some point he would be eligible for release. Leigh was manipulative and intelligent. He could quite possibly hide his disturbed thought process and, until he died, would always pose a threat to his wife and children.

Adoption would be fraught with difficulties, but today perhaps there would be a better option. He really wanted to give Saira one final chance. He could test her commitment to the boys over the next few months, and he could refer her for parenting skills lessons during this time.

It would, he imagined, be a team effort. He hoped that she would take up support offered from within the Muslim community. The refuge staff would assist her too, and she would probably need counselling. At some point, she would need to be relocated, but this was for another day. All he wanted this afternoon was for the reunion between Saira and her children to go smoothly and for Saira to get in touch with the rest of her family.

In a friendly manner, he called out to Bill, demanding he venture out of his office and talk to him. This was no way to address a senior, but Bill was not your bog standard manager in any sense and Wayne, as a locum, was generally more polite to him than the others.

Bill didn't act in the least bit perturbed. He was glad to be wanted and seemed genuinely pleased to hear that Leigh was behind bars, at least for now. Since the Ofsted inspection, everyone had noted that Bill had shown more interest in the job. The two men agreed instantly on a potential plan. Safety was of paramount importance, and the relocation of Saira and her children hundreds of miles away would probably be the safest outcome. And this was free, unlike being in the care system. Paying out hundreds of pounds a week to private foster carers ruined his budget!

"Excellent work!" his manager enthused. He was always doling out the praise, figuring that this cost him nothing. He added, "I'm happy to chair a meeting with our solicitors and the guardian ad litem to discuss the various legal options."

Wayne bounded down the stairs, feeling elated. For once, he ignored the grim prison-like foyer – the dirty industrial poor quality carpet tiles, the fingermarks all over the glass doors to the reception area – for he was on a high. It was all about changing children's destinies for the better and his mission to save Kyle and Brandon was nearly complete.

A forlorn-looking Saira looked up hopefully as Wayne walked back into the interview room.

"You know that I haven't seen my boys for about a year now," she told him. "I miss them so much. Do you still see them?"

Wayne nodded.

"Can I write to them now, and you could give them the letter please?"

She told Wayne that she felt embarrassed that she had no money to buy them gifts, but she hoped to get a job as a hairdresser again, as soon as she had sorted herself out.

He interrupted her. "It's OK. I always said I would help you if you left Leigh."

With a wide smile, Wayne told her that he knew that Kyle and

Brandon would love to receive a letter from her. He studied her face carefully, watching her reaction to what he had to tell her. That she would be seeing them after school in a few hours, and that she could tell them for herself how much she had missed them.

She looked ecstatic and shocked. But this immediately gave way to panic. "But I don't know how to get there. I don't even know which school they are at." The questions were being hurtled without him having a chance to respond. "Or where they live."

Leigh had worked his particular brand of magic, destroying every ounce of Saira's confidence.

It was clear that Saira would take some months to build her self-reliance back up. Much as he would have enjoyed assisted her, realistically, his job was very much about assessing and managing risk to children. Saira needed befriending. And he could see how much trouble David was in for befriending his clients! Despite this, he had cleared his afternoon to start the process.

"Come back here at 2.15pm. I am taking you." Wayne told her, purposely ignoring her feelings of self-doubt.

Elated too that Saira had escaped, he was finding it hard to hide his own enthusiasm for the rushed plan of action. He explained that Kyle and Brandon would be brought after school to the café in their local park. Saira would have an opportunity to meet Brenda and Ian too, and Wayne would be in the background, just in case she needed any support with any difficult questions the boys may pose.

With a reunion such as this, Wayne had felt it should last a maximum of an hour and a half. He promised Saira that he would drop her back at the refuge afterwards. He explained that if all went well, they could set up phone calls between her and the children before the next visit. It was made clear to Saira that every meeting would be evaluated by their foster carers and himself. He would be taking the lead too from Kyle and Brandon as to how often they wanted to see their mother.

With all the arrangements set up, there was one last thing that Wayne felt was needed. A year was a long time. The boys may be nervous, and if she could hand them a gift each, this would be more natural. It didn't need to be expensive. He knew that in principle, he could approach Bill and request ten pounds from the Children Act Section 17 petty cash budget.

But what a waste of time and energy that begging process would be! Bill was bound to say no to this reasonable request. And this negative response would be reinforced if he asked any of the other managers too. He could only imagine the tiresome and repetitive lecture that he would receive about government cuts to the social care sector. That there was no money allocated for luxury items like this. That foster carers should pay for these gifts. That they were being paid enough money. On and on.

All of this bartering about money felt wrong on so many levels. Social work practice was supposed to be about the child. But as always, the little things that could make a difference were overlooked.

But would Brandon and Kyle even care if their adored mother arrived empty-handed? Was he focusing on the minutiae? But imagining their joy brought back painful memories for Wayne. As he chatted with Saira about the impending visit, everything from years ago resurfaced for him. His memories were razor sharp.

Wayne had been seven years old when his father had walked out on his family. He had spent the rest of his childhood wondering what he had done wrong. He would have treasured even the smallest gift. Even a birthday card would have meant something. But there had been nothing. He didn't need counselling sessions to tell him why he wasn't able to trust men. To form lasting relationships.

Not known for his generosity, he spontaneously reached into his wallet and handed her a ten-pound note.

"Take this," he told her. "Go to Asda next door now, and choose a small gift for them both. A magazine but not chocolates. They will melt in the car." Wayne could be so directive, but he was giving Saira a test. Would she return on time that afternoon. And if she did, would it be empty-handed?

"Thank you, Wayne. I will pay you back when I get my benefits sorted out," she offered, instinctively hugging him. They said their temporary farewells and he reminded her to come back at 2.15 on the dot.

Feeling lifted after that unpleasant meeting in McDonald's,

Wayne bounded back up the stairs. Coming across other colleagues in the neighbouring area teams, he stopped them in the corridor to announce his wonderful news. An abused, broken mother had resurfaced that morning and would be reunited that afternoon with her children. He had other work to be getting on with, but he felt it was not so unreasonable to bask for just a few moments on what he had personally achieved for the Leigh children.

Earlier in the week, Kyle and Brandon's future had looked bleak. He had realised that it would be highly unlikely that any adopter would proceed once they were made aware just how dangerous their father was.

But Leigh was now locked in a police cell and there were plans in the early stages of formation. As their allocated social worker for a year, Wayne had desperately tried to avoid the likelihood of Kyle and Brandon having to spend their entire childhood in the care system. But things were very different now. And the option of Saira caring for them alone would hopefully be the best outcome for them.

Whilst Saira remained in the Fenton area, he would monitor her closely, to see whether she could maintain positive change on a long-term basis. He barely knew Kyle and Brandon, but he did care for them. He prayed that Saira could put her horrific experiences behind her. Everything counted on this, for he knew that if the boys could have their adored mother put them to bed every night, his work was done.

Nineteen

After twenty minutes spent relating his victory against Leigh to anyone forced to listen, Wayne eventually sloped off back to his own room. On entering, he was struck again by the unusual quietness. In all the years in social work, he had never become accustomed to the irritating sounds of the phones constantly ringing out. 365 days of the year, the demand on social workers never ceased, with professionals and family members understandably demanding an instant solution to an unsatisfactory situation. However committed he was, however much he loved the job, sometimes it was just too much.

Perhaps this silence indicated that the world had become a better place, and no one abused children anymore. He could go home and put his feet up, ending his career on a high note! But he thrived on the buzz and gravitated towards Bill's office to eavesdrop on a heated discussion. He could hear Siobhan sounding agitated and could guess the gist of it. That baby Ellie's future was still unresolved.

In all the excitement about Saira, he had temporarily forgotten that the last time he had seen David, he was not acting like himself at all. He noted that his shoulder bag was missing, giving the indication he had gone out. The two men were quite close, and it had been Wayne that had encouraged him to take the prescribed anti-depressants. Not that they appeared to be making any difference to his low mood.

It saddened Wayne greatly to watch his friend's life literally fall apart these last six months. He picked up the whereabouts book for clues as to where he had gone but it came as no surprise that David's column was void of any client's name. The column reserved to put the estimated time due back to the office had been left blank too.

This had to be the most dysfunctional team he had ever worked in and he wondered why he liked it here so much! Putting the kettle on, he offered Deirdre a drink. This was good of him, considering it was usually difficult to make conversation with her. She was so reserved. Perhaps that was too generous an observation. The others found her positively aloof. Wayne felt sorry for the children in the care system who were unfortunate enough to be saddled with her. Was life not hard enough for them already?

It was obvious why Deirdre never joined in with the constant complaints relating to Bill's management style. The lack of supervision sessions or the cancelling of the fortnightly team meetings, for example, meant that she could be left largely to her own devices. They had all noted her last period of "sickness" lasting a full month, which had been unchallenged by their supervisor. She was clearly creating for herself an "administrator" position, and she must have been under the illusion that undertaking regular home visits was optional!

As Wayne carried her tea across to her, he watched as she pushed her papers around her desk in a determined fashion. It was unforgivable. Couldn't she grasp what social work was all about? She should be getting out there, and engaging kids, assessing risk and trying her best to keep them safe. It was time that Deirdre's name was added to his next whistle-blowing report.

He sat down and sipped his coffee, needing some head space to dwell on what he had learnt from Saira's visit to the office. Far from naïve, Wayne had never underestimated Mr Leigh's ability to harm the children emotionally, but now he had learnt that his client had originally planned to torch him too. He knew that child protection work was unpredictable and at times even dangerous, but over the years, had become blasé. He shouldn't have taken this risk, especially as procedures were in place to undertake joint home visits, should it be required.

Wayne had an excellent memory, and recalled the exact details of when he had first come across Leigh. The scene he had faced in the twins' bedroom was vivid in his mind. He had been vocal in his concern that the children were not being cared for properly. He could picture the wardrobe which had been locked – without asking permission, he had turned the key. He had noticed it contained nothing but some empty crisp packets. He had wondered whether the children had spent time being locked in there.

He remembered everything. The alarm bells were most definitely ringing loudly. He had stripped the duvets off the beds and had raised concerns that there were no sheets underneath. He vaguely recalled how he had directed both parents to clean up the room. He remembered something too about the previous social worker's file notes.

The case notes had recorded that the family support team workers had delivered sets of bedding weeks earlier. He couldn't remember everything about the inspection, but knew that he had gone about his investigation in his true passive aggressive style. He had probably harangued the parents as to where these items were.

At the time, Wayne hadn't felt any fear, just an overwhelming sadness that the boys and Saira had to live with Leigh, and a sense of deep frustration that no one had done anything earlier. Even if there had been suitable bedding, and the house had been clean, it would have made no difference to the outcome. Standing in that depressing house, he could sense what a dreadful childhood they were enduring. He had made the decision that these young boys were going to spend their last few nights with their parents.

Usually Wayne relied on his gut feelings. He was a confident practitioner but he had been over-confident on this case. He couldn't afford this luxury anymore. Just how many times had he visited the Leigh home without a colleague to accompany him? Maybe two or three times. Every single time he had visited that house alone, he had unknowingly placed himself in grave danger. He thought he hadn't needed the view of a manager to guide him. Regular supervision was something that Bill had not prioritised, but on this occasion, he could have benefitted.

There had been times when Wayne had tried to intervene. One meeting stood out. It had been in the court waiting room, and in front of the couple and the children's guardian ad litem he had asked to speak to Saira privately. The incident was clear in his mind. They had requested that the officials kept guard outside. Taking this opportunity, they explained to Saira what was at stake if she didn't go to a refuge and take up support. To their disappointment, she was spotted immediately afterwards divulging the nature of the conversation to her husband in the foyer.

He couldn't have physically dragged Saira away from Leigh. Perhaps he could have allocated more time to her. But even if he spent many extra unpaid hours a week, would it have made any difference to the outcome? Saira had been brave fleeing for her own safety. He had chosen social work as a profession for a reason and thrived on the ability that he had to rescue people from significant danger. But on this occasion, Saira had not only saved her own life, she had potentially saved his too!

Thank goodness Saira had found the padlock key the previous morning. He sighed deeply and shook his head slowly. She would probably be traumatised for life and would need counselling. Unusually for Wayne, he felt quite shaken too. He made a conscious decision to learn from this and take greater care. Even if the majority of his colleagues were abysmal, at least taking one of them with him would mean another professional to disempower clients such as this abusive character. To alter the dynamics of a potentially intimidating visit. Someone, however useless, to vouch for you in these circumstances.

That first time Wayne had gone out to see the Leighs stood out. The two of them had been alone upstairs. Events could have turned out differently. For instance, Leigh may have been so furious with his questioning, that he may have attempted to push him down the stairs! This had definitely taught him a lesson. Not to be cocky. Never again to go out alone on a child protection investigation.

He acknowledged that most workers in the pressured front line made mistakes at some level and he was no exception. However hard they all worked, it just wasn't possible to cover every angle when caseloads were so high. Furthermore, constantly having to risk assess meant someone, somewhere was considered lower priority. Children and their families were let down every single minute of every single day. It was part and parcel of the job.

It was doing him no good thinking about Mark Leigh, and it helped him to be diverted by the current tug of war case, no doubt still causing acute anxiety to all concerned. In Ellie's case, Wayne, like the others, was troubled by David's substandard social work practice. They had all gleaned that this heartache could have been easily avoided.

Yotunde moved across the room to discuss the crisis. She too was appalled and disappointed at what she had learnt. At the time of Tracey's pre-birth assessment David should have consulted with Fenton's own childcare legal team, just to run the case past them. The procedures in this particular regard were there for a reason and made sense. The obvious alarm bells would have rung, and the natural chain of events would have been triggered. She recalled warning her colleague at the time, but he hadn't taken her comments seriously.

The comradeship the job offered was appealing to Wayne. The two social workers both agreed that it had been extremely short-sighted of David to put all his trust in Tracey, just because she had appeared reasonable and co-operative at the time. Yotunde was a dedicated and capable worker and hated witnessing poor practice. She sounded angry, recalling how David had been celebrating that Tracey had willingly signed a worthless scrap of paper signing away her rights. They both blamed Bill too of course. He was supposed to be supervising all his staff on a regular basis.

This wasn't the only error by all accounts. Wayne told Yotunde that he had been called upon to help David create Ellie's life story book. It had been obvious that his colleague knew little about her extended family. It had been shocking and now he wished he had challenged him properly. The childcare law principles were clear in this regard. Any relatives should be offered the opportunity to be assessed as potential carers for the child themselves. Children had the right to a family life where possible. All this would have entailed was a brief viability assessment.

"I'm sure that Tracey's sister would have liked to have been considered to care for her niece!" Yotunde said, her bitterness evident in her tone.

Wayne finished his coffee, and looked over to the abandoned milkshake on his colleague's desk. He doubted that David would show his face again today. He wasn't going to call and check up on him. If he wanted to ruin his own family life, that was up to him. But to go around ruining others was unforgivable. From Wayne's understanding, David's actions, or rather lack of them, would surely be seen as amounting to gross misconduct. Once this reached senior management by way of a barrage of formal complaints, he would instantly be suspended. A report containing minutiae of this anonymised case would be published on the internet.

From what information David had shared with Wayne, he knew that his wealthy parents had distanced themselves from him and had stopped giving him any financial support. He knew for a fact that David was isolated from his friends and had started drinking alone in the evenings. They both agreed that instead of pestering the Baums for a friendship they didn't require, he should have focused his energies on fighting Gina to see his own young children. The facts were clear and there was no excusing this substandard conduct. His name needed to be removed from the social work register.

But the reality was that Bill would probably cover the errors over, to protect himself. The instance of when Bill had torn up Mark Leigh's grievance letter came to mind. That's how seriously he took his management role!

But Ellie's case was a different set of circumstances altogether. Bill wasn't that inept, surely? How could he fail to realise that David's judgement had been impaired on so many levels? Either way, Ellie's prospective adopters were educated people and would most definitely make a complaint on a higher level.

Given the conflict between Siobhan and David, it was best that David was out of the office. Wayne glanced at his watch. It was only 11.30am, and between Mr Leigh planning to murder him and the row in McDonald's, that was quite enough drama for the rest of the day. He began handwriting his notes on Saira's office visit ready to drop in the typing tray. There was always so much to do.

Twenty

MEANWHILE IN BILL'S OFFICE, SIOBHAN SAT MOTIONLESS as he skimmed Ellie's file. Preoccupied as usual with the dreaded wait for the Ofsted inspection report, he struggled initially to get a grip of what on earth had happened. He sighed as he handed it back to his social worker. He liked his desk clear so he could read his newspaper later. But something had been triggered in this case for him. It was relatively unusual for a client to turn themselves around in such a short space of time. And in this regard, there seemed no way of moving Ellie's case to a satisfactory conclusion. Unusually, he found himself stimulated by this particular dilemma.

He leant back in his chair and began rambling to Siobhan about a case he had heard about reaching the press some years earlier. It involved foster carers who were attached to their two charges. When they heard the news from their social worker that there were plans to have the children adopted, they went on the run to Ireland. Rather animated, he launched into some detail, telling her how there had been a massive police search. It had ended with the director of the local authority being forced to make a statement promising that the foster carers could keep the children.

This true story only brought about more anxiety for Siobhan. Would Melissa and Dan take Ellie and flee? Bill sighed. He had no answers, and felt somewhat for Siobhan. Despite this, he would under no circumstances be agreeing to accompany her to tell the Baums the news. He had lied to the Ofsted inspectors and had made out that he often went out with his social workers. He was of the strong opinion that he would not do the dirty work. Those years of being a social worker were over. He pushed paper now and counted off the days until his retirement.

With Siobhan readily admitting that she was out of her depth, there was only one thing for it. Bill stepped out and persuaded Wayne to join the meeting.

There wasn't enough space to fit two chairs in the windowless glorified cupboard so, without asking, he perched himself on Bill's desk. Given that the only thing on it was a biro and a brand new pad of paper, there was plenty of space! The scene gave the impression it was his first morning at his new job. The absence of a diary, overstuffed client files and fluorescent post-it notes attached to the bottom of the computer screen said it all.

"So can you help devise a strategy so that Ellie is introduced to Tracey?" Siobhan begged Wayne, sounding weary.

But before he had a chance to reply, Bill butted in.

"Where's David?" he queried, sounding rather annoyed. "I will talk to him. Get him to take back responsibility for this nightmare case."

He was trying to be helpful but there was nothing productive so far in any of his suggestions and, in any event, David's current whereabouts were unknown. But Bill was holding his own. Again, he voiced his concern that David should not have lumbered Siobhan and himself with such a time-consuming and severely problematic case.

"Look, I am the manager round here," he announced, adding, "if I tell David to take the case back, that's what must happen!" He glanced at them both, expecting them to be impressed, but there was no reaction.

"We will have to do it without David," they both responded, covering up for David and trying to move things forward.

Bill suggested that Siobhan try and avoid contacting the Baums or any member of their extended family until after the formal planning meeting. It had been booked in for 4pm that afternoon. The meeting was later than she would have liked but with Melissa and Dan's designated officer on holiday, the duty manager was only free then. By which stage, the three of them were united in their fear that they could have a baby abduction on their hands!

With this pressure, Wayne instantly went into overdrive. He felt rather proud of himself, realising, not for the first time, that he was a natural leader. Siobhan had considered most of the mitigating factors, but she certainly didn't have the experience to deal with this on her own. Listening to her, he realised this wasn't even about having experience. David had put her in an impossible position.

But now was not the time to dwell on what procedures hadn't been followed. They both watched as Siobhan, placing her head in her hands, declared, "I can't cope with all this!"

Bill looked uneasy with this show of emotion and looked away from her. So it was left, as usual, to Wayne to deal with the situation at hand. He told her kindly that this was not her fault and he would help her co-work the case.

With Wayne now in charge, the meeting became more structured. He grabbed Bill's empty pad of paper and wrote down several bullet points, then began addressing each one of them methodically. He started with the facts.

The statutory requirements on what was expected from fostering-to-adopt applicants in these circumstances were clear. So much so, that during their own six-month in-depth assessment, their own designated social worker would have explored with them whether in these circumstances they would be able to hand a child over to their parents, should this situation arise. In this event, they would be required to fully co-operate with the local authority's care plan. This would realistically involve transporting their foster child to meet his or her parents and being proactive at every stage of the introductions.

"But this is now irrelevant," Siobhan added impatiently. "Of course the Baums were going to agree to whatever their social worker put to them. They were desperate for a baby."

"You have a point, of course," Wayne replied. "Rightly or wrongly, these are extenuating circumstances, and there is little point in asking them to drive Ellie over an hour each way to Harlton Wells." He added, "No one in their position would be willing to sit with Tracey, encouraging the bonding process!" He shook his head slowly, telling them, "You can forget that idea!"

"We could ask if a prison guard could take Ellie from the Baums' car and hand her over?" Bill was trying so hard to be helpful, adding, "They could wait in the car park for her to be returned?"

The two social workers stared at him in disbelief. Even arranging for Tracey to see Ellie for an hour in the contact room was a logistical nightmare in itself. Furthermore, this ludicrous plan demonstrated that their manager wasn't engaged in any real sense.

However skilled Wayne was, there were no solutions, only other scenarios to contemplate. The conversation went on for another half an hour. If Melissa and Dan would not be well enough, or prepared to hand over Ellie, would there be anyone else to replace them? It wouldn't be viable to ask their parents to do it either.

"To all intents and purposes, Ellie is their granddaughter,." Wayne added in his usual forceful style. "This is out of the question."

There was an alternative option. That Ellie would be removed today, and placed with emergency foster carers who would be able to undertake the visits to the prison and supervise and encourage the bonding process. But this too wasn't at all suitable. Ellie was prone to anxiety due to her drug dependency at birth. In any event, placement moves were considered extremely bad for attachments. This plan, whilst it made practical sense, had to be ruled out too.

Bill then suggested abandoning the usual procedures that would have involved about ten days of staged introductions to a new carer.

"Tracey is the biological mother," he said, stating the obvious. "We are totally within our rights to turn up unannounced and take the child!"

He added that he knew for sure that there were spare car seats in the storage cupboard to fit a six-month-old baby. Obviously Siobhan would need money for nappies and baby food for the journey – this could be given out of petty cash. He made it sound so simplistic, akin to an uncomfortable matter of knocking on a neighbour's door, explaining that a parcel had arrived for them, and by accident they had opened it and claimed it!

Bill didn't pick up on the vibes and leaned back in his chair, putting his hands behind his head. He thought he had nailed it and this could be approved later at the emergency planning meeting. But the two social workers glanced at each other, both thinking alike. Their manager was a waste of space and the Baums were decent human beings. Most importantly, Ellie was in the middle of this. An innocent five-month-old baby, certainly not an object.

"Would you like your daughter snatched from you, Bill?" Wayne spoke out, accusingly.

His manager shrugged. Why did his team feel they could speak to him like this? He didn't have children, and he wasn't going to rise to Wayne's bait. He needed his locum far too much to manage the constant duty emergencies. Instead he listened as Wayne raised yet another potential problem. What would happen if Tracey didn't bond with Ellie, or couldn't manage such responsibilities? Would she simply be dropped back to the Baums?

"Look, we can't be seen to be pandering to a foster couple." Bill was losing patience, and added harshly, "They aren't going to hand her over easily, that's for sure. What I suggest is the following: Siobhan goes to court and applies for an interim care order." He loved this side of the job, directing his juniors. "Then you can go in, if necessary with the police, and just get the kid out of there!"

They could see that Bill was trying to make an effort, but his familiar detached aura was never very far away. This matter was urgent and they were wasting precious time involving him in this wretched crisis. Wayne liked solutions and he was frustrated that he couldn't resolve this dilemma either. No one could.

The day was dragging terribly and Siobhan just wanted it over so she could get to her gym class before dinner. Over the last three years, she had just about got by, pestering her other colleagues for input into complex case problems. By nature, she wasn't a strong character. The previous day Tracey had made an impression on her and she anticipated that she had the skills and love to make a good mother. Furthermore, Siobhan hadn't appreciated how either foster carer had spoken to her on the phone. Of course, she had fully acknowledged that they were distressed. But together with David's persistent haranguing, the job was just completely intolerable.

The past few days had usurped all her energy. She could see that it just wasn't worth her principles to reunite Ellie with her birth mother. It was just too much aggravation.

The discussion paused for a moment as Deirdre knocked on

the door to Bill's office. She was quite possibly the laziest social worker in Fenton Childcare Services, so something must have happened for her to have got off her chair. "It's the governor of Harlton Wells prison wanting to speak to you, Siobhan."

Several minutes later, an elated Siobhan returned to the room. Beaming, she announced the latest development – that the mother-and-baby unit was full. The governor had just accepted a new inmate. The prisoner was considered higher priority given that she was currently breastfeeding. She was a teenager who had an existing bond.

"What a result!" Siobhan found herself laughing with relief, adding, "Now that was a close call. Crisis over!"

Bill appeared pleased too. This meant he could take an extended cigarette break and be left alone. But Wayne remained unconvinced that the matter was over. He put forward the notion that the prison service may have a duty to transport Tracey to an alternative mother-and-baby unit. He pointed out that her solicitor may raise this reason for a negative assessment as a breach of Tracey's human rights.

But Siobhan wasn't overly concerned. After all, she had anticipated this, and had been informed by the governor that there were only eight other mother-and-baby units in the country and there were waiting lists for all of them. The prisons couldn't just create a bed in the units when there wasn't one.

Further issues around Tracey's sentence were dissected briefly. Given that she still needed to serve another year it would be highly unlikely that the courts would release her on licence at this point. There would be no possibility of being offered a community sentence instead. Furthermore, everyone agreed that any appeal process would take too long to go through the courts.

Siobhan was now on a roll. "So there is literally nothing that Tracey's solicitor can do about it." She sounded bright and clearly relieved. "And that mentor can shut her mouth now too. Raising Tracey's hopes and causing all this upset. Interfering bitch!"

No one challenged her offensive language. With the matter being so fraught, they were all just glad it was concluded. Wayne's phone was ringing out, and he excused himself. Siobhan remained in Bill's office and shut the door. She didn't want Wayne to overhear the conversation or he may make her do the right thing.

The matter wasn't exactly finished. She told her manager that she was absolutely exhausted by all this drama, and had no intention of driving that long distance to Harlton Wells prison to tell Tracey the news in person. She couldn't face telling her that the reassessment was futile. It hadn't been really. It was just extremely bad luck that the bed had suddenly been taken! She argued strongly that she was convinced that Tracey would have been told that she wouldn't be reunited with her baby and moving into the specialist unit.

Bill didn't intervene. Tracey, like the rest of the cases that he took overall responsibility for, was nothing to him. Besides, he too was relieved that everything appeared to be under control now. He had felt part of the team, and this positive solution left him with a satisfied feeling. It was lunchtime, and after his cigarette break it would be time for his walk across to Asda to pick up his lunch. He would leave her to write up her findings and email it to Adreen. The last thing anyone wanted was for Tracey's solicitor to mount an appeal on the decision. This had to be the final correspondence between them.

Informing Tracey's father would be overlooked for now too. As another innocent party in all this sorrow, it would have been the right thing to tell him that he now would not enjoy watching his granddaughter grow up. He had sounded so pleasant and supportive on the telephone. He had been through so much, losing his wife at such a young age, and the hell he had suffered, watching his daughter succumb to drug addiction. He had left two voice messages for Siobhan asking for an urgent update whilst she had been in Bill's office. But informing Tracey's family wouldn't even make it onto Siobhan's to-do list.

Before she did anything else, there was someone more important who needed to be put out of his turmoil. As Siobhan dialled David's mobile, she explained that the outcome was just. Technically, a goodbye visit should be offered to Tracey, but as she was no longer her client, this could wait. "It's all sorted," she practically screamed. "You can calm down now."

David was quite literally shouting with relief. He questioned whether the family courts still had the date free for Ellie's final

Adoption Hearing in a week's time. Siobhan doubted very much that the Baums had cancelled the slot themselves the previous day, the horrendous state they had both been in. Even if the adoption hearing was delayed, this would be a small price to pay for an unbelievable stroke of luck at the final hour!

The rather curt tone of the email that Siobhan had sent to Tracey's solicitor showed just how fickle she could be. One moment she was fighting for Tracey, the next, she couldn't care less. She was in a rush too, for David was waiting for her, as arranged, in the car park. She had accepted the offer that he would drive them both to the Baums to share the wonderful news. He greeted her with a hug and a sparse looking bunch of pale yellow carnations as an apology for his behaviour earlier that morning. She pretended not to spot the £1.00 price tag still attached and accepted them graciously.

Laughing and joking, they now drove off in the direction of Mosforth, their earlier argument well and truly behind them. David had phoned ahead and spoken to Melissa's mother. Hopefully by the time they turned up, things may have calmed down and he could explain. He was relying on the fact that they too would be so thankful they could put the past few days behind them. After all, David thought naïvely, they were his good friends!

Twenty-one

The visit to Melissa and Dan's home had gone relatively well in David's eyes. He had sensed that the entire extended family were just so relieved that the nightmare was over, that they were accepting of what he had to say.

The two colleagues had discussed the impending visit in the car and had agreed that it was best to tell the truth. He was convinced the family would be grateful to them. That once they knew the full story, they would understand how hard he had fought for them. Calmly he explained that he had found it impossible to tell them just how bad the situation was. But he had directed Siobhan to undertake the reassessment in order to protect Ellie.

It was sad how unaware he was of how unprofessional he had been in their eyes. He sounded ridiculously childlike and selfish when he stupidly admitted that he had felt too stressed to take their calls!

Melissa was sitting in her dressing gown. She had been unable to get dressed in days. She was dosed up on tranquilisers, and her taut expression said it all. She searched his face for answers but there were none forthcoming. Not the ones she wanted to hear. Just pathetic excuses for an individual who was paid by the tax payer to do a critical job.

Next to her, holding her hand, was Dan, the sleeping baby in his arms. He had physically recovered from the violent vomiting episodes but hadn't slept properly and was emotionally shaken. Still, he wasn't risking David trying to grab their child. The last two days had taught them both something – not to trust anyone to protect their daughter. His expression had hardened too. They had been naïve to befriend this useless social worker, but to be fair, David had pushed himself onto them. All they had ever heard were nightmare stories of adoptions going wrong, of social workers not doing their job. But up to a few days ago, they had only praise for this lonely social worker, who had clearly messed up in his own parenting.

Everything had been going so well. Perhaps too well. Dan glanced at his wife. She had had a total meltdown, and as he was lying on the hospital trolley too sick to call her, he had decided to try not to beat himself up. This useless excuse for a social worker had pushed himself on them, turning up all the time. They knew it had been unprofessional of him, but they had both been grateful and had felt sorry for him.

Whilst David wittered on, Dan struggled to look at him, with his earnest way of offering meaningless platitudes. He glanced at his watch several times, indicating he just wanted him and the frizzy-haired colleague to get out of their house. They all just wanted to be left alone with Ellie to try somehow to recover from the worst two days of their entire lives.

David didn't quite read the signs right. He took it that Melissa was still feeling the effects of the sedation. Her parents were in the house but kept well away. She had barely spoken other than to say that she was very frightened that Dan could have had a heart attack, from the sheer stress they had all endured those last forty-eight hours. The atmosphere was quite tense, akin to visiting when someone had recently died. But both he and Siobhan felt it was understandable. In their opinion, they both seemed satisfied with the outcome of Tracey's assessment and how social care had conducted themselves.

In the end, the mood was one of reassurance and calm. It was a superficial interpretation of harrowing events. Two good people who had thought they were going to have their daughter snatched from them until an hour before. But David and Siobhan appeared to be celebrating. They felt light-hearted. In their own bubble, they chose not to read the Baums' negative body language towards them both. Dan had simply reiterated that they just wanted to move on. No more stress and aggravation.

The Baums had already decided on what they considered the most sensible path for the time being. They would keep their criticism of David and the entire Fenton Local Authority to themselves. The court hearing would now go ahead as planned. They were both so close to finality, the family court judge stamping that absolutely crucial rubber seal on the legal documents. Ellie would finally become their daughter in every sense and they could start their lives again as a family.

Those last few days had been unbearable. In that short time span, they had seen through David. He was not their friend at all. He was a selfish, troubled and ineffectual loser. He was not fit to hold a social work position. Only once they were safe legally would they tell him what they thought of him. They would also tell him that he was never to make contact with them again.

Meanwhile, Siobhan had been rather inspired by her meeting with Tracey. She had managed to step outside her comfort zone and fight for her daughter. She was really very brave. Unlike her, who at the age of thirty still lived at home with her parents. She wondered for a moment what would have happened if she had met Tracey outside of work. They would probably have got on very well. She gravitated towards people with a spirit to them.

The car journey back to the office had been a wonderful opportunity to relish David's company. There were no distractions and he paid her so much attention. Furthermore, he was back to his usual humorous self. It was while she was in the toilets at work that she suddenly made a decision that was most unlike her. She would risk the ultimate rejection.

She phoned her mother and told her that she wouldn't be home for dinner and that she may be staying with a friend overnight. Her plan was simple. She would pick up a couple of bottles of wine and go round to David's flat that evening. She had been there many times before, and knew there was a takeaway pizza place round the corner.

There needed to be a plan. She would have to leave work early, claiming a dental appointment. She had enjoyed some time to herself yesterday, and was now becoming a dab hand at skiving. It was quite addictive!

There was, Siobhan knew, the matter of making herself look more presentable. She took a good look at herself in the mirror. It wasn't pleasing. She really needed to make more effort. She hoped it was just that the lighting wasn't complimentary. But the truth was, she knew she looked a sight. Her eyebrows were bushy and her hair the usual soft and unsightly frizz. She was going to have to address this first.

There was the small matter of her workload to consider first. Karina, the single mother with bi-polar disorder. She was very fragile but could probably wait. The sibling group who were placed in separate foster homes desperate to see each other. It had been two months now. Another few days wouldn't make a difference.

Then there were the demands from an eccentric and tight-fisted uncle. His nephew was in the care system and there was an established arrangement whereby he gave him supper once a fortnight. But now he was haranguing her to be paid for his expenses!

How much could it possibly be to share out the contents of a packet of fish fingers? She had been to the pestering uncle's home. It was actually quite nice. He also drove a BMW. Quite an old model, but still a BMW. Yet another time waster who thought nothing of getting her to run around trying to get £1.50 signed off. Declan, her endearing and sensitive client, enjoyed going, and she hoped he would never get to hear all this.

It was all too much for one day. At 4pm, she couldn't take any more, and walked out of the building into blazing sunshine.

She stopped off on route to David's flat. There was no time to hunt around for a decent hairdresser's. Before she knew it, she pulled over and stepped inside a rather shabby one. The place was empty and doubled up as a beauty salon too. The décor was dated and worn, but a young beautician welcomed her with a warm smile and said she had plenty of time to help her with whatever treatments she wanted. Siobhan thought for a moment of the healthy state of her current bank account. As she didn't pay any rent to her parents, she could certainly afford the odd splurge of indulgence.

It made sense for all the staff to work on their only client at the same time. Feeling cheerful and energised, Siobhan gave the go ahead for the beautician to do anything that was needed. She explained that she was meeting someone later that evening, and she needed to make an impression.

There was the leave-in hair protein treatment, the eyebrow waxing and tint. The bikini and under-arm wax. A manicure and a pedicure. The blow dry made her features softer. Her hair was now unrecognisable. It shone and fell behind her ears softly. A hundred and forty pounds later, she left, leaving generous tips and promising to visit again soon for more treatments.

She could get quite used to this, but she needed to arrive before dinner time and still had one last job. To purchase new underwear.

David was surprised to hear Siobhan's voice on his intercom system. He had already eaten his tuna sandwich, and was enjoying a documentary. This was the first night he was able to relax and he wasn't enthused to hear her buoyant tone. He had spent all day with her and without the others around, he found her quite a bore. Still, she had worked so hard on Ellie's case, and he didn't want to be rude. He buzzed her in, hoping she wouldn't stay long.

"What have you done to yourself? You look different. Your hair ..." He was taken aback at this transformation.

There was no way she was going to admit that this effort had been for him. She downplayed it, saying the appointment was pre-booked and had been a thirtieth birthday gift from a friend.

She held out the steaming pizza, and a bottle of red wine, which David readily took from her.

"I'm sorry again for how I treated you," he said, adding, "you look very nice." They chatted easily as David took two plates out and passed her a wine glass. She was really looking not so bad tonight. He couldn't describe her as attractive, but her new hairstyle made such a difference. Her eyes looked defined with the eyebrows shaped, and her make up suited her.

"Let's phone Wayne. Tell him to come over?" he suggested, knowing full well that he would probably be at home cooking for his dull mother. But Siobhan didn't appear keen.

David located another bottle of wine, and with two now

consumed, they both relaxed on the one sofa. It was a small studio flat with not a shred of personality within its four bright white walls. The talk was not of work for a change, but of previous relationships. Siobhan wondered whether to make out she had had many boyfriends, but of course this wasn't true. There had only been one real relationship, she told him. But the truth was the sex hadn't been great, and she hadn't had a date for six years.

"I am too drunk to drive home, can I stay over?" she suddenly asked, trying to sound intoxicated, but actually she was quite sober. This was so unlike her and she had already planned to say she was joking if he laughed. But instead, he reached towards her. There was no fragrant perfume, in fact he wasn't even sure he fancied her. But he moved closer and kissed her.

Within seconds, his hands swiftly moved to caress her breasts at first on top of her blouse and then almost seamlessly he removed her bra and was pressing with his index finger on her nipples.

It was like she had been hit with high voltage electricity and she trembled as his expert hands moved further down to rub against her crotch.

Suddenly she pulled back from him. She had really wanted him. But sex repulsed her. It was the same as usual. The memories. Having to read the details of those innocent children who had been subjected to horrific systematic sexual abuse. The hours she had to spend interviewing the gang of perpetrators for their pre-sentence reports. If only they had pleaded guilty. Even now, years later, she could never talk about it.

Her anger now was fuelled towards her old team manager. She had explicitly told him that she couldn't face undertaking the sex offenders training. He had put her under pressure, what with the shortage of trained probation workers skilled in that field.

"What the hell are we doing? I'm sorry. We work together," was the best she could come up with. To soften the blow, she added insincerely, "It's not you. It's me. I am a real screw-up these days."

She left the flat swiftly, unable to look him in the eye. How mortifying this was going to be in the morning!

Twenty-two

Wednesday 21st July 2004

It hadn't been a good afternoon at that godforsaken joke of a social work team and as usual Deirdre Turner was exhausted by it all.

There was plenty about her that made her look older than her sixty-two years. For some unknown reason, she wore a wig, and her rather drab clothing gave the impression that she didn't care for herself. But this wasn't true. She had never been a vivacious type, but since the threats, she had felt it safer to have a low profile.

Spending so much of her free time on her own, she wasn't aware that her expression was so sullen. All she was focused on was getting by. Life hadn't always been like this. For instance, before the stalking, she had enjoyed going to the hairdresser's and out for lunch with friends. But the impact of what that violent client had achieved sadly trickled down into absolutely every aspect of her new life.

Despite relocating to Fenton, things were not much easier. She had found a new salon, but came to dread the fickle questions that served to fill in those uncomfortable silences, scared that if she did relax and open up, she may slip up, and disclose the terrifying truth of what had happened to her. She trusted no one and if anything, the anxiety increased due to being so isolated. More time to think, more time alone. Eventually she made the decision. It was both easier and safer to wear a wig.

Set in her ways, Deirdre filled her spare time cooking, and was used to eating on her own. With the radio as her constant companion, she kept abreast of current affairs and had long ago become used to her life outside of work. To her colleagues and outsiders, she looked rather tired and perhaps unloved. But Deirdre had far more pressing things to worry about than what she looked like. She blamed her broken sleep on the demons she tried so hard to escape from. Her life was becoming an existence and it hurt to think of the special times with her girlfriend and close friends a hundred or so miles away.

She was convinced she had Obsessive Compulsive Disorder triggered by what had happened. For instance, she would never leave her flat without checking that her personal alarm was safely stored in her pocket. She ensured the zip was open at all times. Each night she would go through a repetitive process of automatically checking the batteries were working. Then there was the spare one that she kept in her handbag, weighing it down.

There was nothing she could do. This was the way things were now. Darren Lawton had ruined his own life, but he had dragged her down with him. She would never be free.

The world was unjust and Deirdre saw herself very much as a victim. She had always lived as a law-abiding citizen and had been punished for her only crime – choosing to become a social worker.

It was too hard to fight the pessimism. Her parents were no longer alive, and with her siblings living overseas, she allowed everything to overwhelm her. When the incident had taken place she was in her late fifties, but now she had left it far too late to start a new career. It felt like a pointless exercise competing against younger, potentially more vibrant applicants to seek alternative employment. She felt she had no transferable skills to offer, and had come to the conclusion that she would have to remain working in the only job she was trained for.

There was one option but she hadn't felt it practical. If she took a large pay cut, she could work as a carer perhaps. But without significant savings, she had no choice but to continue dragging herself to this godforsaken job every day. In this respect, she had more in common with Bill than she would like. She too was just passing time until her local authority pension could kick in.

At work, she knew she appeared aloof. Her colleagues would have polite exchanges, or perhaps discuss a case that she had had previous involvement with, but that would be about it. She had even snubbed them all by refusing to attend the annual Christmas team meal. She didn't blame them for not reaching out to her. They weren't to know what had happened.

It had been six years since Deirdre had been forced to relocate. Before the threats to murder her, she had taken her job at childcare services seriously and had been dedicated. She would liken it to wading through the contents of a skip. The laborious job of processing each damaged item would take many hundreds of hours. And no article, however insignificant it looked, could be ignored. It had to slot into a bigger picture. Someone's life was being ruined. Aspirations would never be met. Finally, just as the dregs would be left at the bottom of the crate, the cycle would begin all over again.

How Deirdre wished she hadn't been on duty that fateful day in August 1998. As ever, she had been thinking of her overstretched colleagues when she had left the office in a hurry, calling out that she would ring if she needed assistance. Naïvely, she had assumed that she would be safe. After all, the impending visit would take place on a busy hospital ward, and she would be surrounded by staff. She wasn't to know that she would be meeting a well-known property developer with a dark and vindictive side to him.

The aftermath of what had taken place was still very much present and had aged her. The bitterness had seeped in quickly afterwards. It knew no boundaries and at times the crushing fear rested so heavily on her shoulders that she could almost feel it. This terrible burden had managed to engrain itself in every aspect of her life. She was now subdued, and lived an isolated life. She partly blamed herself. She should never have gone out alone on that child protection investigation.

In view of the way she had been treated, she felt she owed her profession nothing. She had to protect herself. She had learnt to excuse her behaviour in a thousand different ways, and this distorted thought process included trying to avoid undertaking home visits wherever possible. Every time she sat at home on sick leave, her workload remained uncovered. Hardened by her experiences, she didn't care anymore that she was in a position of power. By doing the very minimum, she might as well have been colluding with the abusers. It wasn't fair on the children and their families that she was trusted by Fenton Childcare Services to assist. They were reliant on her, and had done nothing wrong either.

She always knew she wouldn't get away with this indefinitely. Having been off sick for the past few weeks, she had missed the Ofsted inspectors storming the building. She had, however, overheard the others talking, worried about the outcome. Apparently, they had been sniffing about Area Team Three too much for Bill's liking.

It was yesterday lunchtime when Bill bumped into her in the Asda café next door to the office. He had been pleased to see her back in the office. She was lazy and impossible to manage. She was probably better than nothing, but she never completed tasks so it was marginal! He had been meaning to speak with her the moment she walked back in, but the crisis with the "tug of war baby" had taken priority. When he invited Deirdre to join him at his table, she felt it would be too rude of her to refuse.

There had been a development, and Deirdre was in a foul mood. Bill had been copied into an email received several hours earlier from the "silent assassin". In her brusque manner, the district area manager with a nasty reputation had demanded a meeting. No prizes for what this was about! It certainly wouldn't be to praise her performance. Her poor practice was being called into question. At this point, Deirdre knew what needed to be done. She needed Bill, however useless, to protect her. He would have to make allowances for her.

All Bill could talk about was the Ofsted inspection report that was due out any day. He was naturally expecting a negative outcome. Talking with his mouth full of the egg mayonnaise sandwich, he told her that he had been present when the inspectors arrived and was alarmed when they headed straight for absent Deirdre's filing cabinet.

There was no diverting them and they had taken every single

file and spent a full day analysing Deirdre's incomplete paperwork. Naturally, things were missing. That was the least of it. Visits were not completed within the obligatory timescales and cases were closed when they shouldn't have been. He launched into another matter. Ofsted had complained that a foster carer had not been reimbursed for purchasing emergency items for a newborn baby on Deirdre's caseload – £400 of expenses which they were perfectly entitled to. Rightly Bill questioned her now as to why this reimbursement hadn't been organised.

There was silence coming from Deirdre as she looked around the busy café. She could hardly recall the matter. In any event, this was certainly not the place to have this discussion. She stared at her now empty plate. It was time to tell her manager the truth. But not here.

It was best to try and change the subject and she encouraged him to talk about the successful outcome of the baby Ellie case the previous day. He told her that he had personally managed the conflict and that he was rather proud of his team leadership skills! He didn't seem aware that any member of the public could have been listening into this highly confidential conversation. He shared with Deirdre how much it suited him to have been promoted to manager, and with this senior role, he was able to distance himself from clients. Unlike Deirdre, Bill was transparent. Undertaking managerial tasks as opposed to the obligatory home visits was his thing!

The two colleagues had many things in common. He too was done with face to face work and was not a team player. There had been plenty of unpleasant experiences involving intimidating clients over the years. Looking back, he told Deirdre that he had grown to resent being put upon and the general local authority politics. In fact, his career choice had been a colossal mistake!

He too sounded bitter. He shared an experience many years earlier to demonstrate just how much aggravation he had had to put up with. A vengeful client had attempted to run him over in the staff car park. Sounding resentful, he relayed that he had reported this incident to the police, hopeful that they would be able to press charges. But he had learnt that the CCTV images had been too grainy to do anything with them. Suddenly, Deirdre felt uncomfortable, the familiar anxiety revisiting her. She breathed in and out slowly, practiced techniques to avoid suffering from a panic attack.

Bill picked up on Deirdre's agitation and asked if she was feeling OK. She sighed loudly. She should have told him about the violent threats when she had moved to his team. She offered that there was something she wanted to talk about, but this needed to be communicated within the privacy of his own office with the door firmly shut.

They walked back to the building together, chatting easily. Bill was enthusing about his allotment fruitions and Deirdre, trying to encourage the friendship, asked if he could spare any onions for her cooking. There seemed no urgency for either of them to return to deal with their workloads. Children suffering abuse, parents struggling to cope. All of them screaming out to be helped. But Bill and Deirdre were engrossed in the benefits of growing vegetables!

In the confines of his poky room, Deirdre sank into the uncomfortable plastic chair, her voice low in order that no one could overhear her.

"I have been relocated under the victim protection scheme," she announced miserably. "You mustn't share this with anyone. I have had to change my identity," she added quietly.

One would expect a manager to be shocked. At the very least, perhaps to be curious. But there was little in the way of interest other than a brief nod and insincere-sounding sympathy for what she had been through. He recalled that he had relayed half an hour earlier how he too had been subjected to an incident in the staff car park. This was a traumatising vocation. Everyone knew that. Being subjected to violent threats was considered very much part and parcel of the job. He had tried to sound sympathetic, but as usual he had a somewhat detached aura about him.

It wasn't a personal thing. He wasn't interested in any of his staff. Deirdre Turner specifically was a drain on his already stretched team. But now he understood her more. Her poor work ethic all made sense. The excessive periods of "stress-related work problems" cited on the stack of doctors' notes. And, of course, the mighty resistance to undertake home visits wherever possible.

The rather unappealing woman sitting before him was clearly beset with problems. But it wasn't for him to start effectively counselling her. She was the one who was ruining this Ofsted inspection, he was convinced. His job would be on the line. He certainly didn't feel obliged to ask questions. He wouldn't want to encourage any offloading on him.

So instead of offering sympathy, he briefly acknowledged her misfortune, but gave her a warning that she really had to start focusing on her work and be more thorough. "Dawn Smithers is on to you!" he told her, referring of course to the "silent assassin". It was always best to blame his own vicious line manager.

"The families on your caseload," he told her firmly, trying to hold her eye contact, "they depend on you, Deirdre." He was feeling the lethargy that always hit him after lunch and just couldn't find the energy to spell out what needed to happen. To his credit, after each lengthy sickness period he had spent time going through in some detail all that was expected from a child protection frontline worker. Nothing had ever changed and he was sick of repeating his mantra.

She sounded so flat and it was having an effect on his own mood. So he got up, giving the signal that the chat had ended. All meetings needed to be pre-booked with him and certainly it had been good of him to befriend her in Asda over lunch. With that, he promised to bring in the onions in the morning, ending the conversation on an affable note. He then grabbed a cigarette and his lighter. It was definitely time for a smoking break!

When Bill returned he noted that his workers were glued to the computer screens. The endless paperwork, no doubt, was dragging them down. In the early days they had all been conscientious. They had barely taken a lunch break and the team had practically run itself. But ten years down the line, most of his good social workers had already left him.

He stared at Deirdre, pushing her papers around her desk as usual. How had she even come to him? He had never interviewed her – he had just been dumped with her, probably through the rolling recruitment drive. This wasn't fair. She was clearly fragile, and the best way to deal with her was to allocate her the worst cases and hope she would quit.

Yotunde, sitting next to her, was banging away at her keyboard. She was too strong a character for him, constantly arguing and refusing to back down. It didn't cross his mind that she was fighting to help her vulnerable clients achieve their best! But as her team manager, he had the upper hand. He took pleasure from the fact that he had turned down her transfer request form three times. She could shove the form in front of his face as many times as she wanted. He wasn't signing it!

Someone, he was convinced now, had been back-stabbing him. It was David, Wayne or Yotunde. Why else had the inspectors targeted his team? There was definitely a certain amount of whistle-blowing going on.

He watched David at work. What had happened to him? He used to be a fine worker. Who exactly had encouraged him to have sex with his social work student? He had brought it all upon himself. The only member of staff he had a certain amount of respect for was Wayne. He unofficially managed the team and Bill had no issue with that. He even nurtured it. Wayne didn't appear to care who managed him as long as he raked in the extortionate locum fees.

Then there was Siobhan, immature and clingy. Yet she appeared to like being left alone to book her aerobics classes and such like! He knew he should book in supervision with her too, tell her how to conduct herself in the office. But she would probably be long gone soon, hopefully within the year. He would be forced to fill in all those tireless job references. Hadn't he enough to do? For sure, all he was going to be left with were the Deirdres of the world. Where the hell was that other chronic skiver Carmel? Refusing to take his calls. It was a disgrace how she got away with it.

Deirdre set herself the task of organising the payment to the rightly-angry foster carer. It had been over a year. Bill's lack of interest saddened her. She was a fool to imagine any other outcome. Why would her ineffectual manager care about her? She recognised, though, that his words were harsh but fair. But what double standards coming from him! She hadn't wanted to share more details in any event. It was safer this way. Hopefully it would go some way to excuse any errors made on her part. As for the warning, she realised disparagingly that she needed the money. Building enthusiasm for a job she hated for six long years? That would be absolutely impossible!

Twenty-three

Thursday July 22nd 2004, 9am

It was unusual for Deirdre to be first into the team room, but she had no choice. With that vile bully of a district manager on her back, she had to force herself to make an effort. Thankfully she had heard that the "silent assassin" was in Tenerife for a week so she had a small window to try to redeem herself somewhat.

She switched on her computer and, like any frontline social worker she had ever met, dreaded the almighty presence of predictable new email notifications. They never seemed to stop filtering through.Some of them pestered her for solutions, most of them demanded an urgent response. The generic theme throughout them all was the various levels of dissatisfaction with the service they were receiving from her. Why did they have to make it so personal?

The bombarding technique was oppressive, clawing all over her to do something. Child protection midwives, the police, health visitors and such like. Professionals complaining that phone calls hadn't been returned. One was from a competent foster carer, requesting she undertake a visit this week. The children had been placed there some weeks before and were, in Deirdre's opinion, perfectly fine. The carer had disputed this, and requested a one-to-one, perhaps to take them to the park, or for something to eat. To engage them properly!

What a nerve the carer had! This wasn't an urgent matter of a potential placement breakdown. What was she? Superwoman? There was never ever any time to do direct work. She relied on the very people paid to do this. Deirdre had nothing against this individual. She was delightful and committed to her charges. But she wasn't going to make exceptions to her rule.

A tip Deirdre learnt years ago was not to fuel dialogue with strong characters. There wasn't any point. This experienced foster carer wouldn't be fobbed off with gratitude and would hound her for a date and time. Quite simply, spending quality time with children on her caseload just for the sake of it never usually made it onto her to-do list. In this regard, her strategy was always the same. Not to respond!

One matter Deirdre couldn't ignore was having to co-ordinate the Looked After Children review meetings. Children in the care system were by law given the chance to have their personal views acknowledged. It was actually Deirdre's job to represent them, but she couldn't just create more time in her working day. The logistics of getting so many people in one place within timescales were near impossible. They were professionals just like her with jam-packed diaries. What she needed was a full-time secretary. In fact, she considered, most of her job could be done by having a junior trailing behind her.

She began by making a list, but everything seemed so urgent. Where would she start? There was just too much of everything being thrown at her, every single second of her working day. She threw her pen down in frustration and watched it roll off the desk. There was no energy in her to pick it up. The pressure was utterly unrealistic and intolerable.

No one else had arrived yet and it was safe to relax back in her chair and shut her eyes. She tried hard to visualise that she was somewhere else. Anywhere else would do. But it was always the same. The usual negative feelings surrounded her, gathering pace, attacking her soul.

For how many years had a large part of her waking hours been stolen from her by having to turn up at this 1970s dump of a building? Sighing, she got up to look out of the filthy window.

From the first floor she was drawn to the unsightly yellow industrial bins at the back door of the 5 takeaway. With 20/20 vision, she could even spot the rat poison boxes positioned at equal distances from each other.

She loathed everything about this insalubrious precinct. It wasn't just the district offices that were dated and dirty. She couldn't see any advantages to the offices being right in the heart of down-at-heel Fenton town centre. Dotted about in between the vacant shops, the barbers and the snooker hall, every registered charity in Britain competed with each other for business.

The view depressed her further, so she moved back to her desk and sat down again. She ignored the phones ringing out and instead stared at the clock. It was 9.04am. The cloudless skies and promises of a pleasant day cruelly taunted her, and she questioned again and again, why did it have to happen to her? As usual, there were no answers. She had just been plain unlucky.

It had been after midnight the night before, when she had forced herself to close her extremely compelling detective novel. Now she was tired, but no more exhausted than any other working day. Time passed quicker if she concentrated on her work, so she tried again to start her working day. This time she opened post that hadn't been touched since she had returned from sick leave.

Hopefully she would have a surge of energy after having her breakfast. No one could argue that the role was incredibly challenging and often soul destroying. With the constant talk of local authority cuts to the childcare budgets, she asked herself whether her job could actually get any worse.

Fenton Local Authority had a bad reputation. Positioned right in the heart of one of the largest council estates in the city, it was known for its deprivation and lower social work salaries than its neighbourhood authorities. They were chronically understaffed, and children and young adults had to be seriously at risk before cases were even opened. Fenton's counsellors always talked a good game but couldn't deliver promises. The only jewel in its childcare services had been its flagship Sure Start centre. And that had only been open for a year before the constant funding crisis forced its closure last summer. Nothing was ever going to improve. Deirdre was convinced of this.

Her colleagues would soon arrive. She had no idea how they could have such cheerful dispositions. Siobhan, with her frizzy hair and inappropriate gym attire, was irritating and immature. Deirdre would watch her, circling job applications and booking aerobic classes. She would probably be gone by the end of the year, but hopefully Wayne would stay. It was peculiar how the council always found money to waste on indefinite locum contracts, yet penny pinched on practically everything else.

Her team was shrinking, which didn't help the workload distribution either. Between Yotunde, David and Wayne, they held the team together, and to be fair, they weren't unfriendly towards her. How Carmel got away with such skiving was beyond her. It had been a full year since she had been signed off with stress. This wasn't fair. After three weeks of being on the sick too, the "silent assassin" had hounded Deirdre every single day, demanding medical evidence and a staged return date.

What was left of the Area Team Three would begin to trickle in soon. She would always be on guard, ensuring she was aloof but polite to them, and she rarely allowed herself to join in with the team banter. It was only Yotunde who made slightly more effort. She had often wondered whether it would be safe to confide in her too, but the fewer people that knew, the better.

She certainly wouldn't be telling Siobhan, what with her constant questions for Wayne and David. It was pathetic how she was, in effect, almost parented by them. She appeared to be unable to make her own decisions and never stopped wittering on about her latest topic, purchasing a puppy. What did a thirty-one-year old who had never left home know about raising children? She still seemed a child herself!

None of this was Deirdre's problem. She looked after herself and as long as no one depended on her, this was good enough. She detested needy people and considered herself far too savvy to be lured in by threats to undertake additional work. In anticipation of this, she would often pretend that she hadn't realised that her work mobile was turned on silent!

Interrupting her bitter thoughts, the impeccably-dressed Wayne bounded into the room wearing one of his signature bright white linen shirts teamed nicely with beige chinos and a tan belt. Buzzing with positive energy, he was too fashion conscious for Fenton District offices, and would have slotted in well in a West End London media agency. How he stood out amongst them all, his polyester-clad team leader and what they all in social work called "the ugly flat shoes brigade". She felt a slight irritation mixed with a hint of jealousy watching him. It was just too early in the morning for such fervour.

They exchanged superficial pleasantries whilst she waited for him to wash out the filthy mugs left in the washing-up bowl from the previous afternoon. She estimated that, as a locum, he ended up with an additional £4,000 in his back pocket, for exactly the same role as a permanent member of the team. So it was only fair that this unpleasant task lay with him.

But Wayne was rightly preoccupied with the urgent nature of the job. Due to staff shortages, his team had been told to cover the duty inquiries that day. Yesterday a reminder email had been circulated and her colleagues had duly treated this notification seriously and had made a note in their diaries. Deirdre hadn't even read it.

As diligent as ever, Wayne dropped his leather satchel round the back of his chair, and headed towards the fax machine. The duty rotas added to the impossible pressures. The fax machine worked all hours, spewing out its wafer-thin paper. Two or three new referrals were already stacked up on the plastic rack, with one sheet having fallen onto the carpet. As Wayne bent down to pick it up, he rescued another one which had fallen into the wire mesh basket below. "I keep telling everyone," he said, sounding exasperated. "The bin shouldn't be anywhere near the fax machine." He didn't want to sound like he was lecturing Deirdre but she needed to be told.

"The cleaners keep moving it back under the table. It's so dangerous!"

Moving the receptacle to the far corner of the room, he thought that he might as well be talking to himself. After all, Deirdre wouldn't lose any sleep if vital information concerning the immediate welfare of children was lost forever. This wasn't a good environment to be in. He had worked as a locum in multiple neighbouring authorities and he had never come across a team manager who was so bone idle. It was negligent behaviour and it was sickening that Yotunde's and his whistle-blowing efforts hadn't been acted on.

Even when Bill was in his office, he was rarely present in the full sense of the word. He actively encouraged his experienced workers to take on the task of prioritising incoming child protection duty referrals. As long as the job got done, he was satisfied. More than capable of the task, Wayne knew that the others would arrive within the next quarter of an hour. They would then divvy up the referrals, and begin the task of unravelling the often lifelong damage inflicted on innocent children every second of every single day.

The only good news was that the school summer holidays were nearly upon them all. With teachers not present on a day-to-day basis to monitor and report abuse, the rate of referrals tended to decrease significantly until the new term began in early September. But for today, it was business as usual, and the sound of the fax machine whirling into motion indicated that yet another notification was about to come through.

The distinctive sound appeared to make no impact on Deirdre, who had her protracted breakfast routine to prepare for. Reaching into her rucksack to retrieve her Tupperware container, she was rudely interrupted by Wayne almost shouting, "Oh my God!"

Deirdre stared at him. He was clutching the fax paper in his hands as if his life depended on it. Why did he always have to be so dramatic? It was so attention-seeking.

"Right, Deirdre!" Wayne spoke firmly. "You are coming with me. We are leaving now!"

"What's the urgency?" She didn't attempt to hide her annoyance at the prospect of undertaking a home visit so early in the morning. She hadn't eaten yet. Furthermore, she didn't appreciate being told what to do, especially by a locum.

She caught herself just in the nick of time. She couldn't afford to make her lack of interest too obvious, especially as Bill's unpleasant warning still resonated. And there was that meeting with the "silent assassin" to prepare for. So she asked for the address of the property in question, and offered to fill in the whereabouts book.

But Wayne gestured with his hand to stop. "There's no time for that!" he called out. "This is an emergency!"

Unlike Wayne, Deirdre wasn't generally an excitable character. She was actually quite fond of him, but had always thought of him as rather over-confident. She had come across this type of forceful personality many times over the years and it took all her energy to fight against it. Nevertheless, it was worth an attempt.

"The others will be here any minute," she said, her voice sounding weary. "One of them will go with you!"

But he was insistent. "I've got no time for your delaying tactics," he told her sharply, walking towards her desk and thrusting the fax near her face.

Deidre read the contents out loud.

"Caller states he is a neighbour. He has witnessed all the family going out, leaving a small child/possibly baby alone in the property for over an hour."

The untidy handwriting screamed out more than enough information to warrant an emergency visit. She gathered her bag and stuffed her notepad into it. This was dreadful. No baby should be home alone for any length of time. She was about to tell Wayne that it was a good job he had arrived when he did, when she spotted a serious error in the duty referral. "What the hell?" Her voice was now raised. "This call was logged at 8.43am. Why has it only been sent through now at 9.05am?" she queried, sounding agitated too. The conversation continued between them as Deirdre found herself running to keep up with her frantic colleague as he surged ahead, dashing down the corridor and hurtling down the stairs.

"There had better be a good reason why it has taken over fifteen minutes to send the scantest referral across to us," she said. To her surprise she found herself engaged. However detached she had become, she couldn't contemplate the appalling thought that a young child could be at immediate risk of fatal harm.

"How many times have that thick lot at the contact centre been spoken to about the referrals taking too long to process!" Wayne mouthed off furiously. He gave the impression that he was way above his meagre status as a locum social worker. Wayne's leadership qualities had never been in question. He encouraged others to give out criticism where due, and it was certainly addictive!

"I've met them at the multidisciplinary training session. Not a brain cell between them." Deirdre was enjoying the interaction. Acting out of character, she found herself in full flow. "How long can it possibly take to jot down a street name and number?"

"Perhaps the neighbour didn't know how to spell his own address!" Wayne offered, sniggering. "And that certainly wouldn't be a first!"

"As with many cases referred to social care, the caller has helpfully chosen to remain anonymous!" Deirdre said sarcastically.

Wayne nodded. Poles apart in their work ethics, the two workers both knew that without background information on a family, it was near impossible to assess the level of risk without barging in.

They swiped their security passes to exit the building, with Wayne dramatically declaring, "If no one answers the door I am not hanging about. We will call 999." Deirdre ran after him, all the while wondering why he needed to state the obvious!

It had been a mistake not to have eaten breakfast at home that morning. She was worried that it might be some time before they would be returning to the office. She hoped the child wouldn't need to be taken for a medical. Hanging around the local hospital was always such a drag.

Her fears escalated. There would be the phoning round, trying to find a relative able to pick the child up. It could even be worse than that. It may fall upon her to secure a foster placement. All of this would be so time-consuming.

There was little she could do to fight her constant negative thoughts. She realised that she had become set in her ways and struggled with the impromptu disturbance to her day. She had her paperwork to do and now everything would be delayed. Unfit, she was breathless as she ran the extra hundred yards towards the furthest end of the car park to where Wayne's sparking Golf GTI was stationed. She smiled to herself. Of course, it would not do for the locum's pride and joy to be scratched by careless drivers.

Complimenting Wayne on how spotless the interior of the

car was, Deirdre eased herself into the leather passenger seat, imagining that this was akin to travelling in airline business class. Experiencing the air conditioning system was also a rare treat for her. At least she could travel in style to the Barnham Hill Estate. Furthermore, she was grateful that Wayne claimed to know exactly where they were going.

Denby Walk was situated just over a mile away, at the heart of the sprawling Barnham Hill Estate. Thankfully, they would reach their destination shortly and hopefully there would be a perfectly reasonable explanation for events. She would then be able to return calmly to address her all-important breakfast routine.

There was only one necessary requirement before Wayne drove off. He took his mileage pad and logged the necessary details to be reimbursed for the trip. Whilst this process had only taken a moment, Deirdre was unimpressed. She might have guessed what Wayne's other priority was, what double standards her money-grasping colleague had. She didn't bother querying why this task couldn't be backdated later in the day, as she could only make an accurate guess that he would be fiddling the figures and the maths wouldn't add up!

As Wayne swung left out of the car park, he narrowly missed the traffic lights and stopped abruptly. Every second counted and he swore profusely and tapped the steering wheel as he waited impatiently for the filter to change to green. "We are an emergency service!" he announced. Unlike Deirdre, who was just mildly concerned about what she may discover on arrival at the property, Wayne obviously felt incredibly stressed. "We should be able to drive through red lights where necessary!" he ranted.

Deirdre stared out of the window. She had lost interest in social work years ago, and certainly didn't thrive on the power it seemed to give Wayne. Still, she didn't want the baby to come to any harm. They estimated that there were only two more sets of traffic lights, and if they weren't delayed, they would arrive at their destination within five to seven minutes. Hopefully they would find the child safe and well.

They parked outside 25 Denby Walk and rushed out of the car, half expecting to find an insecure property and having to kick their way through piles of debris searching for an abandoned baby. Much as this outcome was unwanted, from experience, it would be the most likely scenario.

Instead they were surprised to discover that the semi-detached brick 1960s property had been well maintained. Someone had even planted yellow and orange marigolds down both sides of the short path that led to a red front door. This was odd. They both wondered if they had been given the wrong address. Still, Wayne wasted no time and impatiently banged loudly using the brass knocker.

A black woman dressed in traditional bright Caribbean clothing opened the door, gingerly holding what they both assumed to be her granddaughter. Mortified, the social workers fell silent, for they knew exactly what had led them to this house. The Barnham Hill Estate was a predominantly white neighbourhood. What they were witnessing first hand was vicious racism.

Deirdre spoke up first. "I am so sorry. There has been a mistake," she offered humbly, feeling incredibly uncomfortable. She then turned to leave, but her colleague appeared to have other ideas and was lingering.

In her opinion, it was totally unnecessary to upset the innocent grandmother and there was no need to tell her why they had arrived at the property. She stood behind him, shocked that Wayne was becoming more involved than she felt the visit warranted. She now had no choice but to follow him into the hallway, as Wayne took the lead, explaining the nature of the malicious referral.

All the while the clearly well cared for contented baby stared at them curiously. Her blameless grandmother looked alarmed when Wayne announced that they were both social workers. Deirdre stared at him, willing him to shut the hell up. At least, though, his carefully chosen words were kindly spoken and he apologised profoundly for disturbing her. He told her gently that she had done nothing wrong and she should not be worried in any way.

His magnetic charm always worked, and he managed to get a sad smile out of the lady after promising that they wouldn't be returning. There had been no need to undertake a full check of the property, and they were in and out of the house within five minutes. As they walked back down the path, they both glanced at the houses opposite. They knew what they were looking for.

Both skilled workers, they queried whether the racist caller had enjoyed watching events unfurl from his or her bedroom window. But it was impossible to tell in the bright sunshine which, if any, curtains were twitching. They quickly climbed back into Wayne's car, and drove round the corner before he stopped to analyse the visit.

"Well, that was the quickest child protection investigation ever!" Wayne announced, trying to be light-hearted. But the encounter with the grandmother had left both of them feeling deeply saddened.

What they had both been embroiled in was shameful. They discussed between themselves whether it was illegal to make malicious referrals.

Sharing the frustration, Wayne felt himself warming towards Deirdre. She was surprisingly rather pleasant company. "We were right to go into the house," he announced firmly, reading her thoughts correctly.

He certainly wasn't going to justify the way he had handled the investigation to anyone, especially not to a colleague who spent her time hiding away from clients! Deirdre found herself nodding. It was too much energy to disagree. What was done was done. Certainly, she couldn't see the benefit in analysing it further. Besides, she was now really hungry.

This was odd behaviour from Wayne. He always got himself so involved. She was perplexed as to why he had stopped his car to engage in this dialogue. Surely he could talk as well as drive! There was nothing delaying them returning to the office. Apart from his precious fax referrals that he treated so seriously!

Deirdre now recalled that Wayne had promised the grandmother something else – a written apology. Something that would never have crossed her mind.

"Are you really going to write an apology letter?" she queried, adding, "It's not our fault."

Her detachment from her frontline duties was back. It was almost as if she was watching something on television. A drama that wasn't based on fact. She felt her colleague was overreacting but had more sense than to admit it.

"Of course I am going to write to her," he told her, clearly still affected. "I am so distressed that these racist malicious referrals happen so frequently."

"Of course. It's just that no one ever apologises to us!" Deirdre said, sounding rather bemused. The familiar signs of a potential panic attack were about to descend, embracing her tightly. Anxiety was sweeping through her and she could feel herself perspiring.

The nauseousness was probably because she was hungry. But she knew what to do, and she put her head as low down as she could, and tried to focus on breathing deeply. There were so many triggers that she didn't know what the exact cause was. It might have been Wayne's forceful tone towards her in the office. She knew she had been negligent in ignoring the incoming faxes and didn't blame him on this account.

It could have been the fact that there hadn't been time to fill in the whereabouts book, thus creating a potential risk to themselves. For all they knew, the malicious referral could have led them to a house where a violent criminal was waiting for them. Or quite simply, it may have just been the fear in the unsuspecting loving grandmother's eyes. It didn't really matter what triggered the bad memories. The recollection of what had happened to her at the hands of Darren Lawton had never subsided. She had allowed it to eat at her whole being. She would never be free to lead a normal life.

Twenty-four

"Are you OK?"

"Yes, I just can't stand this job!" The moroseness was back as she stared out of the car window.

"I hadn't noticed!"

Deirdre's tiresome negativity was grating on him at that precise moment. The frustration left over from the home visit consumed him still. It was proving impossible to shake off the image of the loving grandmother, clutching her charge in her arms, bewildered at child protection social workers suddenly turning up like that. What would they want with her? He knew he would always remember seeing the real fear in her eyes.

He had a full duty day ahead of him, and had no idea what type of other referrals he would have to rush out to. But the recollection of this premeditated racist incident left him feeling sad. Did he really need to listen to Deirdre's whinging at just this moment? His colleague was a professional skiver and therefore had absolutely no reason for complaining.

"It has literally ruined my life!" she whined on. "I can't take any more."

He sighed impatiently as he glanced across at his miserable passenger. What the hell was wrong with her now? Clearly being forced to undertake an emergency home visit was all too much for her! Or maybe she was out of sorts having had her breakfast routine interrupted! But Wayne had always prided himself that he was essentially a good sort. His very reason for existing was to reach out to as many individuals as he could in his lifetime. To motivate and evoke positive change. He hoped one day to be rewarded with a suitable honour, perhaps an OBE recognising his achievements. But right now, it was just dreary workshy Deirdre Turner, offloading.

"Has anything happened in particular?" he asked warily, feeling like a free counsellor. His goodwill only stretched so far – he would give her the length of the journey, roughly ten minutes at most. But once they arrived back in the office, he needed to deal with the emergencies.

"Six years ago I had to relocate to escape from a threatening client!" she finally blurted out. On purpose she didn't identify which city she had come from. It was safer that way.

"I get threatened all the time." He minimised what she had just divulged and offered his own experience. "Take that bastard Mr Leigh for example. I heard last week that he was planning to murder me!" As usual he sounded overconfident. But in this instance he was rather proud of himself as he regaled the story. "But apparently his plan became too complicated to execute!" He knew that he could be rather arrogant and it was a mistake to think that he would always be untouchable. He had, as usual, kept himself busy since hearing the news the previous week that his client posed a serious threat. The risk was minimal currently and he hadn't dwelled on the information given to him by the police.

"No, this is serious, this wasn't your run-of-the-mill client," she replied, tentatively at first.

Wayne was forced to turn his attention back to her, and soon she was divulging more. "The client was a wealthy property developer. Apparently I humiliated him!" The words tumbled out and she had to focus properly so that she didn't reveal the man's name.

Certainly a client finding out where their social worker lived was alarming. To be stalked or similar was extremely frightening. Deirdre didn't seem the type to exaggerate and when she told him that certain things had started to happen, slashed tyres and the like, he felt for her. Her drawn features and the way she always presented at work now made sense. His colleague was most definitely telling the truth.

He had never liked Deirdre. No one did. It wasn't fair that she refused to take her work seriously and this had a domino effect on everyone else. They all tolerated her but enough was enough. The latest group effort to whistle-blow had been specific in the concerns. The team had been unanimous that they had been left with no choice. Yotunde had added the final sentence to end on a strong note. She had written, "Kids could potentially be killed by abusers if she continued as their social worker." They had all talked about the repercussions if Deirdre found out it was them. It could, of course, be anyone who had come into contact with her professionally. They decided that if she accused them they would admit it. She was a disgrace and they were done with her.

But he was stuck with her for another five or so minutes and what she was telling him was simply fascinating. He made a conscious effort to change his tone to a more sympathetic one.

"So what happened?" he asked her, his eyes wide open.

As ever, Wayne appeared to thrive on traumas. With his own social life nonexistent, he threw himself into helping others. But he was genuinely now concerned too.

Deirdre began recounting how six years ago she had the misfortune to become involved with removing a baby boy from his father and how he had set about ensuring she feared for her life as retribution. She told Wayne the moment her life changed. How she had been caught off guard in the grounds of her own flat.

It was already dark when she returned from her weekly shop. Innocently parking in her allocated space in the car park, she was so preoccupied unloading the carrier bags that she didn't notice a vehicle parked next to her. Slamming the boot shut, she walked past the silver Audi to get to the flat entrance. The driver had his windows down and calmly said he had a message for her. "I would watch your back if I were you. Darren wants you dead!"

Within seconds he had reversed and sped off. Petrified, it took Deirdre several moments to process what had just taken place. During this time, she was unable to consider that she needed to memorise the vehicle number plate. She dropped her shopping on the ground and searched for someone who had perhaps witnessed this. It was a relatively large block of flats, and she hoped someone had spotted something, but the surrounding area was deserted.

The police, to be fair, arrived within the hour, but it was hopeless. Every resident was questioned but no one had seen anything relevant. Crucially, she was told that no CCTV cameras trailed the car park, and there was nothing they could do to follow this up. In the end, she was given a crime number and a panic button.

That evening the terrorising intimidation laid itself into her already fragile mentality, only dissipating temporarily after she consumed two large glasses of gin and tonic. She made a decision there and then that she would not disclose any of the details to her well-meaning friends. And that included her new girlfriend and anyone at her LGBT social group that were such a significant part of her life.

The very next day she secured an emergency appointment with her GP practice. She badly needed to talk to someone. For a start there was her overwhelming fear of returning to her workplace. Naïvely, she assumed that her doctor would make time for her, perhaps to offer some practical suggestions as to how to move forward. She was bitterly disappointed, to be abruptly dismissed with a sick note and a course of anti-anxiety medication.

The medication appeared to only take the edge off her anxiety. A sticking plaster on a gaping wound. Struggling to sleep, at 3am, she resorted to calling the local Samaritans. It was the second time that week that she talked about how much she missed her work, her friends and the children on her caseload. She had been dedicated to her clients in those days and now felt fearful and vulnerable. It seemed ironic that she gave of herself so much, but now found herself alone, forced to rely on anonymous volunteers.

There was no doubt in her mind that she had been followed and her first thought was for her girlfriend. She couldn't continue acting normally and within days of the incident, she ended the relationship, giving no explanation. It wasn't fair to drag her into this danger. There were several essential trips she needed to make, for instance to purchase a new telephone, but mostly, she barricaded herself into her flat until she had decided what to do. Several friends tried checking up on her, some even pushed notes through her letterbox. They noticed her red car was gone and assumed she had gone away. The truth was that she had parked it two miles away for safety. Eventually they all gave up.

Every week she duly faxed across another sick note to her dispassionate team manager. On the third week, she sent both a resignation letter and her work mobile phone by recorded delivery. She provided no explanation. The only option available was to, in effect, disappear. Hopefully then she would be safe.

Desperate, she chose an uncle and aunt to confide in. Sympathetic, they invited her to live with them as a temporary arrangement. They lived in a suburb outside of Fenton in the north of England and told her generously that they would be glad of the company.

She had no dependants or bulky furniture to worry about, so the relocation only took just under five weeks, including selling her car for scrap, and in doing so, ridding herself of her number plate, which she was convinced Darren had memorised.

She planned her relocation meticulously and booked a small rental van to undertake the journey up north. With her surname now changed by deed poll, and her post redirected to a PO Box address, surely it would be impossible for Darren or his connections to find her.

The move was planned for midweek. That way her neighbours would be out at work. Alone, she began the physically demanding process of heaving her suitcases and computer equipment down the two flights of stairs, shoving them into the vehicle. Finally, she posted the two sets of keys through her own letterbox. It was frustrating that she would need to forgo a £500 flat deposit, but what could she do? The last thing she wanted was questions asked about her whereabouts.

The adrenalin charging, she ran into the van, locking the doors internally. There was no time to put on her seat belt as it felt more vital to check the car park one final time as she placed her foot on the accelerator and hurtled off. There was no relief even then, as she found herself glancing in her rear mirror every few seconds until eventually the M1 sign came into view.

After this traumatic experience, the last thing she ever wanted to do was to continue working in the child protection arena. But unfortunately, it was the only thing she was qualified to do. She had never been ambitious enough to take new courses or perhaps a master's degree. Until her meeting with Darren Lawton, there had never been a problem. She realised now that this had been a huge mistake. She had no transferable skills to fall back on. Sadly she came to the conclusion that she had no choice. She would have to apply to work at the nearest children's services.

"This is why I am here!" Deirdre paused for a breath.

"OK, we are here now," Wayne announced, conscious that they had already been in his now static car for some minutes sitting, engrossed. But she had been in full flow and didn't appear to be in any rush to finish. He would generously allocate her ten more minutes.

"I suppose you removed his kid? For some reason most people take issue with this!" he mocked harshly.

Deirdre nodded.

"Now tell me more about the client," he demanded, trying to take control of the conversation. Multi-tasking, he dutifully completed his mileage form details as he continued speaking. "And I will tell you honestly if you have anything to fear!"

Acutely aware that Wayne hadn't even met Darren Lawton, Deirdre thought it was odd that he was offering to pass judgement on such a serious risk assessment. However, it felt good to open up. She momentarily put aside her hunger pangs as she summarised the events of March 1998.

The background to the case was straightforward. Deirdre had been on duty the day that a self-made successful property developer abused his eight-month-old baby boy.

"I hate the wealthy clients! They are always the worst to deal with," Wayne butted in forcefully.

"Yes, he thought he would be treated better than other child abusers." She nodded enthusiastically. "That in essence was the whole problem." She paused, clearly still affected by revisiting the events.

"Go on."

Deirdre would hazard a guess that she had been involved in

over a hundred child protection investigations in her career, but this one had been horrendous. Time hadn't lessened her sharp memory and she was grateful to have this opportunity to share the details.

Darren Lawton worked from home and had been looking after his son whilst his wife was out. The phone rang. It was his bank manager. Usually on good terms, they had played at the private golf club together. But now there was bad news. Following their meeting several months earlier, the payment terms on the multiple loans and mortgages had been breached and was he planning to put the company into liquidation and apply for a winding up order.

"How do you know all this?"

"Because it all came out in the court case and national newspapers covered the story. Can you let me continue?"

Restless, she explained that Darren had tried persuading the manager to buy him more time. She could almost visualise him looking around his magnificent home set in its own grounds as he reeled in shock. He had worked hard in the early years, and his reputation in Wexley was crucial to him.

The trial had lasted three full days and Deirdre had been there for the entire period. The bank manager had sworn on the bible that Darren had begged him for more time to pay the debts back. Appearing a credible witness, he referred to his notes and directed his responses to the judge. His version of events made sense. They were both struggling to hear each other above the sounds of Ben whimpering loudly. The child had initially been clawing at him for attention. Indeed, in the earlier part of the conversation, Darren could be heard attempting to soothe him. But soon afterwards, he had obviously lost patience with him. Apologising in advance for using foul language, the witness stated that Darren raised his voice, stating, "Fucking get off me, Ben, get away from me!"

It was established that what had probably happened was that whilst trying to hold the receiver in one hand and Ben in the other, Darren had snapped, either dragging Ben or throwing him across the room. The bank manager held up well to the cross examination. He had been concerned that child's crying suddenly morphed into screaming before he heard a now-panicked Darren shout, "Oh God no. Are you OK? Daddy's really sorry!" before slamming the phone down.

"So this Darren fellow has a vile temper, clearly. But this was all years ago." Wayne was struggling to understand the relevance of all of this.

"Can I just finish? Then you will understand everything," she told him impatiently.

She spoke quickly, continuing the story from where she had left off. Michele, Darren's now ex-wife, gave evidence at the hearing too. She told the court that when she returned home from playing tennis about half an hour later, she found Ben hysterical. When she picked him up, she discovered to her horror that his right arm was hanging loosely and he had the beginnings of a black eye. Screaming hysterically, she demanded her husband drive them immediately to A and E.

On arrival, the medical staff queried how such an accident had taken place. Darren's story changed several times, and his timeline of events was not consistent with the injuries sustained.

"So I assume there was no time for Darren to concoct a pack of lies?" Wayne enquired. "It's interesting the wife didn't back him up."

There was nothing that Wayne loved more than a human interest element. This was partly the reason why he thrived on his job so much. By now the two colleagues had reached the entrance to their office building, but remained outside talking.

"Apparently when I was called to the hospital to investigate, I humiliated him with all the questioning." Her tone was cutting as she recalled everything.

There had been an ugly scene in the A and E small side room. Ben and his mother had gone to another department to have his arm put in plaster. Darren was told to wait behind. The police and the child protection nurse had arrived. Stony-faced, Deirdre had confidently led the interview and got straight to the point. Ben's dislocated shoulder and black eye amounted to a non-accidental injury. She informed Darren that he would not be permitted to see Ben until the court decided otherwise. There would be a causation hearing, she told him firmly. And then the next "insult". She hadn't been afraid to inform him that she would not be arranging any visits with Ben in the interim. In the circumstances, even supervised contact at this stage was deemed too much of a risk.

Deirdre relayed Darren's shocked reaction as the police announced that they were charging him with GBH. At the time, she hadn't felt particularly intimidated. After all, it wasn't a normal week if some client wasn't abusive in their tone towards her. She did, however, register the threats. "No one crosses me, I will sue you for slander." There was more, but she laughed it off at the time. "You will regret what you have done. I'm telling you. Watch your back."

"How did you know that it wasn't Darren's wife who had injured the child?" Wayne always considered the family dynamics. Nothing was ever straightforward in child protection work.

"Because as part of my investigation, I called the tennis club and they had CCTV of her at around the time of the injury."

"Quite the detective, aren't you!" Wayne laughed. Deirdre looked rather taken aback. Wayne realised just in time that he was being too harsh on her. He softened his tone, adding, "Actually, I am very impressed with your initiative. I wouldn't have thought to do that."

What a story! He now bombarded her with questions, such as what Darren's home was like, and whether it was set in its own grounds. He asked too whether she remembered what car he had driven. Whilst Wayne had freely admitted that he hated well-off clients, he very much enjoyed seeing where they all lived! He imagined that as a property developer, their family home would have been magnificent.

But to his disappointment, Deirdre was unable to answer. She explained that she had only met Darren twice. The first time had been in the hospital emergency department, and the next morning, she had immediately transferred the case to the court team. The next time she had come face to face with Darren was when he was called to give evidence at the trial.

It hadn't been a pleasant experience being cross-examined in the witness box but Deirdre classed herself as a competent and experienced officer. Besides, she had kept meticulous notes of the investigation, and had followed all the necessary safeguarding procedures. In the court setting, it had been relatively easy to avoid Darren's piercing stares, and of course she had no idea how events were going to escalate.

All in all, the three-year custody sentence had been an extremely satisfactory outcome for Deirdre. More news provided the icing on the cake. Michele had found him in the court café and told him that she had become romantically involved with her tennis coach and had filed for divorce and full custody of their child.

"So he lost everything really," Wayne interrupted. "Mind you, he was the one to throw an eight-month-old baby across the room. Serves him right."

Deirdre continued to describe what had happened after the court case. With Darren being a property developer, it probably hadn't been difficult to find out where she was living. Odd things started to stress her out, and with hindsight, the signs were there. One morning, she found all her car tyres had been slashed. The following day she noticed a deep scratch mark running down the side of her passenger door. Then the silent calls started in the middle of the night. Of course there was never any hard proof.

"I see where you are coming from," Wayne offered, now feeling uncomfortable. He didn't want to share that he too would have felt scared.

"Surely you got relocation costs and compensation?" Wayne queried, adding, "I hope you instructed a solicitor from the Union?"

"No. I never received a penny. I was treated like dirt by the senior management." This was Deirdre's real bugbear. She had assumed naïvely that she would be protected by some sort of witness scheme, but this request was turned down by the police, who stated that the concerns were not deemed high enough risk.

Furthermore, she told Wayne that she had failed to make the move to the Fenton area a positive one, and that the nightmares never relented. She now lived a very quiet life and felt set in her ways. She had some family members living in the surrounding areas, and they knew the truth. But absolutely no one else knew. And it had to stay that way.

She continued to offload, telling Wayne how dedicated she used to be to her charges. How she used to avoid participating in the constant discussions relating to the salary freezes. She had felt at the time that it was a waste of energy. A negative force. Instead, she had made the decision to work extra shifts on the emergency out of hours team to boost her income. She was clearly still hurt by how they had treated her so poorly.

"Did your team give you a goodbye party?" Wayne asked, trying to end their chat on a lighter note.

"You are joking, aren't you?" she replied sadly. There hadn't even been an offer to meet in a pub after work for a drink. She recalled how one day an A4 blue card with its signature small grease mark on its envelope was pushed through her letterbox. By its uneven distribution of weight, it gave a strong indication of the coinage within. She had opened it carefully, emptying the spoils onto the kitchen worktop. Disgusted, it hadn't taken her long to count out the measly £13.70!

It had taken even less time for her to read the many good luck messages. How they lacked substance. There was plenty of space for everyone in her building to write more, but they had clearly chosen not to. Tearing it up, she finally realised these people had just been her colleagues, not her friends. She had spent seventeen years with some of them and they couldn't even reach into their wallets and give her a decent whip-round. What a waste of time it had been to invest in them. She decided not to share these details with Wayne. Maintaining what dignity she had left felt crucial.

Wayne smiled at her. Everything she had said made sense. It explained why Deirdre was so withdrawn and miserable.

"It's been six years, Deirdre," he said, trying to sound reassuring. "I think you are safe now, but I think it's a good idea to book to see a therapist." He hesitated, but then decided to take it further. Could she contact her old girlfriend, to explain what had happened? But she shook her head firmly. It had been for the best to sever all contact. Darren's threats had been clear. That wherever she tried to escape to, he would find her and kill her.

It was now 10.30am and Wayne needed to continue working through the referrals. He couldn't just leave it all to the others. He felt for Deirdre who was clearly needier than she let on. She was just better at hiding it. It had been wrong for him to snigger behind her back. He decided too, that he would persuade the others to befriend her. To encourage her to feel part of the team at the very least. It infuriated them all how she neglected her caseload. But if the whistle-blowing attempt didn't work, they were stuck with her.

Just now, he needed to consider himself. He had laughed Mr Leigh's threats off over the past year. Listening to Deirdre, he wondered now whether he had been naïve. Leigh was perfectly capable of creating hell for him too. He certainly had the intelligence and the incentive to stalk him.

As he slung his leather briefcase strap across the back of his chair, about to sit down at his desk, something dawned on him. His efforts to assist Deirdre had given him food for thought. He wondered whether he could submit his own claim for relocation on the basis that he was at risk from Mr Leigh. He even had evidence from the police statement that backed him up. Perhaps Fenton Local Authority might be more sympathetic to compensation. What a marvellous idea. If he succeeded, he would potentially be able to relocate to London in what could be an extremely lucrative move for him!

Twenty-five

"Don't bother sitting down!" Yotunde called out to Wayne, the moment he entered the room. She ignored Deirdre. "Get yourself downstairs now and book an interview room!"

As ever a team player, Wayne didn't appear to mind being dictated to. With the pressure of the job being so acute, manners were often deemed a luxury, with social workers often finding themselves forgoing the usual etiquette.

"A four-year-old girl is about to be brought in by the police," Siobhan interrupted, sounding panicked. She had no time to fill in the gaps. "It's terrible," she announced, "battered by her stepdad."

"We need to book a medical," Wayne replied, grabbing his phone to action this. But as he was holding, the whirring sound of an incoming fax indicated to him that his team would be facing multiple emergencies that day.

His intuition was spot on. Things were beyond crisis point downstairs. The receptionist had rung Yotunde, alerting her to a harrowing scenario played out behind the safety of the protective glass.

One of the typists rushed into the room out of breath. "The waiting room is full of crying children!" she blurted out, sounding upset.

The situation indeed was full on, even for inner city social care standards. At ten o'clock that morning, a subdued boy of eleven years old had presented with his younger siblings, a toddler and a five-year-old brother in tow. Wearing his school uniform, he told the staff that he had been given strict orders to look after them for the week. Apparently their mother was offered a free trip with her new boyfriend! No surprises that her mobile phone was switched off when attempts were made to contact her.

Wayne covered his mouth and shook his head silently as he absorbed the sorry facts. He knew what he had to do and would galvanise his team into the familiar process of sourcing emergency foster carers. But Yotunde's and Siobhan's solemn faces revealed that there was more.

The telephones rang constantly to inform them all that a troubled teenage boy had just arrived, having run away from home. He had self-harmed using a penknife and his clothing was drenched in blood. Several social workers from the other neighbouring teams barged into their room, expressing their concern too. David had been dealing with this, and now ran in, requesting back-up. Panicking at what he had been dealing with, he demanded someone go out and purchase plasters and bandages. "A kid is covered in blood downstairs!" he reported. Fuming, he added, "No one has bothered to replenish the first aid kit!"

It was obvious that these current emergencies were too much for one team to deal with. The other social workers were making big noises, but when asked if they could step in and assist, even just for a short period, they quickly made their excuses and sloped off back to their rooms.

The pressure was untenable. They were always so short-staffed but right now, they were unable to offer a safe environment to the sibling group if this teenage boy was in the same room as them. They briefly discussed bringing the children upstairs into the office to separate them. But they weren't exactly able to offer a babysitting service. This was all unsafe practice. Exactly where was their useless manager when they needed him?

Deirdre shocked them once again with her lack of interest. Naturally her colleagues had reached their limit with her. Oblivious, she seemed engrossed in removing her Tupperware bowl from her rucksack and emptying out the little polythene bags containing the ingredients for her muesli mix.

"What now?" She scowled as she clocked her four colleagues

staring at her. One by one, they turned on her.

"Can you go downstairs please?" Yotunde told her as pleasantly as she could manage given the acute circumstances.

Taking a directional approach, Yotunde said, "You make a start with the sibling group and I will help David with the self-harmer."

"I have already been out on a visit," was all Deirdre offered. She had reached saturation point too. Her overbearing colleagues were only her equals and she tried standing her ground. She told them calmly, "I will go downstairs when I am ready!" Deirdre knew her limits and if she didn't eat soon, she would become quite light-headed. It had never entered her head that perhaps she should have eaten her breakfast before coming into work!

"We are sick of this, Deirdre!" Siobhan told her unkindly.

"This is the workload. Just pull your weight!"

"Don't speak to me like that!" Deirdre fired back instantly. "I have to write up my notes from the malicious home visit before anything else!" she insisted.

"You need to take your responsibilities seriously!" David told her, raising his voice.

"The notes can wait!" Yotunde reiterated, as she dialled for police backup. This was totally unacceptable behaviour and it was entirely Bill's fault for not dismissing her. Deirdre, like Carmel, was not fit for purpose.

"Where the fuck is Bill?" It was Siobhan's turn now to raise her voice above the others, her stress evident.

"Can you get downstairs?" Wayne gestured with his hands, his patience clearly being tested.

"We will need everyone?" David said, addressing the whole group but staring at Deirdre intently.

"The police are on their way," Yotunde said, as she hurriedly got up from her chair and made her way out of the door. She turned back briefly. "These kids will be petrified. Now get downstairs," she demanded of Deirdre as her parting shot.

It was true to say that even the most experienced officers would struggle with trying to deal with such multiple challenging scenarios at one time. It would be impossible to get through the paperwork let alone identify several sets of foster carers urgently.

The search would need to begin for suitable relatives in the first instance. Ideally each family group needed two members of staff to safely co-work. There was layer upon layer of bureaucracy to get through in breakneck speed. Without other social workers stepping in, it would be near impossible to support the children simultaneously.

There was only one person who Deirdre Turner was focused on. Herself. It was her human right to have a couple of minutes to eat before dealing with more full on trauma. Privately fuming, she pushed her cereal bowl away and got up. This kind of pressure amounted to bullying in the workplace and was unacceptable in her eyes. She wished she hadn't bothered confiding in Wayne, as he wasn't supporting her. They were all supposed to be social workers. Why couldn't they all see that she was suffering from severe anxiety? She needed a more passive role within the office. This much was obvious.

For the second time that morning, Wayne started to run down the corridor. Visions of terrified children haunted him as he moved to attend to the multiple emergencies playing out downstairs. Approximately an hour earlier, his self-obsessed colleague had taken up his precious time, banging on about something from six years ago. Deirdre's traumas felt so irrelevant now. He had listened to her, feeling trapped, droning on and on. There was only his good natured self to blame for giving her so much of his precious time. He had been too generous in spirit to shut her up.

Today they desperately needed extra hands. Even Carmel would have been something. However, she was preoccupied, skiving for the past twelve months. Typical of this joke authority that no one had investigated thoroughly or provided a locum to take her place. Between the four of them, Bill, David, Carmel and Deirdre, they were a total drain on the entire team. They personified why social work had a bad name. He considered, not for the first time, what it must be like in a "normal" job. Perhaps a sales job when your colleagues let you down and you don't reach your monthly targets. Unpleasant, but children's lives weren't at stake. Innocent families weren't destroyed by not hitting targets. Here on the frontline, he had what he perceived to be a worthwhile and responsible vocation.

How could he do this when he was surrounded by these ineffectual and troubled colleagues?

Something made Wayne turn round. Typical of Deirdre's lackadaisical style, she was lagging behind. "Hurry up!" he told her, as kindly as he could muster.

"I need the toilet. Am I allowed?" she responded in her familiar sarcastic tone.

"Be as quick as you can," were his last words to her.

In a split second she had made her decision. She returned to her desk for the last time. There were items that she needed from her top drawer. She pushed her favourite hand cream into her bag. She wasn't leaving her expensive Tupperware container either, and locked the four corners of the lid tight so it wouldn't leak. Entirely focused on the job in hand, she ripped down the A4 poster containing information about the union reps. She would be needing that too. She was nearly ready. She needed her ID badge in order to exit the building, but as for her work diary, she flung it on Bill's desk, scrawling a message on a post-it note that read simply, "I've quit!" Sorting out her appointments and reallocating her cases would give him something to do!

Her pension would be an issue, but she was frugal and would continue to be. She would have to take a menial job, anything rather than subjecting herself to this horrendous torment for another second. A wave of relief swept through her as she realised that there would be benefits to this rash decision. There would be no disciplinary with the "silent assassin" to prepare for. No explaining to do. She smiled as she realised that she would never have to see that vile district manager ever again.

Everyone was busy in the waiting room as Deirdre exited through the back door. She ignored Bill who was finishing a cigarette in the designated smoking area and ran to her vehicle. There was an urgency to escape whilst she was feeling in control. Still her shoulders slumped as she drove out of the car park for what she was determined to be the very last time.

The last thing on her mind was the children she was paid to protect. The traumatised sibling group who had been cruelly dumped by their mother and instructed not to come home for several days. The four-year-old girl who had been viciously assaulted and would never return to her mother's care. The teenage boy so desperate for someone to listen to him that he had taken to cutting himself in front of the horrified administration staff.

None of this was Deirdre's problem. She was consumed only with her own needs. How she had been such a fool to continue in social work. She had got herself into a terrible rut and now she berated herself yet again that six years of her life had been taken. She needed to be her own best friend at this moment and tried to tell herself it was all over, and she would move on to other things.

When it was safe to do so, she pulled over, turned the engine off and dialled the phone number. She had paid enough in her subscriptions over the years and was entitled to be taken seriously.

"Someone will take the can for this," she told her union representative, impressed with the firmness of her voice. Appreciating the sympathetic ear, she added, "I will be suing Fenton Local Authority for damages!"

Twenty-six

Thursday July 22nd 2004, 2pm

When Deirdre walked out, Bill made no attempt to contact her. With his hardened approach to everything, he simply moved on. In his view, any social worker was utterly replaceable. He recognised in her the same apathetic and bitter tones that he was familiar with. She was a liability and would definitely not be missed.

He had realised for some time that he exerted no useful influence over the remaining team members and reverted back to leaving them to their own devices. They were too dominant and it was easier to give in to them.

It was after his extended lunch break in Asda that he returned to his poky "cupboard" to find the "silent assassin" seated in his chair, scrutinising his work diary! His filing cabinet and desk drawers had been pulled wide, in her attempt to find evidence. What a mess she had made!

It was obvious what had precipitated such an invasion of his work space. A disgruntled client had probably made a complaint to an MP about his performance. An individual with a vendetta against him may be threatening to sue Fenton Local Authority. Things like that had happened to him in the past, and he squirmed slightly as he recalled the previous disciplinary hearings he had been so unfairly subjected to.

The truth was he simply didn't care that much anymore. As long as he was suspended on full pay, things would get resolved somehow as usual. He always enjoyed his long periods of suspension, with each day his own to do as he wished. There was his allotment to attend to for a start.

The wheels of Fenton complaints bureaucracy turned slowly which always worked in his favour. However, he knew he needed to feign some level of concern and would have to speak to his union representative with a matter of urgency. It went without saying that he would have to fervently fight any allegation. His healthy pension counted on it. So he made some form of protest at this unwarranted intrusion, but his objections were met by the "silent assassin" with an equally obvious lack of concern. Dawn Smithers piercing grey eyes bored into his skull.

She smiled as she demanded his identification badge and escorted him past his colleagues and out of the building. The process was extremely slick, and he was itching to get back to his garden and soak up the remains of the late afternoon sun.

Twenty-seven

Epilogue

JANUARY 1ST 2005

SIX MONTHS LATER

AFTER LENGTHY ASSESSMENTS WERE CONCLUDED, SAIRA WAS deemed by Wayne to be "good enough" to care for Kyle and Brandon independently. For safety purposes they were moved to a new home over a hundred miles away.

Mark Leigh pleaded guilty to all charges. He remained on remand and received a four-year custodial sentence. It wasn't long enough, but for now they were all safe.

Melissa and Dan got to celebrate Ellie becoming their legal daughter in a moving court adoption ceremony. The atmosphere was one of celebration as the smiling judge posed happily for photographs with the elated new parents and their close relatives. Afterwards, they all tumbled out into the corridor. A proud family that only had eyes for Ellie. The cards, flowers and hugs that social workers often humbly receive at this significant point were absent, as they unexpectedly turned on David with some harsh truths.

Ellie's new family had made a sensible decision to wait until their daughter officially belonged to them before having their say. Still fragile after their recent horrific experience, they didn't need the added aggravation of making a formal complaint. In any event, they had lost all faith in the system.

The timing of their vent had been planned for maximum effect and bystanders in the waiting area couldn't help but overhear the accusations.

"You failed to do your job properly!" Dan practically spat at their former "friend".

"You are an absolute selfish screw-up!" Melissa's soft brown eyes had welled up, the tears threatening to ruin her carefully applied mascara. Her facial features contorted, she spelt out each syllable, her tone cold and measured as if she had practised the line many times. It was a great shame that she had to restrain herself from slapping him incredibly hard across the face.

The explosion of vicious verbal abuse continued. But it was something that he knew he deserved. Still, he was somewhat appalled that they had conducted themselves like this in such a public arena. He remained silent as he looked around him, waiting for the moment to pass. Surely there would be nothing else they could add? But there was more. Dan coldly told him that the invitation to the belated adoption party was rescinded, and warned David never to contact any of them ever again.

Melissa's sister now butted in, "I pity the poor families that get you as their social worker!" she told him curtly, before swiftly turning her back on him and storming off to join her relatives.

A mortified David stood still, not knowing what to do. The court ushers and a security guard rushed over, intervening with somewhat encouraging news. The CCTV showed the family heading out of the building. Still visibly shaken, David decided to take a seat and wait before leaving the vicinity too. The cutting admonishments had washed over him; only Melissa's had been internalised. He was left with a deep sense of sadness with the realisation that he would never see this vivacious and beautiful woman again.

Siobhan and the Baums' fostering-to-adopt link worker witnessed this very personal attack on their colleague. Purposely, they hadn't chosen to intervene. Ellie's adoptive family had behaved inappropriately but their comments were valid. David Lindley had failed to follow procedures and had let everyone down, including the child, her mother and her maternal grandfather. He was simply unsafe to practise as a social worker.

Tracey Mellor made a lasting impression on impressionable Siobhan. It had been shocking to see a client transform themselves within such a short timeframe. Her memories of that prison visit remained with her and eventually she realised why. If Tracey could turn her life round, then she would learn from this experience and try and take steps to become more independent.

With this newly found strength, she made tentative steps about leaving home, planning to move out of the bedroom that she had slept in her entire life. Whilst inspired, she made an appointment for counselling to address her sexual difficulties. The matter of her unbearable job was harder to deal with. For like her other colleagues, she too felt trapped with little in the way of transferrable skills. She remains in her current team, but regularly vows to leave the social work profession as soon as possible.

Unlike Siobhan, David continued to lack any initiative to deal with his family problems. He spent most of the Christmas break isolated from his parents and friends. His alcohol dependency is concerning and to date he has not made an application to the family courts to see his children.

As the months dragged on, Deirdre realised that her options were limited. She had no energy to sue the department and given the circumstances, the safest and most realistic plan was to apply for a job in a call centre. The trauma she suffered at the hands of Darren Lawton continues to affect her on a daily basis.

Yotunde gained employment in the charity sector. Working in the Young Carers Project involved undertaking direct work with children and their families in an empowering way. Accepting a lesser wage was a price worth paying. She vowed never to return to the local authority in any capacity.

Living up to Fenton Childcare Services' appalling reputation, the multiple formal complaints made against Bill strangely got "lost" in the system. Due to these gross errors, "silent assassin" struggled to dismiss him. Luckily for him, he was given one more "final" warning, and shamelessly returned to head up Area Team Three just before Christmas.

Wayne continued to live with his irritating and needy mother. He recently came to accept that he could well spend his entire life without a partner. There was one benefit to his lack of social interaction outside of work – it freed him up to pursue his lifetime goal, to hurtle around, believing that he was saving lives. This inimitable knowledge boosts his spirits every single day.

After the Christmas holidays he returned to work to receive some news. He noted the postmark and ripped open the envelope.

"Hi Wayne,
I am loving my new job as a hairdresser and it should only be a couple of months before the boys start play therapy.

I will be on the witness protection scheme once Mark is released from prison so I hope we will be safe. We will all be given new identities and it will be hard to get used to being called a different name.

Kyle and Brandon are doing as well as can be expected and have settled into their new school. They are as close as ever. Ian and Brenda, their foster carers, come to see them every month, which is really important. They are good people and have been so kind to us.

I am so grateful to you for believing in me. The new social worker pops in from time to time and I receive help from the Sure Start team.

We all miss you.

Saira, Kyle and Brandon."

Heartened, he reread it, feeling the warmth of this uplifting news. The brief letter represented everything he ever stood for, giving vulnerable families unwavering support at a critical time of their lives. He had fought hard to rescue Kyle and Brandon, and against the odds, he had succeeded in giving them a right to a family life with their mother. Saira had included her address so he would write back.

He glanced round the room, taking in the grim surroundings. The ugly 1980s Formica desks, the dirty coffee cups. Files piled up on every surface. Within these four walls, for some strange reason, he felt secure. Engaging families had become his life. Within his overstuffed filing cabinet was his whole being. Every single client mattered to him.

There would never be any recognition for his efforts in the form of an OBE or an equivalent. It was about coming to terms with this fact. This magnificent news was enough to keep him going at what he clearly excelled at. At that very second, he felt complete.

Acknowledgements

A special thank you to Dominic Savage, my incredibly patient editor and friend. My deepest gratitude for the professional help and dedication given to me by internal layout designer, Chenile Keogh and the book cover designer, Andrew Brown. It's quite a challenge to mention anyone else when I am a pseudonym! So my apologies if you didn't make the cut! Hopefully it's safe to mention Gerry, PW, Jonny, Nad, Si, and Mish. I am so grateful for your input and get ready for the sequel!

My love as always goes to my devoted husband and children.

Printed in Great Britain
by Amazon

28254932R00148